The Total Transference and the Complete Counter-Transference

The Total Transference and the Complete Counter-Transference

The Kleinian Psychoanalytic Approach with More Disturbed Patients

Robert Waska, MFT, PhD

JASON ARONSON
Lanham • Boulder • New York • Toronto • Plymouth, UK

Published by Jason Aronson
An imprint of Rowman & Littlefield Publishers, Inc.
A wholly owned subsidiary of The Rowman & Littlefield Publishing Group, Inc.
4501 Forbes Boulevard, Suite 200, Lanham, Maryland 20706
http://www.rowmanlittlefield.com

Estover Road, Plymouth PL6 7PY, United Kingdom

British Library Cataloguing in Publication Information Available

Library of Congress Cataloging-in-Publication Data

Waska, Robert T.
The total transference and the complete counter-transference : the Kleinian psychoanalytic approach with more disturbed patients / Robert Waska.
p. cm.
Includes bibliographical references and index.
ISBN 978-0-7657-0875-5 (cloth : alk. paper) — ISBN 978-0-7657-0876-2 (ebook)
1. Psychoanalysis. 2. Transference (Psychology). 3. Countertransference (Psychology). 4. Klein, Melanie. I. Title.
RC506.W376 2012
616.89'17–dc23
2011038479

™ The paper used in this publication meets the minimum requirements of American National Standard for Information Sciences Permanence of Paper for Printed Library Materials, ANSI/NISO Z39.48-1992.

Printed in the United States of America

Contents

Acknowledgments

I have dedicated the last twenty-six years to the close and focused examination of how individuals unconsciously relate to themselves and to their world. I have accomplished this by extending value to exactly what goes on in the therapeutic relationship. This loyalty to the importance of transference, counter-transference, and phantasy is at the bedrock of Kleinian theory and technique. This approach seeks to understand the essence of the patient's internal conflicts between self and other and offers the patient an opportunity to redefine and rebuild those fundamental problems of love, hate, and knowledge. The transference and the counter-transference provide the most effective vehicle to learning how the patient places themselves in their internal world and the nature of their unconscious desires and anxieties.

In working with patients, I have gained a great respect for their struggles and how everyone, in their own way, is trying to find a foothold in the unpredictable and often threatening inner experience we call life. Sometimes, I am able to help my patients learn more about themselves and assist them in fashioning a new way of thinking and feeling about themselves which eventually leads to greater fulfillment and sense of inclusion in the world.

Sometimes, this goal goes unfinished or never is achieved. But, even in the more disappointing moments of psychoanalytic treatment, I believe the effort alone can be healing for some patients. I thank all my patients for giving me a greater appreciation for the complexity of the human spirit and the intensity of the universal conflicts that we all walk through at some point, to some degree. I strive to never give up on anyone and I work toward a willingness to help every person who enters my office regardless of how damaged, difficult, or disturbed they feel or present. Ideally, by my sticking it out, sometimes they are able and willing to stick it out as well. As a result, they can begin to risk change and growth.

I wish to thank the following journals for allowing me to use some material previously published in their volumes. Chapter One has appeared in the *Journal of the Brazilian Psychoanalytic Society*, Chapter Two has appeared in *Psychodynamic Practice*, and Chapter Six has appeared in the *American Journal of Psychoanalysis*.

All clinical material has been disguised to protect the confidentiality of the patient and any identifying details have been altered to become applicable to most patients dealing with similar internal and external conflicts or situations.

1. Chapter One has previously been published as Waska, R. (2010). The As-If Way of Life Versus the As-Is Way of Life: Confusions Between Servant, Master, and Self, *Journal of the Brazilian Psychoanalytic Society*, 12: (2).

2. Chapter Two has previously been published as Waska, R. (2011). Low Frequency Psychoanalytic Engagement with a Depressive Patient: The Beginning Phase of Treatment from a Kleinian Approach, *Psychodynamic Practice*, 17: (2), 159–173.

3. Chapter Six has previously been published as Waska, R. (2011). Striving Toward Useful Interpretation While Managing Counter-Transference Enactments: Encounters with a Thick-Skinned Narcissist, *The American Journal of Psychoanalysis*, 71: (3), 246–263.

Finally, I would like to thank my wife for her help, support, and loving presence. We met about the same time I began my career in psychology and she has been a constant inspiration. Also, she has been a faithful friend who is willing to field some of my counter-transference confusions and offer some clarity. She remains the incredible balance in my life. As Freud, Melanie Klein, and many others have said, there is work but there must also be love and play. She is all of that and more.

Preface

The book takes the reader "into the trenches" with the author as he describes his psychoanalytic work with a variety of patients with very thorny and complex conditions. The reader becomes familiar with the clinical and theoretical difficulties psychoanalysts encounter in their day-to-day practice with such patients, especially the counter-transference reactions so common with patients who rely on certain rigid defense systems. The book provides a wealth of in-depth clinical material that shows what actually happens in the room when faced with severe personality disorders, chronic depressive conditions, pathological phantasies of grief and loss, and destructive states of narcissism. Each chapter provides a vivid look into the moment to moment workings of psychoanalytic treatment in the context of the contemporary focus on understanding projective identification, enactment, acting out, and the careful and thoughtful interpretive working through of these complex clinical situations. Because of the troubling and hard to manage counter-transference situations with such difficult to reach patients, much of the book also addresses how to notice, learn from, and utilize these volatile moments. The reader will develop a better insight into these transference and counter-transference problems that often result in various enactments and therapeutic standoffs unless examined and understood. Indeed, once properly understood, what once was fertile ground for the analyst's acting out can become a bridge to better translating and interpreting the patient's core anxieties and providing a therapeutic experience of change and growth.

While presented from a Kleinian viewpoint, the book is written in a very inclusive and flexible manner that brings together a variety of analytic thought and provides easy access to the reader unfamiliar with Kleinian theory. In addition, the author's Kleinian approach is readily accessible by means of a rich mixture of theory and clinical exploration of the moment-to-moment therapeutic situation and the use of a wealth of detailed verbatim case material. It is rare that a book offers so much actual "he said, she said" clinical data which engages the reader to the material and brings psychoanalytic theory alive.

Important technical questions of how the modern psychoanalytic practitioner works within the transference, how he/she monitors the counter-transference, and how he/she makes interpretations are fleshed out in each chapter in this genuine, user-friendly, experience-near atmosphere. However, the reader will find out how to specifically work within the transference and counter-transference matrix when meeting with patients that create more tricky and brittle relational standoffs.

This volume shows the therapeutic power the modern Kleinian approach can have with patients throughout the diagnostic spectrum. By attending to the interpersonal, transactional, and intra-psychic levels of transference, counter-transference and unconscious phantasy with consistent here-and-now and in-the-moment interpretation, the Kleinian method can be therapeutically successful with severely neurotic, borderline, and narcissistic patients, By making the goal of psychoanalytic treatment the gradual establishment of analyst contact, a broader range of patients can be helped and understood.

Introduction

In chapter one, the author looks at how issues of idealization, envy, the death instinct, and pathological projective identification cycles can intersect to produce a constant and desperate search for total knowledge and perfect love followed by constant disappointment and rejection. Case material follows one patient who was intent on becoming the ideal beacon for the object, providing the perfect match for the object's desires, only to empty himself out so profoundly as to feel hollow except for the winds of contempt and loneliness that remained. To accept the self as-is and gamble on the depressive position mixture of love, hate, and knowledge that can mean loss and difference is too unbearable for some patients and results in their reliance on an as-if personality defense in which the object is seduced with falsehoods and control. A manic search for immediate love and proof of one's uniqueness is the vicious side effect. Unlike the classic definition of the as-if character who tries to keep everything quite stagnant, this variety of internal conflict involves a manic striving for expansion and relational motion in order to prevent an ever looming collapse, rejection, and loss. Psychoanalytic treatment is shown to offer relief and transformation, regardless of frequency, as long as a consistent goal of analytic contact and transference interpretation is maintained.

In chapter two, one extensive case report is used to explore the clinical reality of working in private practice and often seeing patients only once a week because of managed care restrictions, financial hardships, and the limits of family and employment. Some patients are seen on the analytic couch and others are seen sitting up. The level of pathology ranges from very fragmented borderline or narcissistic profiles to entrenched neurotic issues. Instead of trying to create various artificial distinctions between psychoanalysis and psychotherapy based on frequency of visits or use of couch, the author demonstrates the practice of low-frequency psychoanalysis from a Kleinian perspective based on exploration of the transference and phantasy conflicts as the defining criteria.

While some patients are unable or unwilling to step into the difficult and uncharted explorations that psychoanalytic work entails, the author shows how the effort to establish analytic contact with each individual can pay off and provide valuable support, containment, and growth for most patients under most circumstances. The patient may display great resistance to the challenge of psychoanalytic treatment, subtly inviting the analyst through projective identification processes to succumb to counter-transference despair and the idea that one must give up the psychoanalytic quest and settle for something less valuable or complex because of frequency, diagnosis, or length of treatment. In response, the author uses one difficult case to show how the basic principles of the Kleinian approach are applicable to almost all our clinical encounters in the day-to-day private practice setting. The case material utilized includes issues of intense pre-depressive anxieties, distorted oedipal conflicts, and persecutory phantasies regarding caretaking and pleasing the demanding and dependent object to prevent crippling loss and guilt.

In chapter three, the author discusses a particular type of depressive phantasy some patients have. When working intensely with patients in a psychoanalytic setting, one eventually comes to notice a set of individuals who appear to exist with dead or dying objects that they desperately try to revitalize, reconstitute, or restore. To let go of these mummified objects is to give up desire and hope and instead face isolation and desolation. The mummy ideal may be a meager morsel of what one really wants or needs but it is seen as better than nothing. Some of these patients dress up their phantasy corpse with denial, false optimism, and manic control in order to feel like everything is always OK and everyone is always happy and conflict free.

However, it becomes clear when working with such patients that they are simply trying to prop up a dead object that they feel responsible for killing off with poisonous love and hunger. So, they try to pretend to have a live, healthy, and positive object by their side instead of having to face the aloneness of being with a corpse, a disappointment, or someone they have hurt.

Another strategy such patients take is to resign themselves to being handcuffed to a decaying, broken object in the hopes that one day they can revive the object enough for it to finally love them and pay attention to them. This creates an eternal graveside vigil, and a strong resistance to mourning because that would necessitate a good-bye, a separation, and an individuation that would push them into an eternal void and aloneness. They are sure that facing the truth of their objects in all of its good and bad aspects will mean the complete lack of love and the realization of guilt, aggression, and loss. Such patients are able to admit to caring for a corpse, but refuse to bury it.

Clinical difficulties are explored with case material. The case material is presented not so much to show a new theoretical concept but to illustrate the actual nuts-and-bolts clinical reality of how a Kleinian analyst really works with these types of patients. This is more of a window into the day-to-day clinical unfolding of the Kleinian psychoanalytic approach with a particular variety of patient.

Chapter four examines patients who spend their lives trying to protect, enhance, defend, and honor their objects. However, in examining their unconscious phantasies and conflicts it becomes obvious that this apparently loving and protective effort is coupled with a more controlling and demeaning perception of their objects as weak and powerless, always in need of some sort of handout. Also, these patients show thinly veiled feelings of envy, superiority, and hatred toward their beloved objects for which they in turn feel very guilty. Then, they worry about retaliation or consequence of some variety. These phantasies include terrible damage or neglect to the object and/or damage and punishment to the self. The underlying aggressive feelings that fuel these phantasies include viewing the object as greedy, neglectful, ignorant, inferior, and hurtful. In fact, the patient seems to be angry at their object, wanting to be properly cared for and loved by the object instead of having to be a nursemaid all the time but is reluctant and guilty to ask for that. To be equals is desired but a state of mind that is avoided as well as it means giving up the ability to be the controlling savior, having the upper hand, and having to meet on an equal playing field.

Also, to feel like an equal the patient would feel vulnerable to the same critical eye they have had, now feeling inferior and powerless themselves. So, underneath this patient's seemingly pious and generous way of relating lies a more critical, looking for flaws, controlling manner. This is combined with a sense of great loss and desire for a protecting and caring parental object. But, the aggressive control of this, through projective maneuvers, is the overriding defense. With excessive reliance on projective identification, a harsh and critical spotlight is alternatively focused on the self and then on the object and then on the self. Expectation and judgment is acute. Persecutory guilt, a fear of primitive loss, and a desperate, hungry need are all elements of this patient's internal chaos. Case material from one psychoanalytic treatment is used for illustration.

While Part One of this text shows the complicated issues encountered with patients in the depressive position, Part Two shifts to a focus on patients operating more in the narcissistic realm of experience, often a more paranoid-schizoid state of mind.

In chapter five, case material is used to illustrate the difficulties encountered in psychoanalytic work with thick-skinned narcissistic patients. The rigid and complex phantasy states and defenses regarding envy, greed, need, and loss are explored. The intense reliance on projective identification, denial, and splitting shape the transference into a formidable barrier from which the patient neutralizes all feeling states. This type of transference creates a special counter-transference tension that must be addressed to avoid various enactments. The theoretical aspects of envy are addressed and the destructive and libidinal conflicts of envy and narcissism are discussed. The clinical and technical approach to narcissist's underlying struggle between the life and death instincts and the conflicts between love, hate, and knowledge are illustrated in the case material.

The clinical report shows the tricky nature of working with such narcissistic pathology and the painful realization that no matter how much we may try, sometimes the patient's phantasy state will not allow change and their internal conflicts will prevent the establishment of any meaningful analytic contact. However, the analytic method can still provide some possible relief for such patients. For some it may be lasting and other more temporary.

Narcissistic patients tend to push the analyst to work harder than usual to contain, understand, translate, and utilize their counter-transference states. This is because of the unusually extreme reliance on denial, devaluation, projective identification, and control that these individuals exhibit. Defenses against loss, envy, greed, and dependence create difficult transference states in which symbolic or creative material is flattened, stripped, and neutralized. Feelings are out of the question.

Chapter six continues this exploration of the narcissistic lack of connection to self and other that endures in the transference as well as in all aspects of these patients' lives. With thick-skinned narcissistic patients (Rosenfeld 1987), there is a subtle lack of engagement, an underbelly of control, and a complete uncoupling of feeling or link between self and object. Envy is often a cornerstone of such difficult clinical problems and is part of an internal desolation that fuels an emotional firebombing of any awareness of interest in self or other.

Case material is used to show how confusing, alarming, and demanding narcissistic patients can be, trying the very essence of the analytic process. These troubled individuals enter treatment looking for help, wanting a quick fix to their suffering, but resist the deeper understanding, learning, and change that psychoanalytic treatment offers.

In chapter seven, one psychoanalytic case is utilized to explore the dynamics of patients who declare themselves to be special in some way and who insist, either indirectly or in an openly demanding manner, that the analyst "do" something for them and help them achieve their special destiny. They want the analyst to help them find out why they are being denied this privileged position in life, this attention and love, and this unique status. This type of depressed, anxious, and often paranoid patient is impulsive and in the transference puts themselves and the analyst into a high-pressure climate in which someone needs to take some type of immediate action, produce some type of outcome, find some sort of solution, or create some type of quick fix.

In working with these difficult-to-appease patients, one finds a great deal of resistance to mourning. They do not want to face the cruel and frustrating reality that they are not so great and one's objects have been less than stellar. Indeed, there is a great fear of being overcome by the useless nature of the self and the persecutory nature of others if this idealized and privileged version of life is not obtained. The development from paranoid to depressive functioning is fought off with excessive reliance on projective identification and the demanding dream of being properly parented once and for all.

Transference states are rigid and relentless at times, creating rocky counter-transference moments. The creation of successful analytic contact is often temporary and prone to rupture, as it presents a threat to the patient's wish for ideal change and their avoidance of real but less than perfect versions of self and other.

In chapter eight, case material is used to illustrate the Kleinian approach to working with patients struggling in the area between the paranoid-schizoid position and the depressive position. They are unconsciously focused on avoiding a devastating loss of a persecutory nature in which they would face the absence of a caring, supportive object. They would be without someone who saw them as unique and special. To allow their in this painful loss brings on a primitive state of mourning that involves persecutory experiences of having no value, being invisible, and being without identity. It is a lack of love but ultimately a lack of meaning.

Through confusing messages from caretakers and/or from their own internal coping mechanisms, these patients rely on a rigid defensive structure of entitlement and the vision of greatness being around the corner. They see themselves as one day being very special and having a privileged destiny. This is a fragile phantasy barely stuck together with intense reliance on projective identification and splitting, which creates paranoia, idealization, and devaluation cycles. Many of these hard-to-reach cases involve various forms of acting out, including early termination and sometimes create counter-transference enactments by the analyst. This chapter utilizes an analytic case that, although very difficult and rocky, proved to be successful as the result of consistent focus on transference phantasies and the patient's core conflicts regarding persecutory mourning.

In chapter nine, the reader learns from in-depth clinical material how difficult it can be for the analyst to engage a more severe narcissistic personality, especially with more brittle borderline features. Working from a Kleinian perspective, the author shares his counter-transference entanglements that were part of a mutual acting out of the patient's archaic and pathological object relational phantasies. Due to the patient's excessive reliance on manic devaluation, splitting, and projective identification, the analyst was exposed to strong emotional pulls to step into various persecutory roles involving withholding and sadistic objects combined with helpless, abandoned objects. While the analyst repeatedly tried to regain his therapeutic balance when this counter-transference acting out emerged, the complex and intense nature of the patient's narcissistic stance provoked a less than optimal analytic response throughout the treatment.

Being used by the patient was a difficult role for the analyst to tolerate, especially when it seemed obvious that the patient merely wanted to use the treatment as a method of regaining lost power, security, and control before discarding the analyst. This made it difficult for the analyst to remember that there may be a small, healthy, and desperate part of the patient that actually did feel remorse, actually did want change, and actually did want to take ownership of their actions.

When the coarse and selfish aspects of the more destructive narcissist (Rosenfeld 1987) patient are more present in the transference, it is not easy to stay balanced in the counter-transference and remember that there may be a more libidinal aspect of the narcissism (Rosenfeld 1987) operating in the shadows, desperately needing patience, trust, and containment. Sometimes, there is nothing we can do. Regardless of how on our toes we are clinically, the treatment is headed toward an iceberg. However, if we continue to study our own therapeutic disasters and those created by the patient within the total transference situation (Joseph 1985), we may be able to build a better more cohesive bridge toward analytic contact (Waska 2007) and perhaps find ways to maintain analytic contact even under these more harsh conditions.

Part One

Disturbances of the Depressive Position

Chapter One

The As-If Way of Life Versus the As-Is Way of Life: Confusions between Servant, Master, and Self

J was an intelligent young man in his early twenties who came to me for help with "a lifelong tendency of not approaching women in a healthy manner." He described a predictable feeling of noticing something special about a woman, including memories of female classmates back when he was only eight years of age, and then immediately "really falling for her." He would develop elaborate daydreams and desires about how the both of them could live happily ever after. J usually ended up feeling very much "head over heels" for the girl long before he ever got to know her or be friends with her. So, by the time he finally asked the girl out for a cup of coffee, he was ready to profess his undying love for her. He would try and hold back but felt "this was simply being dishonest and that he should reveal what was truly in his heart and mind rather than pretend that he didn't feel anything."

This immediate gushing of emotion usually got J into trouble in terms of the girl feeling surprised and overwhelmed, even "a bit creepy about him." J would write these women long romantic letters, explaining all his feelings and usually he would discuss in the letter and later in person all the conflict he felt about whether he should pour out his soul or try and get to know her and see where it went.

From my counter-transference feelings, I interpreted that he told me about mailing the love letters in an anxious and even regretful way so he may be wanting me to take over and tell him if it is ok or not. But, that would now mean he is throwing himself at me and letting me lead him around just as he ends up feeling the women do. J said, "I do think I get myself into trouble by giving them the letters. I need to keep those letters and not send them." Here, he was able to take my interpretations regarding his sudden transference repeat of dependency and over-reliance on the object for knowledge and fulfillment and stop to reflect on his own mind and opinions. For a moment, his as-if compliance shifted to an as-is state of mind. However, I also thought this was too good to be completely true and that his remark was also meant to placate and please me, telling me what he thought I needed to hear. I also made that interpretation and realized I would need to listen very closely at all times to how J used me and what he wanted for me to feel and think throughout our time together.

Also interpreting from my counter-transference, I said that J seemed both excited yet desperate to get to each woman immediately before she vanished, to somehow immediately own her, or perhaps both. So, my first counter-transference based interpretation was what Roth (2001) calls a direct comment on the transference dynamic and the possible enactment process. This last interpretation regarding his need to get to each woman so desperately was more of what Roth (2001) calls a level 1 comment on the nature of his phantasy beliefs about self and object.

In response, J said, "I feel some kind of adrenaline. A passion takes over and I need her. I want her and I feel it is destiny somehow. I want to know everything about her, spend time with her, and give her everything. But, I know from experience that this rush to happiness can be disastrous to the relationship. But, again, I feel frustrated. It seems false to try and hold back." So, I interpreted that J wanted this pure, honest, and immediate harmony and union with his special object but was starting to realize that somehow this way of launching himself at the object was ruining the object and reducing his chances for unity. Here, I was interpreting the destructive and possessive aspects of the projective identification process he relied on so much.

J said he thought it would probably be better to slow down and calm down. I said, "I think you say that partly because you have given it some thought and think it might be the right thing to do, at least on paper. And, I think you also say that to please me again. But, I think you can barely tolerate holding yourself back. We need to end today but we must find out what makes it so difficult to not have instant love and immediate reassurance. It looks very painful." J said, "It is true I don't want to change that because I want to be with her and I want her to be with me. So, you are right. I am trying to do the right thing and maybe wanting to please you too. But, I am going to try even if it is an artificial effort for now. So, J was going to artificially "calm down and move a bit slower until he could figure out what was going on."

J's method of injecting himself into the object so quickly and hoping for a magical blissful state but then wondering what happened when it crumbled was quickly replicated in the transference. J came to a session almost an hour early once and when I asked him about it, he said he wasn't really sure what time it was because he never wore a watch. On the surface, the reason was because he couldn't afford one and he could easily find out the time in most situations without his own watch. But, my sense about it was that on a deeper level his lack of ownership represented a "free and easy, don't need to be tied down to convention" type of lifestyle that left him feeling special, unique, and unencumbered but also detached and lacking a method of effectively relating to others. I asked him what sort of feelings he went though as he sat in the waiting room for so long. He said that at first he wondered if he had the right time and maybe he had misjudged the time. After a while, he wondered if I had forgotten the appointment. J said he was anxious at first because he "really valued the time, the chance to talk, and the opportunity to find things out" but as time went along he started to worry that he "would lose that precious time and not be able to have the full chance to explore things since the sessions were relatively short already."

I said, "You sound like you were looking forward to how we could be together and what you would get from it and then you started to be anxious and irritated that I would not be giving you everything you wanted. You look forward to it with a lot of excitement and then it begins to crumble?" J said, "Yes. I felt I was going to lose out on what I was looking forward to. This is important so I don't want to only be left with some of it. I want all of it."

This type of transference hunger, sense of disappointment, and emotional demand was repeated when I invited J to come more frequently. J said, "After you offered me more sessions, I had a few different reactions. At first, I felt deeply touched. I felt you must really care about me and want to help me. That made me feel very good. But, then I thought that maybe it means you think I am really sick and see me as having terrible psychological problems. That made me feel scared and worried. I also started to think that maybe you wanted me to come in more often so you could make more money off of me. You wanted to fill the time up in your schedule book. That made me suspicious and not want to come in."

This absorb/reject type of transference also emerged when J told me how he "was so intrigued with the things that he was learning in therapy and how much he is finding out." He told me that "after the sessions lately, I have left in a state of near euphoria, really feeling hopeful and full of positive energy. But, later that night or the next day, I started to think about how the more I dwell on everything by talking about it with you, the more depressed I feel. So, I can't see the point of how this will help me. It feels more like it will only bring me down and remind me of my problems."

I said, "Maybe you want us to be perfect together so fast and so strongly that you end up feeling suffocated or disappointed." He said, "That is what happened with Mary over the weekend. I asked her over for dinner. We have been coworkers for almost a year and I think she realized it was a date when I took her to the movie two weeks ago. I spent all day cleaning up my apartment, making a special dinner, and getting ready. We had a good time and then we watched some television and eventually started making out. We had sex and then we went to bed. I was on cloud nine. But, around two in the morning, she got up and told me she had to go back home and make sure she had everything ready for some special work assignment the next day. She gave me a kiss and said, 'thanks.' I couldn't believe it! 'Thanks,' like I had given her a stick of gum. I felt used and resentful. I still do. I know she doesn't express her feelings too openly but this was like a slap in the face. I feel really disappointed and confused."

Because J seemed very confused at what Mary's actions meant and that he had hoped she was feeling one way about him and now she seemed to feel another way that really upset him, I chose to start with an interpretation aimed at exploring that anxiety. I said, "It seems you are really trying to know what her feelings are but can't figure it out. You want something close and special but you can't tell if it is there or if she is just using you for a good time?" J said, "Well, maybe not using me for a good time, but treating us like lukewarm when I want something special and on fire. But, I know more and more that I have a problem with that so I am trying to not react and freak her out."

When I mentioned how he seems to want to know what his object feels and how the object feels about him, J picked up on the notion of wanting to know. J told me, "I have always wanted to have full knowledge about things and I always want to understand everything I can about whatever it is. So, when I was interested in poetry during college, I researched everything about it that I could, joined the poetry society, read about it, and went to various clubs and societies. Once I thought I knew enough about the topic, I dropped it and moved on. I felt I had it under my belt and knew it in-and-out so I wasn't really interested in it anymore."

I said, "It sounds like you used poetry for your own needs and when you were done, you tossed it aside and moved on. If I were poetry, I might feel used." J laughed and said, "I get it. That is sort of like how I feel with Mary. But, that has been my pattern for my whole life, just figuring out everything I can about it. When I was curious about sailing, I ended up quitting my job and taking a job on a sailboat for the summer and sailing around the Caribbean. I was able to learn everything possible about sailing. They taught me and gave me food and shelter. It was perfect."

I asked if he still sails or is interested in it and he said no. So, I wondered about this desire to own knowledge being more important than having an actual interest in the subject. Here, I was wondering if his desires to possess the insides of the object were so aggressive and his need to own that which seemed out of reach so great that it became the quest above all else. Then, if J felt he won the prize, he no longer valued it and could not take it in as a new object of security. It was only a notch in his belt but not the fulfillment of his own genuine interest.

Again, his as-if desire to own the props and clothing of the perfect one and to capture the love of the object rather than risk seeing if he were to be loved as-is left him empty, unable to keep the knowledge and love that was gained and to feel sustained by it. This manic rush to force an idealized union followed by an envious attack on self and object brought on persecutory anxiety and a despairing collapse. This type of as-if absorb and reject approach is different than the as-if character Deutsch (1942) and Malcolm (1990) write about. They examine a type of patient who strives to maintain a stagnant state of no growth or progress. J represents a subtype of as-if functioning that is more the result of a collapsing or fragmented psychic refuge (Waska 2010a). While desperately searching for a pathological retreat from the ravages of both paranoid and depressive anxieties, but the patient is actually completely exposed to the worst of both. So, J demonstrates the desperate and constantly in motion defensive moves of such a massively conflicted individual.

In discussing this with J, another aspect of his need to know came to light. He told me, "If someone else suggests that I should learn about something, I put all my energy into that and don't stop until I have really mastered it." I said, "Is that so you please us?" J replied, "Yes. I do want to learn about whatever it is. I am interested in it, and I respect the person as an authority in the subject, so I want to take advantage of that opportunity. But, yes. I want to show the person that I am eager to follow their lead."

Exploring the transference aspect of this, I said, "So, maybe I should be cautious about when you are eager to learn here?" J said, "Probably. But, sometimes, I do want to figure out what is going on with me." He went on to say how he remembers going into a small bookstore close to where he lived and not being sure what to buy or read. He asked the old man behind the counter for a recommendation and even though the book he suggested "was by an obscure writer," J went ahead and bought it and read it with vigor. Then, he came back for more recommendations. The impression I had and interpreted was that J so much wanted to partake in the knowledge of the other that he left himself empty of his own ideas and feelings. J left no room for himself to ponder or explore. Because he emptied himself out so entirely and violently in order to take in and take over the object, he was no longer present in his own mind. He had absolutely no idea what he might want to read about. He had the same experience when he went to buy a car, when he went to the market to decide what to possibly cook, and so forth. He reached for the advice and knowledge of the other and shaped himself around it. I interpreted, "in some ways, it sounds like you become the disciple or follower of the person and lose sight of yourself." J said, "I have done that my whole life."

This way of becoming whatever the other likes when it comes to reading, cooking, or driving also emerged when J told me about his lifestyle. J worked at a job that enabled him to help the poor and needy, a cause he felt strong about, but the job paid next to nothing. I was amazed at how J was able to survive on so little. I soon learned that he really never spent almost anything on his own food, clothing, or recreation. He sought out whatever was free and saw his own needs as unimportant. I said, "It is as if you keep your slate clean and wait to be filled up with someone else's identity." J said, "I must admit I agree with you but it also makes me feel a bit creepy because that is what my mother does all the time." I asked him what he meant.

J went on to tell me about how his parents had a son before he was born. When their son was five years old, he was killed by a car. The family was devastated and J's mother went into a deep depression. Two years later, J was born. J said, "She has acted very oddly around me my whole life. She seems to see me as the lighthouse in her life, the thing she always pays attention to and the thing she is most invested in." I said, "You said the word thing instead of person so maybe you feel used, like a thing she uses to replace her terrible loss?" J said, "Exactly. I never felt she was interested in me. I feel like she brightens up every time she sees me and there is this almost erotic or primal attraction she seems to have for me, like she must have me or be with me no matter what." I said, "Which is exactly how you feel around other women, drawn to them in this intense, magical way in which you feel there could be bliss and complete harmony." J said, "Oh dear God. I am acting like my mother. I don't want that." I said, "No. You want your own identity. So, we have to find out why you so quickly sacrifice it and want knowledge about the person, attention from them, and have to prove your love so much that you end up angry and lonely." He nodded in agreement, looking clearly moved.

So, in the transference, he was demonstrating his need to own the object and worship the object but was very disappointed and angry when the object didn't notice all his efforts and pay him back with devotion and allegiance. Some of the motivation for this came out when during another session, J said, "I cannot be alone. I just can't. I am never alone actually. I am never alone because if I am alone I am constantly thinking of being with someone, anyone. So, I am never alone." I interpreted, "So, being alone with yourself feels too overwhelming or empty?" He nodded in agreement and said, "Something to avoid at all cost." He continued, "I don't know myself. I don't know if I even have a self since I usually do anything I can to please the other person or find a way to be like them. I never ever cook for myself but I am happy to cook for my date, my roommates, or anyone else. I never would listen to music if it weren't for people suggesting various artists to me. Then, I go out of my way to buy everything that artist has done. I study it and I try and know everything about them." I said, "So you can impress the person who suggested it?" J replied, "That and I figure if they like it there must be something valuable about it so I want to be a part of it."

At one point in the treatment, J mentioned that he had received some correspondence from his insurance company which included my diagnosis codes. He brought it up and I asked him what sort of reactions or thoughts he had about it. J told me he was immediately worried and hoped I hadn't made a mistake in my assessment of him because he didn't want a misdiagnosis which would end up with him "bounced around from one doctor to another getting the wrong treatment until someone finally makes the correct diagnosis and follows that with the proper treatment." J went on at length about how he knows for every diagnosis there is a particular and proper treatment régime and he wants to make sure he is getting "the proper treatment so he doesn't waste time in getting better."

I interpreted that his feelings about possibly not getting the right treatment from me and my possibly not understanding him or his needs sounded very similar to how he wants an instant, perfect-fit kind of love from the women in his life and when he doesn't feel that it appears instantly or in the way he expected, he feels very anxious, disappointed, and empty. J replied, "Yes. I was angry with you for maybe giving me the wrong diagnosis. That would mean you didn't really know me or understand me. Then, you wouldn't be able to give me what I need."

Here again, there was a blurry confusion between his wanting to have the proper and immediate diagnosis as a trophy or a mechanical "thing" that he could check off on his list of ingredients to constitute his as-if shell versus really allowing himself to take in our relationship and slowly find out if I understood him and knew what his core needs and identity really were. Since his intense reliance on projective identification precluded and prevented a stable as-is personality, J saw me as not being able to figure out who he was with a proper assessment or diagnosis just as he struggled to figure out his own needs, conflicts, joys, and fears.

These elements of his internal conflict continued to emerge in his associations. J told me how he is "always wildly infatuated with women, so much so that I don't really know them. It is more the idea of being in love with somebody. I am so connected with the idea of being with someone that I have no idea who they really are. If and when I ever get to know them enough that we actually get together and have a relationship, I am usually disappointed and quickly pick them apart. I see all their flaws and feel like I don't want to be with someone like that." I interpreted that he was angry with me and others because he sacrifices so much to please us and figure out what he is supposed to do for us that he expects a special offering back in exchange. The object needs to meet his high expectations or he is angry that he gave so much and never was known or loved properly in return. Then, in anger, he attacks the object and picks it apart for all its flaws.

In response, J associated to how he always ends up saying sorry to everyone, apologizing for anything and everything. He said, "I was in the pedestrian crossing the other day and the light was red for the cars. This big truck comes barreling through, right through the red light and nearly hit me. The driver flipped me the finger and I caught myself yelling out SORRY to him." I see myself doing that all the time. I feel really guilty like I have done something fundamentally wrong and bad. But, later, I start thinking about it and realize I have been shorted or denied and I get really angry. No one is ever bending over to be nice to me!" So, here, J was sharing the primitive and corrupted sense of guilt, reparation, and persecution that swirled around in his mind in a very chaotic and confusing manner.

Before J started his treatment, he had applied to the local police academy in the hope to start a career in law enforcement. The more we talked about his aspirations, it seemed clear that he imagined it would be a wonderful opportunity to "help others and make sure I could help get them out of bad situations and do the right thing." I interpreted that this was a thread in the overall pattern of him wanting to make sure he could control the object's happiness and keep his objects content and safe but the personal cost was his constant vigilant efforts to serve and protect. And, at the end of the day, would he feel betrayed if someone didn't "bend over backwards" to serve and protect him?

So, when J told me he got a letter notifying him he was accepted into the academy, he said he wasn't sure if he would accept the job. He said he "realized after a great deal of thought that I might be getting into the career for all the wrong reasons." He talked for awhile about this in a way that sounded insightful but also somewhat removed and intellectual. I interpreted, "I think you are thinking about yourself and wanting to learn more, but it seems sort of academic. I wonder if you want us to be together with our logical, academic hats on, searching together in this very controlled way. It is safe and controlled but cuts you off from feeling much." Here, I was interpreting his rejection of himself in order to please me and protect and serve our relationship over his own thoughts and feelings.

J said, "I think I know what you mean. Sometimes, I feel stuck between sounding a bit stiff and academic as you put it and sounding like a fifth grader with no sense of etiquette." I said, "And if you aren't stiff and controlled when you talk with me, then I might think of you as a dumb fifth grader? I might feel critical of you?" J said, "Yes. I haven't thought of it that way but maybe I am trying to prevent something like that. I want to please you so you don't look down on me." So, here he was associating to the depressive control he used in his as-if transference state, a way to prevent loss and persecution.

In the next session, J brought his acceptance letter up again and told me that after thinking about it some more, he realized he was partly telling me he was going to turn it down so I would be happy. He said, "I am realizing that I am ready to not go to the academy if it means you will be happy with me. In fact, I think I am ready to break it off with my girlfriend, not go to the academy, move out of my problem roommate situation, or get another job if that is what you really need me to do to prove that I am willing to do whatever it takes to improve and make progress."

I said, "You are ready to make the ultimate sacrifice on my behalf to make sure I stay happy and pleased with you." J said, "Yes. To make sure we are making progress and to do what you think is right, I would." I said, "You want so bad to have me love you and accept you that you are ready to sacrifice yourself and your ideas. As a result, I will be happy and want you around but you will be empty and hollow inside." J replied, "I think that is how I live my life. And, part of that is how much I want to make progress. You mentioned before that I seem consumed with goals and progress. It is true. I just want to know how to make progress as fast and effectively as possible so I can learn what I need to."

I said, "You want to own these things called knowledge, progress, and learning. But, you seem to have an iron grip around it and want it NOW so much that you kill off what we are and what we have right now. So, again, I think you want this magic union with these special goals so much that it is only a matter of time before you are disappointed in me and in us. Meanwhile, it is really unclear what on earth these goals are. The progress we are making doesn't count against such a huge intense goal. We are the victim of your wanting it all now."

J said, "I see what you mean. It is true. I don't actually know what it is that I am striving for. It is ironic that I want progress but can't think of what that really even means to me. It reminds me of how if someone tells me or even suggests that I investigate something, like a movie, a book, or a band, I will do everything I can to learn everything about it without ever asking myself if I actually care. But, there seems to be something dangerous or strange about asking that question." I asked for some detail and J said he didn't know.

I interpreted, "perhaps you are worried that if you turn your attention away from me, stop sacrificing for me, and value yourself instead, I might be hurt and upset and not want you anymore." J said, "That makes me think of how I wish I could just do something monumental to once and for all make my mother happy and content. Whatever that might be, I am ready to do it." I said, "Ready to sacrifice your life to save hers." J nodded. In the counter-transference, I thought that it was to save his mother but also to save or resurrect his dead brother. We went on to talk more about his drive for progress and what he called his "quest for knowledge" about whatever subject it might be and the "thirst for progress and achievement" without any real definition of what that might mean.

I interpreted, "you want to replace what we have with this grander, perfect vision. So, you attack what we are or what we have to reach this ideal and then you are left with a fragile image that goes up in smoke and leaves you empty and alone." J agreed and said he "wanted to change that." Again, in the counter-transference, I wondered if he was using us to play out a scenario in which mother so wanted the old dead son back that she didn't bother to see or relate to her new alive son.

A few sessions later, J came in and told me he wanted to start coming in more frequently. Up to now, we had been meeting once a week and he was on the analytic couch. I had suggested an increased frequency but because of his rather extreme financial situation, he declined. As a matter of fact, it wasn't that long ago that J was using food stamps as a supplement to his meager income. But, regarding paying for more sessions, J said he could "find a way to pinch a few pennies and make it happen because he was starting to see the benefits of therapy and wanted to have more of an opportunity to come in and find out more."

Given what we had been exploring prior, I interpreted that he might want to make another sacrifice for my love and was ready to do "whatever it took" to please me. I also interpreted that J might be seeing the increased frequency as a way to make the magical fast paced progress that he dreamed of to get to the mystical goal of perfection. J said, "You are right about how I am constantly seeking some form of perfection, whether in myself or others. But, in this case I don't think I am trying to do that or that I am trying to please you. Well, maybe some of that is mixed in but I feel like I really do want to be able to talk to you more often and try and figure myself out." So, we began meeting twice a week.

J's manic mission to become the best possible object for others so they might notice, desire, and admire him continued to surface along with the parallel fall from grace that was always looming. When projection is so intense and demands of the object are so constant, there is always a brittle and false quality to the patient's internal experience. J told me about how he had gone golfing with his girlfriend and group of coworkers and had been looking forward to it. But, upon arriving at the course, he started to wonder about how he would appear to those around him. At each hole on the course there were five areas of expertise that one could hit their ball from. Given he had only ever played golf five times in his life and he had a sore ankle from a work incident, J told me he knew he "should" be hitting from the second or third area.

But, he said, "I started thinking about it and realized how impressive and cool I would look and feel if I was hitting from the back tees, the fifth level. I thought I could pull it off and I started to feel really good as we made our way to the golf course. Then, I started to get nervous because I didn't want to mess up on those extreme tee boxes and look like a fool. So, then I thought I should probably just play from the second or third level which is about my skill level. As soon as I pictured that, I felt pulled into this crummy loser zone where I thought of myself as a complete failure and a laughing stock to all my friends. I thought I would never live it down. But, then I started to notice that this was the very pattern we had been talking about and working on. So, I tried to pull myself back and calm down. I went ahead and just played from the area that was appropriate for me. Those feelings of failure came up at times during the day, but overall I thought it went pretty good."

I interpreted, "You are worried that we will all forget you or even look down on you if you are just yourself, as-is, without dressing it up and making it special and extra." J agreed and added, "I want to feel special and know you see me that way. Otherwise, I think it is like you said, I feel I am a nothing, an empty vessel with a hollow middle."

As we proceeded in J's psychoanalytic treatment, it became clearer how much he wanted to be special to others and saw himself in an idealized form, providing perfect service to others. However, to do so or have the illusion of doing so, J had to be a piece of carbon paper, only existing to copy what others already have or if they have lost it he would replace it. He tried to take on whatever form the object seemed to want, need, or wish for. It was easy to see this when he tried to "wow" his girlfriend with all the special dinners or shows that he thought she would enjoy, hoping she would then see him as very special because he "knows" her well enough to be able to please her in every way.

It was also easy to see in the transference how he tried to engage me with deep and witty reflections that pulled me in and made me feel lucky to have such a motivated patient who could achieve such special insight. Over time, I began to notice how J tried to achieve this manic perfection or reparation cloaked as a gift in all his affairs. It turned out that J volunteered at a local homeless shelter where he would show up very early three days a week to help serve breakfast. Two of these days were during the week so he did the volunteer work before he went to his job. The third day was Saturday which meant he used up most of every Saturday serving breakfast and lunch and helping clean up the kitchen after both meals.

He told me "the little effort I make pays in great dividends. So many people are affected by my small efforts. It is a great opportunity to help." I also learned that J believed very strongly in the state sponsored organ donor program. He signed up to be listed as an organ donor on his driver's license. But, he went to the extra effort to contact the local government office and investigate if he could not just donate the usual organs but to insist that he be "harvested for everything and anything that could be used for someone in need."

J made such an effort to be this savior by literally giving of his flesh to save the other that I made the interpretation, "you make such a heroic effort to save someone else from death with your body that I wonder if on some level you are trying to save your dead brother and in the process save your mother from her terrible depression. You try and keep me alive by being interesting and wanting to find the magic cure right away. You try and keep your girlfriend smiling and alive with all your gifts and dinners. So, perhaps you are trying to make up for something with your brother and mother and the rest of us."

Here, in using the phrase "make up for something" I was wondering if J was trying to make some sort of manic restitution or reparation. J replied, "I really like doing something that provides more for you than for me. If I can give more than I receive I feel it was a job well done, a cost/reward ratio type of thing. As far as my mother and my brother, I think that must be part of it, even though I am not consciously aware of that. But, I think there must be something there where I am or have volunteered to be the replacement for my brother. That way, I can keep my mother's sanity intact and stop her from such terrible grieving. I think I may have elected to erase my identity in order to take on the needs of others in that situation and many other situations. I don't see anything wrong with it but as you have pointed out I am left with a hollow shell. I may be you now but I have lost me. But, if I can get what I want, so be it."

I said, "you are desperate to heal us all and make us ok. But, the way you just said "get what you want" also shows how powerful you are. It is a way you get what you want. Being the martyr, the rescuer, and the pleaser can be a secret power you have over others, finding a way to make sure we need you and we like you." J replied, "You say that in a way that makes me cringe but I think it is true. I want to be special and I want to make everyone ok so I do what it takes to make that happen."

I interpreted, "but when you can't pull that off, it looks like it is devastating. You end up feeling like you let me down and let me suffer. I am disappointed and you feel forgotten, like a rejected failure." J said, "That is the crash and burn cycle I want to manage or stop." Even though J genuinely wanted to change this pattern, it represented his lifelong defense against unbearable guilt, a sense of totally abandoning his objects, and a persecutory sense of being used and unimportant to the object. He relied on a pathological projective identification process to cope with the sense of being completely ignored and undervalued by his primary objects. He desperately tried to copy himself in their image or what he imagined they might desire. He jettisoned himself in order to make space inside himself to become their puppet, their first aid patch, and their golden surprise.

For awhile, J felt special and perfect, an ideal object of desire. But, he ended up envious of this version of himself (Lopez-Corvo 1994) because he could never partake in it fully as it was never real. He then felt resentful and attacked this ideal self, punching holes in this effigy. Now, he was left with a deflated and useless self and felt empty and scared. This was all part of a pathological organization (Steiner 1990) that he was reluctant to give up as it seemed to offer a meager and temporary respite from what felt like an eternal black hole of dying and disappointed objects that gave him no love, only grief. J's intense reliance on projective identification and the relentless conflicts he felt as a result created an ongoing breach in the wall of this psychic retreat so he only had a meager and temporary respite from the ravages of both paranoid and depressive anxieties (Waska 2006).

Melanie Klein established the important place envy has in normal and pathological development cycles. Kleinians have elaborated these findings and examined the role envy can have when directed at the good object that possesses the desired resources and is willing to share them. Kleinian theory has also examined how the ego can attack the bad object that seems to only want to amass, covet, and hoard the desired resources. Both good and bad objects can be experienced as showing great strength and confidence in their ownership of emotional resources and it is this power that is attacked (Wilson 2009).

J seemed to make intense use of splitting, projective identification, and idealization. He saw himself as either boring and unlovable, always in second place to others or he saw himself as a special, skilled, and unique individual able to quickly gain the favored eye of others if he catered to exactly what they wanted. He also saw others as ordinary and uninteresting, even plain and repulsive or as incredible and alluring but often "completely out of his reach." He would work hard at becoming whatever he thought the object desired and then felt able to capture the heart and mind of the object. But, at some point, he grew angry at having to maintain such a special posture and upset that the object would only love him for being false. So, sometimes this led to an attack on the object as too needy and demanding or as envy of this special impostor he had become, envious of the rewards this charlatan received when the other side of J, the as-is side, felt he could never be loved just for himself. So, he attacked himself and spoiled whatever gains he did make with the object but then he was left alone with the plain, unloved side of himself again and a sense of despair.

So, there had been several sessions where J came in feeling fantastic because he had felt he won my attention by providing me with what I wanted and needed. Through actual enactments with me or through his own phantasy distortion, I in return had seen him as special and interesting. But, there were other moments when he attacked himself out of envy, hating this easily won but false victory and/or attacked me for not providing him with immediate and precise answers and gifts of insight.

J came into a recent session and told me he was thinking of quitting. This was the week after we had discussed his idealization of the analytic process and his desire to come multiple times and "do whatever it took" to find the magical goal and transform his life overnight. He had wanted to "know everything" and was motivated to reach it "as soon as possible." We had examined this manic demand and magical phantasy of instant bliss where we both found the road to nirvana. In that last session, I had interpreted the pain of having to be in the here-and-now and face the slow and sometimes painful gains of learning about himself as-is.

After J announced in this session what sounded like very definite plans to stop his psychoanalytic treatment altogether and immediately, I asked J why he was so suddenly sure it would be right to end it all, especially after he felt so enthusiastic last week. I added that it might be that very enthusiasm that had him so spooked now. J said, "I want to stop because I don't have any exciting topics to bring in. There is nothing special I have to discuss and that makes me anxious. So, I think that stopping might be the answer. If I don't have anything to say, why be here?"

I felt J was being flippant and rejecting. I felt irritated by his comments but I also thought that he was probably feeling desperate without any "special" or "exciting" topics. So, I went with my impression of his core anxiety and interpreted that he was fearful of disappointing me and having nothing to offer me today. J replied, "I am worried about disappointing you and not doing it right." I interpreted that he has very rigid and strong expectations about how we need to be to get along and that he was projecting these onto me and seeing me as impatient and demanding.

J said he was anxious about "not knowing the full and complete arc of the treatment and not knowing exactly what our goals are." I interpreted that he was very uncomfortable being present in the moment with me as-is and it was easier to try and box in the entire course of treatment, check off the goals, and feel in control then to not know how we are doing right now in the moment. J replied, "I feel boring and flat without all that, no direction." I interpreted that he was anxious about me seeing him as mundane and regular instead of special and exciting. He said, "I do feel that. I dread that feeling. I never want to drift into that abbess of the regular and the painfully ordinary."

In the counter-transference, I began to think about J's constant struggle to be the "special beacon" and the "replacement part" for his parents during childhood. So, I interpreted that J may have felt he needed to be special for his mother after the death of his brother. With a great deal of affect, J replied, "I felt I had to be the answer to all their prayers! I had to be the fix for their dead son as well as their dying marriage. I was the glue that held their shitty marriage together! They were always fighting and never getting along. But, they had to stick it out for me. I tried to please them and run interference whenever I could. I was the glue. I was the answer to all their worst nightmares." I said, "You had to give up yourself to become the glue. That must have been a very powerful position for a child to have but one that also left you angry, lonely, and hollow."

J replied, "All of that! I had to be the replacement son for their dead son. That is horrible enough but I had to also be the new and golden reason for them to stay together. They hated each other so much that they would have gone their separate ways if they hadn't felt obligated to pay attention to me." I interpreted that he was trying to provide me, them, and his girlfriend with a special, exciting, healing experience. He had to be unique and then maybe we would all be ok. But, this leaves him angry because no one finds him special and wonderful as-is. He is loved for pretending or for providing, which creates a prize not so sweet.

J replied, "I never felt any love for either one of my parents. I know it sounds strange but I truly never had a moment growing up where I felt a moment of actual love for them. Instead, I only felt a profound deadness, all the time." I interpreted that he has such high expectations of what he needs to do to please his parents, his girlfriend, and now me that he must fear a crippling deadness in himself and in the object if he fails to sparkle us with his magic powers of pleasing. If there is no specialness, he will end up all alone with this overwhelming grief and deadness. Here, I was interpreting a massive and overwhelming anxiety that he was on the run from and trying to control with his manic powers of specialness and knowledge. J agreed and said, "I don't want to end up there."

After a moment, J went on to say, "My girlfriend said she wasn't thrilled with our trip to the golf course because it was so artificial and fake. She said it was atrocious to see all that artificial turf and a world of plastic pleasure as she put it. Now, I am scared because I want to go visit my friend down in Los Angeles and you know how everyone says LA is just a place of fake snobbery, artificial boobs, and pretentious attitudes. So, I am afraid she will judge me and not like what I am doing." I replied, "I think you are describing how trapped you feel, wanting to please but afraid someone is going to catch you being artificial and fake and then you will be rejected. But, you are afraid that you are not good enough just as-is without any props or extras added on.

J said, "I don't want to make her upset or spoil her view of me." I said, "It all sounds so fragile and hard to keep balanced. You are at work, on guard all the time." This fear of being rejected was a duplicate of the transference fear he had voiced at the start of the session. By the end of the session, we had worked through his need to take flight from his persecutory phantasy of failing to please me. We agreed to continue to meet twice a week.

When J came in several days later, he announced he was going to quit after that week was over. I asked him about this sudden action and apparent repeat of last week. He explained that he had spent the weekend toiling in the kitchen making an elaborate dinner for his girlfriend and making sure the house was immaculate. J said he had the idea that they would have a wonderful evening and spend the night talking about "all sorts of special things and really matching each other emotionally." Then, he would go over to her place and spend the night having sex.

When the actual evening was over and J drove her back to her place, she simply said thank you and good night, not offering to have him come in or to spend the night. J told me that when he returned home alone he felt so depressed he thought of killing himself. He said, "I have never felt that way before but I found myself in the kitchen looking at a sharp knife in the drawer and thinking it would be good to end all this suffering."

I said, "You felt so rejected and so disappointed after making all the efforts for dinner. I wonder if you expected her to notice and reciprocate and when she didn't you felt all that special packaging was wasted and unnoticed. You ended up alone and feeling she didn't care about you." J said, "Yes. I thought she would want to be with me and that the special dinner might be the start of something important in our connection." I said, "even though she is pretty upfront about only wanting to be your friend and occasional sex buddy, you continue to see if you can convert her with your special efforts. But, when she remains consistently your friend, you feel like you failed and like she doesn't care about you." J said, "I see what you mean. I do set myself up that way."

J told me that the next day he went over to a friend of his who advised him to drop his girlfriend and "to realize that he is a talented and creative individual who doesn't need to be hemmed in by such petty drama." His friend told him that he should continue to strive for the best in life and not let anyone get in the way. So, afterwards, J wrote a "breakup letter" to her and explained how since she didn't want to have a special relationship with him he felt it was time to break up and move on. I interpreted that he was disappointed with me and his girlfriend for seeming to get in the way of his pursuit for immediate knowledge, joy, and perfection and that he was delivering a breakup letter to me during the session. I said he must feel I was disappointing him. J said, "Well, I feel you are taking away the special qualities I have and I will end up mundane and ordinary. I don't want that. I feel that my natural sensitivity and my desire for heightened emotional experiences are valid so the right choice was to break up with her." I said that he must see me and her as the source of the problem and now he wanted to break up with us, since we are taking that special aspect of him away.

Segal (1993) has written about the life instinct being the thrust for growth and change, the acceptance of dependency, and the tolerance of need. Likewise, Segal explains how the death instinct is demonstrated clinically by the drive to attack and eliminate need, dependency, and difference, thus crushing change, growth, or creativity.

For J, he so wanted to be special and to be able to draw others to him with unique and dazzling power that he felt I and the girlfriend were a threat if we didn't immediately respond or if we treated him as a regular man with regular attributes. To be simply himself, as-is, was a path to neglect, rejection, and boring regularity. So, he envied the split off magical and special image of himself that could attract others with these imagined powers. J dreaded being stuck at this ordinary mortal place of probable loneliness and pain. This is why he tried to kill off his none idealized, regular, as-is identity and wanted to kill off myself and his girlfriend because we wanted to relate to him as a regular man with non-magical powers. He did not want to risk depending on us or needing us in any way.

At the same time, when J felt back in the driver's seat of this manic quest for attention, he hated that he had to become this golden boy forced to make everyone happy, to save his parents, and to essentially beg for love by being a replacement and a hardworking servant. So, this also led him to attack himself and others for being involved in this cruel opera of love, loss, and grief. J used the death instinct to kill off the ordinary, the dependent, and the flawed aspects of himself and others, in order to maintain and worship the special, artistic side of himself that could control the love and attention of others. Now, he could proclaim he was self-sufficient and didn't need his girlfriend or the analysis.

In the counter-transference, I felt frustrated and rejected and dreaded this next and possibly last session. However, I also realized I needed to stand firm in my conviction that our union in the ordinary was worth fighting for, that our work together, as-is, was more valuable than the dark world of best and worst that he existed in, being dragged between idealization, persecution, and devastating loss.

When he arrived for the next session, J lay down and said he was embarrassed at "what a regression had happened" and how I "must think he really slipped backwards." Here, I heard him as worried about my disappointment in him at not being the servant or patient of my desires, that he was letting me down and leaving me sad and upset. Since he normally dealt with this anxiety by trying to be special and unique and demanding that others respond in kind, I interpreted he was angry with the girl and myself for not granting him immediate special love and value, so he threw us away and saw us as the problem. He felt that if he got rid of us he could go back to being a special and talented individual and pursue his happiness. I said he must feel we really slow him down and bring him face to face with what seems like a very foreign and lonely place, his own self as-is. So, here I had interpreted his anxieties, his conflicts, and his defenses all in the context of the transference and of his overall internal phantasy world.

Responding to my comment about his fear of coming face-to-face with himself, as-is, and not the idealized extra shiny version he strives for, J said he "didn't know if he even has a self." He said, "If I strip away all that other stuff and take away what I think others need from me and how I can grab their attention, I don't know if there is really anything that makes me up at all." I interpreted that he is usually so busy trying to take in what others say as a request and then trying to find a way to please us that he is empty inside. J replied, "I tried so hard to please you yesterday and then I got confused with what I probably want so I didn't know what to do or say. Sometimes, I say something to you or agree with what you say and I can't tell if I honestly am expressing my opinion or if I am simply trying to agree with you to avoid any conflict."

Here, he was bringing up the internal fallout of his extreme reliance on projective identification. With patients such as J, they can rely so heavily on relating from an as-if perspective, always keeping themselves empty so as to take in whatever the object may seem to need or demand, that they truly do not have any idea of their own opinion, thought, or feeling. Other times, they may indeed have their own sense of self but severely curtail, censor, and camouflage it in order to cater to the object and protect self or other.

For J, at this point in his treatment, he did not seem to have much capacity to cultivate his own sense of self and when he did manage to find something that resembled his own thought or feeling, he was genuinely unsure if that thought was his own, had been put there by the object, or had been manufactured by him to please the object.

This is an extremely difficult technical situation that makes interpretation very slow going and prone to perversion. It is especially vital to play close attention to the counter-transference in such moments. But, even then, the analyst can feel just as confused or even desperate due to the violent and controlling nature of the patient's projective identification mechanisms. So, when J told me he wasn't sure if what he was saying was really his idea or that he was simply saying something I would enjoy, I too could not tell which was which, what was what, and who was who. We spend some time exploring how when he actually agrees with something I say he genuinely doesn't know if he means it or if he is just complying with something I said. I interpreted, "You have lost yourself trying to be exactly what I need or want. You want to be my glue and a perfect gift to me so I might notice you and see you as special and unique. But, this means you have to destroy the as-is you to be my puppet."

In response, J associated to his childhood. He said, "There was so many times I wanted to tell my parents to stop ignoring me and to be parents instead of neglectful, narcissistic shitheads. There were so many times I just wanted to scream at them to shut the fuck up and stop arguing with each other! I was so sick of having to listen to their fighting and have my life be all about their failed marriage. But, I never said a thing. Nothing. I stayed silent and just mouthed what they needed and went about my day."

I said, "That must have been so painful, lonely, and devastating. And, like you said, you were furious at them for making it be about them and never about you. We have to stop for today but this is why I think we need to meet more often. We need a chance to find you and find your voice." J agreed to continue meeting twice a week. In the few minutes remaining in that session, I interpreted that there is something important about how he wants more from me and asks to meet more often, then quickly rejects me and wants to quit altogether, and then goes back and forth yet again. I interpreted the parallel between the love letters and breakup letters that he sends to his girlfriend and his hot and cold feelings for me. In an insightful moment, J associated to how he "may be finally having the arguments and the fuck yous" with me that he has always wanted to have with parents but never did.

DISCUSSION

Starting with the work of Bion (1962) and continuing in the clinical efforts of many contemporary Kleinians, containment has been a key element in assisting all patients but especially so with the more disturbed. Clinical research has demonstrated how the harder to reach patient lacks their own sense of internal psychic containment due to early infantile conflicts between self and object and therefore tends to move into, envy, attack, or ruthlessly take over the object's own containment abilities. Melanie Klein and her current followers such as Britton (1998) have elaborated on the fundamental psychological importance of knowledge and the impact of self-object conflict regarding knowing and being understood.

Often, containment and conflicts regarding knowledge intersect in either healing or destructive ways. Steiner (2004) notes how the developing ego turns to the object to be emotionally held and understood. This desire includes being paid attention to and accepted for both good attributes and flaws of character. The ego feels loves as-is and without need for immediate reciprocal repayment.

J never felt his objects had the time, capacity, or desire to contain his developmental struggles let alone provide critical self-knowledge to him through their understanding. He never felt known as a separate and unique individual. Indeed, J felt his mother and father needed to use him as an emotional garbage container for their psychological debris. As an adult, J now tried to jettison his less than ideal feelings and thoughts since he felt unable to contain, accept, and understand them and certainly didn't believe there was someone else who could or would. In order to become a perfect attraction to others, he had to void himself. He evacuated himself into a hollow, empty shell without knowledge or containment which left him always feeling near collapse and without any sense of self-security, identity, or self love. And, his projections left the object looking like a disappointing, mundane, yet demanding foe.

The extreme demands J felt from his parents were internalized and now he commanded so much immediate reassurance, healing, and love from the object that no one could live up to his requirements, leaving him feeling validated regarding the desperate, lonely, and combative nature of the world. He tried to magically heal and restore this nightmare existence by grandiose gestures of empathy, charity, and volunteering but this only made him envious of that false self he constructed and resentful he wasn't rewarded more for all the effort and his as-is self was envious of the seeming success of the as-if self.

It was either bliss or despair for J. And, these states of mind fueled his existing anxiety so much that when he demanded instant love, instant insight, or immediate cure from me or from himself, he was unable to stop and allow the space to see what we had already accomplished and the space for future understanding, trust, and learning. He was so much in a rush to reach "the goal" that he could never find the map to that goal, reflect for a moment if that goal was truly what he wanted or needed, or even consider if that goal was actually his or if it was what he envisioned for his object.

In the counter-transference, I had to tolerate being a container who was constantly assaulted by fake and seductive praise which often ensnared me to join him in a manic search for the ultimate source of knowledge and happiness. Next, he tried to fill me as container with demanding devaluation, hopelessness, and obsessive ranting about every detail of the to and fro he had emotionally. I had to constantly find my analytic balance to avoid becoming a compliant container that merely accepted what he offered without ever being curious or challenging. The moments in which I lost my analytic balance were times I became a manipulated, controlled, and overly saturated container without much of a personal identity. I was simply an echo for J, sustaining his pathological view of self and object (Steiner 2000) and now existing as he had in childhood while he took the place of his demanding, broken, and self absorbed parental objects. In those slippery counter-transference moments (Waska 2010a), I was in danger of simply validating the pathological object relational experiences that made up his psychic retreat (Steiner 1993).

As I write this report, J is still engaged in his psychoanalytic treatment at the rate of twice a week on the couch. I call it a psychoanalytic process because of the mode in which I am tending to his internal processes. Much of the work done today by psychoanalysts involves once a week meetings with fairly disturbed individuals unable or unwilling to meet more often for a variety of external and internal reasons. However, a meaningful psychoanalytic treatment can still be conducted provided the analyst attempts to establish Analytic Contact (Waska 2007) throughout the procedure. Analytic contact consists of the analyst always striving to understand and interpret the patient's transference, unconscious phantasies, and internal conflicts. All aspects of the treatment setting and the therapeutic relationship are considered part of the transference/counter-transference matrix. The total transference (Joseph 1985) situation and the complete counter-transference climate (Waska 2010b) are the guiding instruments of the process. When meeting infrequently with patients who demand quick relief to their symptom profile, the analyst may feel pulled into various enactments and into focusing on interactions rather than psychic exploration. Therefore, it is even more crucial to maintain a close focus on the essential elements of the psychoanalytic process and interpret the unconscious dynamics occurring whenever possible.

Oremland (1995) notes how the essential difference between a psychotherapy process and a psychoanalytic process is if the therapist utilizes prescriptive interactions as the mode of intervention or if he uses the technique of interpretation. The first approach is used to overcome, ignore, or manipulate the transference and the second is used to explore, understand, and transform the transference by working through the basic internal conflicts that fuel it. With patients operating more in the paranoid-schizoid position (Klein 1946) or the more unstable or brittle depressive position patients (Klein 1935, 1940), there is often a counter-transference pull to manipulate the transference within the course of various enactments that tend to emerge. But, the primary task of the analyst is to constantly retrace their footing back to the understanding and interpretation of the underlying transference and projective identification process.

Just as we aim to therapeutically help our patients bear their experiences of unbearable guilt (Safan-Gerard 1998), we also strive to help our patients tolerate, bear, examine, and own their intense persecutory anxieties. With J, I used the vehicle of containment and interpretation to consistently offer him my understanding of these phantasies and in doing so, I consistently offered him my hope and belief that there is something beyond these terrible feelings that is soothing and gratifying to both self and object. To do so, I had to show him that I survived his persecutory, envious attacks of control and seduction. I had to show him that I didn't want him to restore me, to feed me, or to sacrifice himself for me. He needed to know I wouldn't retaliate and that I could love him as-is instead of wanting him to distort, starve, or inflate himself for my benefit. By our work in the therapeutic relationship, by working through the transference and his intense use of projective identification, his devotion to the as-if lifestyle could recede and he could test the waters of just being himself, as-is.

Chapter Two

Low-Frequency Psychoanalytic Engagement with a Depressive Patient: The Beginning Phase of Treatment from a Kleinian Approach

Hinshelwood (2004) notes the three key elements of current Kleinian technique to be interpretive interventions aimed at modifying the source and nature of the patient's anxiety, an understanding of the inevitable enactments that emerge as projective identification based transference states infect and shape the analyst's counter-transference, and the effort between patient and analyst to jointly discover and create new knowledge about the patient's internal world and thus promote new ways of thinking and feeling. Of course, the more disturbed patient will react to knowledge and change as something dangerous to either self or other (Waska 2006) and show corresponding transference styles of perverse relating or destructive non-relating.

CASE MATERIAL

I began meeting with K once a week, sitting up, because that was all she would tolerate emotionally and all she could afford financially. Actually, when I suggested to K that she come in more often, she initially worried I must see her as "terribly sick and broken, like someone with a mental problem." But, over time, she did want to attend more but was so in debt that even coming in once a week was money out of her food budget.

K came to see me to "try and change her patterns of feeling uncomfortable around people" and find a solution to her longtime uncertainty about her relationship with her boyfriend. K was thirty-five years old and lived alone but had been dating her boyfriend for almost two years. He told her he wanted to bring the relationship "to the next level and move in together." K told me she realized this made sense, but it scared her and she "didn't want to have to share her space with him."

As we began the psychoanalytic treatment process, K told me she is able to interact with others quite well and is respected in her job and by friends, but she is never truly at ease with anyone and always looks forward to the time when she can be alone and relax. She described how she has to be "on alert and on guard" and can "never really be herself or be 100% relaxed." She said, "I love the time when I get home and can feel completely safe, surrounded by my own things, and have things be exactly the way I want them." The way K told me this conveyed how controlled she felt by others and that "it was a hassle to be 'on' all day" so she enjoyed coming home to no longer having to cater to or be on guard against others.

Here, in the counter-transference, my sense was K was struggling with something depressive but quite primitive. But, there seemed to be a persecutory anxiety of some sort as well. Overall, it seemed she felt very burdened by a harsh depressive obligation to be there for others and this phantasy state eventually slipped more into a paranoid enslavement that she looked forward to escaping from every day by being by herself at home in a very controlled environment.

When I made this interpretation regarding burden and judgment, K said, "Yes. When I get home, I don't have to worry about what I am doing, how people see me, or how I am affecting others. I am off the clock and I can be in my own world where everything is exactly like I like it." So, she seemed to confirm my idea of this fragmented mixture of paranoid-schizoid (Klein 1946) and depressive anxieties (Klein 1935, 1940).

I asked K to tell me about this special private world where she could escape and finally relax. K said, "I just love being by myself in the environment I created. All my stuff is where I put it and I know it will be in that spot next time I look for it. And, I don't have anyone watching me or wondering what I am doing. I can have things exactly like I want them. And, you will think I am a freak maybe, but I like things very organized and just so. I have my pillows in one place, I keep my bed made in a certain way, and I know how many times I have used my towels so I know when to wash them."

In my counter-transference associations, much like a dream state, I began having a mental image of a stark white, pristine personal fortress in which K felt safe and protected from the pressures and chaos of the world, a place where she felt in charge and in control but in a very rigid and probably very brittle way. I thought this was a counter-transference image that emerged from her projective identification based transference (Waska 2010c) in which she was communicating with me by providing a non-verbal experience of what she held so important and critical in her life.

I made this interpretation and she responded, "Yes. I want to feel safe and protected and I can't do that if someone else is there." I asked her if sitting with me felt unsafe. K said she felt nervous and wondered what I was thinking of her. I asked her what came to mind. She said she didn't want me to be confused but she thought she was "talking all over the place and not making too much sense." I said, "You are worried you leave me confused and burdened by your problems?" K said, "I hope not. I want you to help me but I don't even know where to start."

Here, I was interpreting the way K pictured my mind becoming burdened and pulled apart by her sharing and by her vulnerability. She was worried I was feeling like she felt most of the time.

Helping her organize her mind and perhaps showing her I was resilient and able to accept and contain whatever she may have for me, I asked her what the strongest thing on her mind was at that moment. K told me she was upset with "not being able to figure out my relationship with my boyfriend. I know I love him but there is a lot I don't love about him. He is not had a job for a year, after he was laid off from a local computer company. So, he can barely pay his bills and now has credit card debt. If we move in together, I would have to believe he would make the effort to find a job and be able to help with the bills. I don't trust that. Also, and even worse, I can't picture sleeping with him every night."

I said, "You mean sexually?" K said, "Oh no. The sex is fine. I mean I don't like to share my bed with him. First of all, I worry that he is dirty and will bring dirt or crumbs into my bed. You will probably think I am pretty strange but my bed is my sanctuary. My apartment is my special place away from everyone. People are a constant pressure and bother to me. It is a huge relief at the end of the day when I can finally leave behind the bother of having to interact with people, always being on alert or paying attention to what they want, what they say, what they mean, and what they do. And, then in my special hideaway, my bed is the ultimate safety zone where I can feel truly ok and all by myself. But, I have a whole bunch of special rituals or rules about my bed." When her boyfriend sleeps over, K insists he always bathe before getting into her bed because otherwise K "lays awake all night just imagining how he was getting everything so dirty and filthy."

Of course, the bed itself had to have clean sheets and be nicely arranged. K told me she could never leave her apartment if she knew the bed was unmade. Once she was ready to get into bed, K had "special pajamas for sleeping and special socks that fit very tightly." She went on to tell me how important it was for her to "have tightly fitting clothes but especially her socks and pajamas so that she could feel secure and tightly held in."

This is an interesting phenomenon that I have encountered over the years with other patients who were mostly in the borderline or psychotic realm. They needed a concrete body container to prevent them from literally feeling fragmented, leaking, or about to explode.

Therefore, I interpreted that K might be anxious of falling apart and not having anyone or anything to provide her with a sense of being grounded emotionally and physically. I said that she may have no secure sense of emotional and physical boundaries. K said that "might be the case" but added that she remembered always needing that "sense of security" from tight clothing from when she was very young.

Finally, K had a special pair of slippers that she used if she had to get out of bed for a drink of water or to go to the bathroom. These had to be kept on her bedside table so they would not get dirty or be used for any reason other than the quick trip from the bed and back.

From the way K talked about her bed, the importance of it, and the rituals that surrounded it, I felt like she was floating on a little island, trying not to fall into the unknown depths of a dangerous sea. I also envisioned her wrapping herself with all these protective layers and climbing into an embryo-like space capsule, ready for a frightening, endless journey into the great uncharted universe. Finally, I felt there was something sexual yet sad and scary that was being conveyed to me, an invitation to climb into bed with her as she went on about taking a shower, putting on her pajamas, folding back the sheets, and pulling her socks on oh so tight. I also felt I was witnessing the tale of a scared child hiding from something that seemed invasive or abusive, something very dirty that she was trying to avoid.

All of this counter-transference pondering was similar to what Ogden (1996) discusses as reverie but I view it more as the internal counter-transference play (Caper 1996) which emerges as a result of the projective identification cycles so typical with more troubled patients. The leading edge of my internal imagery was the idea of a helpless little girl desperately trying to control her little boat as it floated through such perilous waters. I imagined she had such a death grip on the rudder that the boat was simply going in circles, creating a greater and greater panic.

So, I thought that K's obsessive rules and rituals and her attempt at defense and protection were so full of control and demand that the level of freedom and security she sought was spoiled by the aggressive nature of how things "must be at all times." So, she was a prisoner of that security. The counter-transference play is an aspect of the complete counter-transference (Waska 2010d) which parallels the total transference situation (Joseph 1985). Psychoanalysis is defined by the consistent exploration and working through of these two pivotal aspects of the treatment process, leading to interpretations of phantasy and conflicts regarding internal objects and particular views of the self.

When I interpreted this death grip K had on herself and others, she said she thought "it was interesting" and she "could see how true it was when she thought of how many pieces of the puzzle she has to go through to maintain the safe zone and how easily it can get messed up by her dog jumping up on the bed, her forgetting to put on the right socks, or her forgetting to leave the bed with her special bed slippers." So, we started to explore this way of organizing her anxieties and conflicts but she also was clearly wedded to the rituals in a very concrete manner which didn't allow her to dig too deep into their meaning just yet.

I asked her how this need for control impacted her sleeping with her boyfriend. K explained that she "hated it when someone else was in the bed because she didn't feel free to move around. She thought she could easily wake them up since she tends to thrash around a lot and take a long time to fall asleep. So, she has to force herself to stay really, really quiet and not make a sound, and not disturb them." I interpreted that she sounded very worried about waking the other person and the consequences of that. K told me she thought the other person might become angry. I asked her more about this fear. She said that "sometimes she has woken up her boyfriend and he has been irritated with her." I said, "It sounds like you worry it could get worse so you better not push the envelope." K told me, "I sometimes wonder if he might just get so fed up with me that he would leave. That is my biggest fear of all, that I will be abandoned. I know it sounds extreme or strange but that is the worst thing that could ever happen." I said, "So you do whatever it takes to prevent that." She nodded yes.

This fear of being left was something K said affected her as long as she could remember. But, what was interesting was that she recalled it in terms of losing her precious house that the family lived in. When things were rough with her parents and it looked like they might split up, K would panic and dread losing her bedroom and all the things she had in it as well as the comfort of the home as she knew it. This was similar to when she told me that one of the principal reasons she would never want to move out into a bigger apartment with her boyfriend, apart from having to give up her sacred solitude, was that she would have to give up the view from her living room. She thought it was the best view of downtown possible and made her feel relaxed and happy. K could not envision finding a place with a view just as good or even better. She had found the one that worked for her and she was going to do whatever it took to not lose it.

When K began describing her experiences growing up, I came to wonder if she had created an alternative good parent object in the image of her room to which she could attach and feel secure. This was in response to the more insecure, confusing, and hurtful attachment she had with her parents. Also, there seemed to be a third object created in her mind, usually a concrete object like her bed or the view from her living room, that she felt was a better or safer object to be with than the parent, boyfriend, coworker, or friend that was in her life at the moment.

K told me that her mother was an "angry, unpredictable, and critical woman who made life feel like the edge of a cliff." She went on to describe how her mother constantly picked on and yelled at her father, faulting him for everything. He was "a passive and reserved man" who retreated from the verbal abuse into a bottle. He was an alcoholic who came home "every day and closed the door to the garage where he drank himself silly listening to the radio. I knew I couldn't go in there since he was drunk and so I was left to be with my mother and her tirades." K said that her mother would sometimes be nice and attentive with her but "would withdraw her love and put anger and judgment in its place in a second flat." I said I thought this might be related to her fears of being abandoned. She immediately nodded in the affirmative.

When K described her father's alcoholism in greater detail, I noticed a very interesting and eerie theme. K told me that her bedroom was down the hall from her parents, and that almost every night her father would emerge from his bedroom in a blacked out state of drunkenness and begin wondering down the hallway. K said she could easily see down the hall from where her bed was and always "wondered what he was doing."

Both as a child and now as an adult, K thought of him with a great deal of pity and sorrow, feeling he was "such a sad man, always beat down by mom and never happy. He was always alone and trying to escape her anger by drinking. I feel so bad for him. I feel very sad for him and terrible that he was trapped in his life that way. He seemed so small, broken, and unhappy. I feel very bad for him."

However, the main feeling K had each night as a child when her father emerged in his drunken state was one of curiosity, alert, and a difficult to describe state of "what is he doing??" She would watch him stumble down the hallway and on more than one occasion, he made his way into her room and "ended up curled up on the rug and went to sleep. I just ended up staring at him sleeping on the floor, feeling sorry for him. But, most of the time, I just tried to figure out what was he doing as he stumbled around the house." In the counter-transference, I felt this all to be erotic and suggestive of a possible history of molest or at least some type of emotional boundary crossing that was erotic or perverse in nature. On the other hand, I also wondered if this was her memory of a confusing time when she developed her own set of erotic or perverse phantasies that were not the result of any external abuse but now remained as memories of pity and curiosity. I asked her about these matters and K insisted that there was never any sexual abuse and that she would "never have wanted her father in her bed or even close to her when he was drunk like that. But, he seemed more like a strange lost man trying to make his way around the house in this strange way every night." I also interpreted that her current need to have her bed be an island of safety and solitude seemed to be a repeat of how she sat in her bed as a child wondering what all the strange, scary, and sad situations around her were and how to cope with them. She said that might be but also simply felt "my bed and how I am with it is very important to me and makes me feel good."

This "wanting to know what was going on" was not only a strong element in her memory. While sounding very much like an Oedipal desire to find out what was going on in the parental couple's bedroom, my impression was that it was a more primitive or perverted persecutory quest for knowledge, an attempt to know what the immediate status of the object was, its intent, and the possible consequences to her of those intentions. An example of what I mean emerged when K told me about why she did not want to use the analytic couch. I had recommended that she use it and she said she "could never do that. I would never feel comfortable. I wouldn't know what you are doing. You could be watching me or you could go to sleep and not pay attention. I would never know. I guess the worst part is that you would be watching me. I don't want that to happen."

So, here there was an indication that K's desire for control over knowledge was a defensive effort to not be watched. It seemed a persecutory phantasy in which I would be watching her in an invasive manner and she would be helpless and at my mercy, without the magic control of her bed or any other way to protect herself. I made this interpretation and she told me, "I would feel like you are judging me and making faces. I think you might start thinking things about me and I would never know." I said, "So, by sitting up you can keep an eye on me and make sure I am not judging you or abandoning you by being bored?" She agreed and told me, "I don't want to cause any trouble either and if I can see your face I can tell if you are getting upset." I said, "How might you upset me?" K told me, "If I forget to give you the money for the session, if I am late, if I say the wrong thing, or a dozen of other ways."

I said, "So, you have quickly decided I am someone you have to be careful with and please, in order to avoid any conflict and me getting offended, angry, and tossing you out. I would abandon you." K said, "Yes. I want to make sure to never let that happen." I said, "You don't want me to become like your mother, hot and cold and able to make you feel very lonely and rejected." She said, "Yes. My last therapist asked me why I wasn't angry with my father. Well, I just felt sorry for him, he seemed so beat down by my mother. But, she was the one to avoid, to watch out for."

When K spoke about her father and feeling sorry for him, I felt K was feeling somewhat guilty as well. She also appeared guilty when she arrived late for a couple of her sessions and when she had to reschedule one of them. I asked her about this and she told me she did "feel guilty and didn't want to hurt me. That she imagined if she hurt my feelings I would be angry and then I would not want to see her or I would keep seeing her but in the back of my mind I would think of her in a bad way." This was something K "really wanted to avoid, no matter what." I interpreted that she tried to please me and care for me to avoid these conflicts and threats and that perhaps she wanted to care for me and her father in the way she wanted to be taken care of.

Also, I interpreted that she wanted her father to care for her and love her but he seemed incapable of it so she would have to nurse him and love him like she wished she was loved and cared for. But, there was also this element of mother entering the room and becoming enraged. So, it became very confused, risky, and out of control. She had to try and control it all in every way. K told me, "I think you may be right. Especially the part of how I want to care for people but I never feel cared for. And then you are right again. I want that but I am scared that if I let them care for me, I will only end up disappointed or hurt. So, why bother? People are just a bother and I would always rather be alone, safely tucked in my bed with my world just as I want."

Another way K's feelings of guilt and persecutory anxiety emerged was in the transference when she had to reschedule one visit due to a work obligation. I offered her a late night time and she immediately reacted with discomfort. I asked her what was wrong. She said that she was sure I would be so "burnt out and tired that I would not care about her, ignore what she talked about, and might even fall asleep." I added, "given what you have said before, I think you are also worried I would be angry with you for keeping me up so late and I would maybe want to throw you out, abandon you." K said, "I couldn't have said it better."

Now, I believe this was an accurate line of exploration and we discussed this more at length with good result. But, I also had the same counter-transference feeling as before that there was something erotic, in a persecutory way, about her anxieties. So, I said, "are you uncomfortable meeting me here alone, just you and me late at night like there could be something improper or sexual about it?" K said, "Oh, no. Not at all. I trust you and think you are on the up and up. It is just so late I don't think you would be happy to see me. I go to bed early so I guess I assume you want to, too." Here, again I felt there was both something very childlike and withdrawn about her comment but also something that felt flirty and seductive. So, I was viewing her as operating from a primitive hysterical position, unable to function in the more mature depressive aspect of the oedipal phase (Britton 1989, 1991). She had identified with her father in an invasive manner, feeling the world is invading and judging so she needed to keep herself isolated, not with alcohol but with obsessional control and ritual isolation. She also became the caretaker for father in her mind, able to take over and care for him since he wasn't able or willing to care for her. She denied any anger toward him and projected it outward. She felt a bond with non-human sites, such as her apartment or bed, all symbolic for the parent or lover she wished for but felt unable to connect with without the risk of being abandoned.

Finally, it seemed she fused mother and father in her mind and felt guilty and sorry for her objects but then felt they could easily become angry, rejecting, and out of her control. So, there was a constant undercurrent of sexuality in the room, but it was overshadowed by these other more persecutory and pre-depressive states. At the same time, her foothold in the depressive zone was shaped by more manic phantasies of denial, obsessional control, and magical thinking regarding how to keep the goodness and keep away the badness.

Just as K worried that if she let her boyfriend sleep with her, she could irritate him with all her moving around, wake him up, and make him angry, she worried I would be put off by her fidgeting in the chair. K was obviously quite anxious most of the time and this resulted in her nervously moving about in her chair during most of the session. At one point, she kept looking at me in a concerned way and I asked her what was wrong. She told me "you probably are wondering why I keep moving around, maybe you think I have to go to the bathroom or something. Or, you are just irritated that I won't sit still." I said, "You sound like a little girl who is worried your parent is angry that you won't stop squirming around and sit still. You are having a hard time trusting that I am ok being with you and could accept you for how you are and how you feel without attacking you." K said, "Yes. I am always on alert that way. And, the more I think about how you are critical of me moving around the more I get nervous and end up moving around. I always think people are thinking something about me. That is why I like to get home as soon as possible after work and just be alone. It is so draining to be with others. I feel so much more comfortable by myself. I don't have to worry about if I am doing something wrong or if someone is going to want something from me."

I said, "ever since you started focusing on yourself instead of me and talking and sharing your feelings with me instead of standing guard and monitoring me, you are suddenly not moving around in your chair as much. You seem more at ease with yourself, instead of without yourself."

In talking about her life and her overall goals and dreams, K told me she really wanted to be married and have a family. She said she loves children and wants the warm and happiness "that some people obviously have in a family." But, she said she feels very much in a stalemate debate with herself because of what she pictures she would have to give up. K told me that her privacy is the number one priority. "When someone is over, I am always thinking, what are they doing? If I am in another room and hear them walking around or doing something, I am unable to think of anything else until I can figure out what they are doing!"

In trying to understand this more, it came out that what K meant is that she is mostly worried that they will be "disorganizing, messing up, or getting dirt on something that she has carefully managed to put in a way that she is happy with and knows about." So, if they are making noise in the kitchen, they could be getting the counter dirty, they could be eating the last portion of some food that she carefully set aside for herself, or they could be creating chaos in the neatly organized pantry. This sudden messy invasion, this lack of visual and mental control, and this anxious vision of someone operating with a separate and unknown agenda that will impact K in some terrible way is at the root of the transference, at the base of her phantasy world, and the central theme of our ongoing analytic exploration now in its third month. These elements seemed to be part of a primitive oedipal and pre-oedipal conflict in which she had to know what the other person was doing with their object, their actions, or their thoughts. In other words, what the person was doing with the kitchen, separate from K, what food the person was stealing away from K to have to their own, and what I might be doing privately with my own thoughts (Rusbridger 2004) about K, separate from her knowledge and control of me and my mind, all felt like a persecutory exclusion that made up a constant primitive depressive storm of pre-oedipal and oedipal phantasies.

Examples of some of these very complicated, fragile, and primitive anxieties and phantasies emerged during a recent session. K had left me a phone message saying she wanted to continue coming twice a week but could no longer afford it. She was in debt already and saw no way out anytime soon. So, even coming in once a week put her further into debt but she wanted to keep attending. When she arrived for the session, she asked me if I had received the message and apologized for not being able to continue at twice a week. She went on to explain some of the details of how bad her finances were and how she has "never been in this place before." Listening to the details of her plight, in the counter-transference I was left thinking of how frightening and hopeless this seemed. But, I was then aware of how K did not show any sign of distress. She was simply informing me of the facts.

K went on to say how "tough things have been lately with her boyfriend and how he hasn't worked for over a year and only with her complaining about it has he finally started to look for a job." She went on to say how when "she adds everything up and sees how he is, how his finances are, and how he wants kids right away, there is no way she can envision a future with him." K then said things "took an upturn after we talked over the weekend and we had a good time hanging out." Again, I noticed how much I, in the counter-transference, felt hopeless and depressed over her plight, now both financially and romantically. But, K really hadn't shown much affect at all about either one of these overwhelming situations in her life.

Now, she shifted to another topic. K told me she "knows I have an OCD problem and over the years some of my friends have pointed it out because it is so obvious. But, in the last few months, one aspect of it has really gotten much worse." I asked for details and K told me that when she leaves her apartment, she has always had to double and triple check the locks. K said, "I know I have an OCD problem with all the other stuff but this is the one thing where I actually have to repeat it over and over, like a ritual or counting or something. So, it used to be a couple of re-checks each time but now it is completely out of control. I stand there for five or ten minutes checking the door over and over and over again." I said, "You must be very scared that you will leave and have it be open." She told me how she has countless scenarios of various people, the mailman, the landlord, the neighbors, and so forth who might discover it being unlocked and enter her place and "mess it up." She asked me if I had any tips or advise on what to do about her "door problem."

K reiterated that the door was the only thing she ever double checks. I interpreted, "In fact, there are other ways you double check. I think you felt guilty and worried about my reaction when you called to tell me about cutting down our sessions. That made you want to double check by asking me if I received the message. You wanted to know if I was ok with it or if I was hurt or angry with you." K said, "I am worried about that. I am so broke that I can't do it but I don't want to stop. I should stop completely given my debt but I don't want to." I said, "Maybe you want me to know you are not just carelessly throwing me away, but that you care about our work together. You double checked to make sure I didn't take it personal." She said, "I do that all the time I think. I find myself saying sorry for no reason to everyone. I constantly think about what people might be thinking about my actions or what I say."

I interpreted, "I noticed that you said a lot about how terrible your finances are but you didn't show very much feeling at all about it. Then, you told me of how bad things have gotten with your boyfriend, but with not much feeling attached to it. Then, you told me about the sudden increase in checking your door and you have a lot of feelings about that. I wonder about how you neutralize your worries with money and your worries about your boyfriend to save yourself from facing and sharing the intense feelings you have. But, then all those feelings are threatening to kick down your emotional door. I wonder if you end up feeling so invaded and threatened by those feelings but instead of knowing how to work with them emotionally, you end up feeling like it is a very concrete worry, the door, checking the lock, and having someone break in and mess everything up. But, now, we are here and I am possibly the threat. I am coming through your door of perfectly organized, controlled feelings and may mess it all up?" K said, "I see what you mean. I normally try my best to deny or ignore anything that feels negative, scary, or overwhelming, especially if I don't think I will be able to do anything about it."

So, here I was interpreting the projective identification and splitting in which K tried to separate herself from the difficult feelings she was having with money and romance and the underlying anxieties that were triggered by these problems. By trying to attack the symbolic and the emotional she created a concrete and external threat embodied by the door and the invasion from outside. Indeed, by trying to escape the anxieties of the depressive realm, K ended up trying to cope with the anxieties of the paranoid-schizoid realm.

In responding to my interpretations, K associated to her childhood and told me, "When I was growing up, I always wanted to stop all the pain my father was going through." I asked if she meant his daily drunkenness. K said, "No. What I remember wasn't so much about his drinking. I think I was too young to know what that was and he was drunk so much of the time I thought that was his natural state. What I am talking about is how beat down he seemed all the time. My mother yelled at him, picked on him, and pushed him around so much that I felt really bad for him. I felt so sad to see him hiding in the office every night with his booze."

I interpreted, "it sounds like you ended up feeling guilty that you couldn't save him from all that." K agreed. I added that she may try and still undo that by trying to make me and everyone else happy by catering to whatever she things we need. I said, "You probably do feel very guilty but also feel angry and resentful so when you try and take care of someone whom you care about but also feel angry with, it can leave you very conflicted. That might be part of why you have to control everything with the OCD. Your inner world feels very close to being out of control." K said, "I always do feel very close to being out of control. And, you mentioned anger. I know I carry around lots of anger. Certainly, I now wish both my parents would have acted like decent parents so I didn't have to go through all that. But, I still feel sorry for my father. He still drinks and he still seems like a broken down old man."

Shortly after, K asked me, once again, if I had received her message about cutting back and "if that is ok." I interpreted, "at the beginning today, just like you have to double check your door to avoid trouble, you double checked with me if it is ok to give me a check instead of cash and now you are double or triple checking if I am ok with you cutting back. I think you are very anxious about if you hurt my feelings and if I will be upset and retaliate." K said, "Oh gosh, you are right. Well, I am nervous that you might be angry with me. So, I see what you mean. I guess I want to make sure we are ok and not at odds." I interpreted, "So, you have to spend a lot of time keeping the peace and controlling any conflict or hurt between us. You are standing guard at the door to make sure nothing comes crashing through to mess things up." K said, "I want to make sure no one is feeling bad but you are right, that makes me tired and resentful."

One of the core conflicts K seemed to have was a very primitive depressive struggle over knowledge and the need to always have it. Without knowing what her objects were doing, were going to do, or might do, she felt very anxious. For Melanie Klein and most contemporary followers of her approach, knowledge is considered a powerful component in all emotional situations. Britton (1998) has proposed that love, hate, and knowledge are the three primary instinctual sources of all our motivation, desire, and conflict. He notes we all strive to love and be loved, all feel hateful yet fear being hated, and all want to learn and to feel understood. Klein viewed oedipal development and the resulting depressive position to be greatly influenced by the ability to tolerate knowledge about one's objects and I would add that depressive stability is only possible when one can bear a lack of knowledge about one's objects. K was unable to bear not knowing what was happening around her. She felt driven to know how she was impacting her objects and how they were impacting her. Without this knowledge, she felt alone and abandoned, fearful and uncertain. She felt out of control so she had to resort to a very concrete and literal form of control using obsessive compulsive rituals.

Feldman (1989) notes how successful resolution of oedipal conflicts results in the ability to allow thoughts and feelings to link and reside with each other even if they create anxieties or conflicts. I think K's obsessive compulsive symptoms are the result of the lack of this linking and accepting ability. In fact, as Zeavin (2005) points out, excessive anxiety regarding conflict with one's objects can attack and corrupt these critical links. For K, it was mainly the primitive guilt she felt regarding her father but also her fears and anger toward both parents that made her mental integrity very brittle. Feldman (1989) echoes this when he notes that if the patient's phantasy involves a predominately destructive linkage between the parental couple, there will be a perverse or severely inhibited form of thinking.

As K demonstrates, one form of this perversity can be the extreme control she had to have over her objects and the world at large. Zeavin (2005) notes that knowing and not knowing is a lifelong repetition of tolerating separation, otherness, to realize the exclusiveness and exclusion of the parental couple, to bear loving and hating at the same time, and to accept not knowing what the parental couple is doing at any given time.

For K, this was and still is unacceptable. To not know means she is not standing guard over her father, protecting him from mother. To not know means she is not taking precautions against her mother's critical attacks and the overall threat of total rejection and abandonment by the both of them. I have made the interpretation that she may feel guilty and anxious about her own image of herself suddenly abandoning them. So, I proposed that she can shift from feeling she is the victim to she is the perpetrator and back, creating a constant wave of guilt, persecution, and anxiety.

This idea that she could be abandoned being part of a projective identification cycle in which she feels scared and guilty of abandoning her objects as well came out in a recent session. K told me she would not be coming the following week since she had the holiday week off of work and "just wanted to say no to all her obligations. I just want to do nothing and not have to answer to anyone." I said, "I didn't know I was such a bully. You include me in this feeling that life is nothing but a constant obligation and hassle. Tell me more." K said, "Well, I always feel that way. I go through every day feeling like I have to do something to please people, say what I should, and make the right choices to avoid conflict. It gets really tiring so I just want a break from that next week." I asked K how she felt obligated with me. She told me that she feels she must "always have something important to tell me, something useful to talk about and to work hard at changing myself. But, sometimes I just don't feel like that and don't want to but I don't want to let you down or cause trouble."

Based on my counter-transference feelings, fostered by her very concrete and rigid projective identification mechanism, I became interested in her concerns about filling me up and keeping me afloat. I interpreted, "you seem to see me as quite needy and ready to be down or upset if you don't manage me and find ways to please me. Maybe you want to please me and help me so much that you end up feeling I am demanding you constantly produce something for me." Here, I was interpreted my phantasy of her desire and guilty obligation to care for her broken down father and her projection of a broken down self that she feels too guilty to accept help for so she must assign it to me and others instead.

K responded, "Yes. That is exactly what it feels like. I really feel like I always needed to know what was up with my father, how he was doing, and if he was ok. Now, I still feel that way about him but like you are saying I do feel that way with you and everyone else, too. That is why I just want a break next week from all that so I can rest." I interpreted that she sees those feelings as real and very concrete, not a terrible feeling of guilt but an actual obligation that she must fulfill every day no matter what.

K said it "does feel real and I can't get away from it." She went on to tell me more about her ever watchful eye on her father as a child and now as an adult. K said, "As a kid, I didn't understand that he had a drinking problem but I could tell how sad and depressed he was, how my mother was always yelling at him, and how she was making him feel bad. So, I was always trying to figure out if he was ok emotionally when I was growing up. Now, as an adult, I am always trying to find out if he is drinking to make sure I can be there to help him out if he needs me. He could end up dead if I don't keep an eye out for him. I know it is not really my job but I feel so bad for him. He is such a sad person."

I interpreted that she feels so guilty about his condition, as if it is her fault, that she has to be on watch for him all the time along with making sure I and others are ok, too. I interpreted how she is the perpetual lifeguard always preventing me and others from drowning but that feels like a terrible obligation and maybe sometimes she doesn't care if we drown or float and that makes her feel very guilty. K replied, "Oh yes, very very guilty."

DISCUSSION

The psychoanalytic work with K continues but with the same slow going, difficult pace. Given her struggles with persecutory guilt and the fragmenting fear of being abandoned, she is very reluctant to give up her rigid control over life. Her obsessive need to know what her objects are doing, thinking, and feeling is a desperate and destructive internal organization that defends her from feeling completely at the mercy of her own anger, hunger, and needs, as well as the projected vision of her angry, hungry, and needy objects.

At the same time, K has not been in analytic treatment for very long so her progress so far has been remarkable given her unconscious anxieties and external symptom profile. If K was able to attend more frequently, I believe she would profit more from her analytic experience. However, as with many of our contemporary patients, their internal and external circumstances prevent this from ever happening. Indeed, the odds are great that K might suddenly terminate altogether, as is common with such disturbed patients. But, I do think she has already profited from this analytic opportunity to finally take a closer look at her anxieties and core phantasy conflicts. In doing so in the context of the here-and-now transference situation, K has found the courage to begin contemplating how she could be survive and change the persecutory visions she holds in which she and/or others are the terrible victims to unpredictable chaos and unknowable disaster.

Grotstein (2010a) writes about how psychotherapy is a procedure where the interactions of the patient with their external objects in the real world are highlighted and perhaps explored from a psychodynamic perspective. But, he notes how psychoanalysis remains the unique study and exploration of the patient's internal objects and their unconscious relationship to those objects, including the vessel of the analyst in the transference. Certainly, the analyst will address reality issues and external figures in the patient's life, but always with the idea that they serve some symbolic function as placeholders for deeper phantasy conflicts regarding the internal playhouse of object relations. This is the essence of my approach to patients, regardless of frequency, diagnosis, or length of treatment. Therefore, I am always attending to the moment-to-moment transference climate, the nature of the projective identification systems used, and the pull of those systems on my counter-transference. I am always trying to locate the moment of greatest anxiety within their paranoid-schizoid (Klein 1946) or depressive (Klein 1935, 1940) phantasy state. My goal is to foster insight into the patient's unconscious phantasy world of conflict and thereby help to bring resolution, change, and choice to the inner mindscape.

Segal (1962) notes how the curative factors in psychoanalysis have to do with the achievement of insight regarding the workings of one's own mind and its unconscious cast of characters. The process of Analytic Contact (Waska 2007) which I used with K is a method of clinically understanding the emergence or retreat of the patient's mental awareness and engagement with their core internal conflicts and the ways they may play these out with themselves, with the analyst, and with others. Both analyst and patient can promote and cultivate this process or resist, discourage, and attack this process.

Segal (1962) highlights the crucial importance of this insight, knowledge, and analytic contact occurring in the climate of the transference for it to bring about the deepest and strongest levels of change. By paying very close attention to the moment-to-moment processes of projection and introjections, the analyst can make helpful interpretations that recast the patient's hardened method of coping. Segal (1962) clarifies how the nature of the interpretation will hopefully over time include the patient's feelings, anxieties, and defenses in regards to their place in the present and their replication of past events and phantasies. In this manner, we work with the constant interplay between external reality and internal reality.

Chapter Three

The Graveyard Sentry, Self-Induced Comas, and Building the Better Beast

Some patients encountered in psychoanalytic treatment are involved in chronically destructive relationships with partners who never give them the love or attention they hunger for. This is sometimes in phantasy, sometimes real, and usually a blend of both. These patients feel they must remain silent, not ask for much, and not create conflict because the love they pine for could not only vanish but turn into outright abandonment, rejection, or attack. The desired ideal object always ends up a deficient object, broken and in need of fixing. This tragic figure is viewed as barely able to provide the meager morsels of love that the patient both craves yet feels undeserving. This deficient object is usually propped up and idealized, with its broken features denied or manically glued together with rationalizations and self-sacrificing justifications. As a result, intense resentment, control, and anxiety are also hallmarks of this type of patient.

In analysis, these patients' phantasies reveal objects that are dead, dying, or irreparable. In addition, these objects are extremely unstable and prone to shifting from craving or attentive to unavailable, dismissive, or outright attacking. Therefore, the patient tries to avoid conflict, tries to please/appease, and tries to sacrifice any self-definition to the hopes of being allowed into the good graces of the object and to prevent any possible rejection or abandonment. The hoped for object is often an ideal object, based on the best potential of an object that is proven to be far from ideal. So, a broken, disappointing, or volatile object is, in phantasy, pieced together like a Frankenstein monster puzzle. It is an attempt to use the best pieces of one's memory or the best parts of one's hopeful and ideal wishes for the potential of what could have been.

SIGNIFICANT THEMES

A number of significant themes arise with such patients which compliment as well as contradict each other.

1. The patient is internally linked to an object that is experienced as fragile and in need of being attended to, agreed with, healed, or bolstered to prevent depression or collapse.
2. The patient is internally linked to an object that is experienced as ready to reject, abandon, or attack at a moment's notice unless managed, controlled, and honored.
3. These two objects are one in the same but due to excessive splitting dynamics are not consciously seen as connected. These two aspects of the same unstable object lead the patient to feel constantly anxious, guilty, worried, and seeking to avoid conflict.
4. The primary method to avoid this dreaded conflict and collapse is to forfeit personal identity, goals, independence, and difference. This leads to a frequent presentation of an as-if character, masochistic styles of relating, and passive controlling interactions. Indeed, these patients are often trying to manage, control, and manipulate the object with care, niceness, and loyalty.
5. All these factors lead to a psychic profile of someone who puts themselves into a self-induced emotional coma to prevent harm to self for object as well as being on constant vigil at the object's symbolic gravesite to protect the fragile corpse that needs protection. This sentinel service is also the result of not being able to say good-bye to this dead and disappointing object that the patient once loved but hated and feared as well. Because of the intense internal conflicts regarding the tie to this unstable object and lack of self definition due to over reliance on projective identification processes, there is also tendency to try and build a better version of the object, a sort of zombie or Frankenstein project. This gives the patient some hope and DEADication. So, when they begin working through unresolved grief and loss issues, they often feel very empty, anxious, and bored without their normal state of crisis, drama, and masochistic loyalty. When they find a non-rejecting object or begin to see the analyst as someone they could trust, depend on, and be loved by, they tend to push away and act unsure if they want to trade in their old model for the new model.
6. All these factors emerge from and intensify a deep sense of resentment, envy, hunger, and anxiety that is hidden and split off to protect the self and the object. However, this becomes visible within the transference and usually leaks out in the patient's interpersonal life. These patients often shift from passive victim to resent-

ful, controlling, and demanding. They feel they should be rewarded for their lifelong graveyard services.

The purpose of this chapter and the clinical material which is at the heart of the chapter serve not to break any new theoretical ground per se. Rather, this chapter is meant to show the reader the actual moment-to-moment movements of a Kleinian analyst working with patients suffering from a particular set of conflicts. It is a rare window into the to-and-fro of clinical interactions from a Kleinian perspective. The emphasis is much more on the "he said," "she said" demonstration of the psychoanalytic treatment of one variety of patient and their specific transference matrix.

LITERATURE REVIEW

In 1935, Klein (1935) wrote of the concept of damaged, injured, or dead internal objects that made up the core of a patient's phantasy life and resulting internal conflicts. Klein described these comatose or deceased objects as the result of projective identification processes with primary external figures who were distorted by various paranoid and/or depressive phantasies of love, hate, and the desire for knowledge. In the years preceding these important clinical and theoretical discoveries, the concept of lifeless internal objects has been reexamined and elaborated on by other Kleinian and Freudian analysts.

Andre Green (1983) has outlined his thoughts on the internalization of a depressed rejecting, or unavailable mother, creating what he calls a dead mother syndrome. Emphasizing the internal phantasy experience so much utilized in the clinical setting of Kleinian treatment, Green made sure to explain he was dealing with the psychic death of a mother object, not the actual demise of an external person. One of the characteristics Green described in these "dead mother" patients was separation and intrusion anxiety, very much a part of the anxiety illustrated in some of this chapter's case material. Fear of abandonment, aggressive desire to own and intrude the object, and visions of being taken over are only some of the pattern of psychological issues seen with this group of patients, sometimes from a more paranoid state of mind and sometimes with a primitive depressive quality to them.

In response to Green's pioneering work, which builds on Klein's early discoveries, Ogden (1999) has noted the deadness that can emerge within the transference and counter-transference with these patients. An important extension of the dead mother concept is Lussier's (1999) idea of the dead father. Lussier also points out how much patients can resist the aliveness of new objects, such as the analyst and resist the aliveness of change and growth in favor of maintaining their embalmed internal objects. I would say that these patients also try to add new mummified objects to their collection so that the analyst and the treatment can be deadened or mummified for their collection of unavailable yet always present when needed dead objects. This is similar to Sekoff's (1999) views of how some patients find a sense of security in the certainty of dead or frozen objects versus the uncertainty of life. This view certainly is in line with contemporary Kleinian views on the defensive use of the death instinct (Grotstein 2010) and the creation of pathological organizations (Rosenfeld 1987) or psychic retreats (Steiner 1987) from which the patient feels entombed but in control of threats from both paranoid and depressive anxieties.

O'Shaughnessy (2001) makes the point that during an analysis, it would be critical to gradually differentiate the blank, empty mourning a patient might feel in an inner world of deed objects from the aggressive nature of the death instinct, deliberately choking the life out of objects. The analyst's interpretive focus would be greatly shaped by one or the other. I would add that often these patients bring to bear a complex combination of both issues. O'Shaughnessy (2001) also notes that these patients who are struggling with mummified, damaged, or deadened objects are often intensely identified with their comatose objects via excessive reliance on projective identification dynamics.

Diamond (2004) has investigated the difficulties of attachment in some patients and linked this with Klein's notion of the paranoid-schizoid and depressive positions. Diamond has studied the possible interplay of projective identification and experiences of withdrawn, unavailable, and unstable parental objects, leading to confusions between self and object. These situations bring about fixation and identification with the mummified, lost, or damaged object and prevent healthy mourning.

Betty Joseph (1989) has elaborated on the Kleinian notion of relational guilt, resentment, and anxiety over the phantasy of eternal coma states and deadened or dying objects that must be cared for perpetually. Joseph has studied the moment-to-moment nuances of the transference with such difficult to reach patients who resist the idea of their objects or themselves ever waking up from their crypt like emotional fortress.

Neuenschwander (2006) has discussed this graveyard fortress as one of the more entrenched pathological organizations we see in clinical practice. Other recent Kleinians writing about this phenomenon include Andkjaer's (2004) work on the legacy of irreparable object's in the life of a famous artist and Steiner's (2004) reexamination of an early case of Freud's and the impact of damaged or dead objects that are being dug up in the emotional graveyard for possible reanimation. Finally, Rey (1988) has written extensively about how some of our patients specifically bring their dead, dying, or mummified objects to us for revival. I (Waska 2010d) would add that these patients also may approach us in the transference seeking assistance in keeping these objects buried out of either intense guilt and/or persecutory anxieties of zombie objects returning for revenge over imagined grievances.

CASE MATERIAL

Marsha had been unhappy in her marriage for many years. She and her husband had raised several children and built a home. While there had been many happy moments in the relationship, Marsha felt "things were never really on track and she and Jack (her husband) were never on the same page." She came to see me feeling things had "really deteriorated even more and he is completely unavailable emotionally. But, I cannot imagine ever leaving him and I think his condition must be my fault somehow."

When Marsha mentioned "his condition," she was referring to how Jack had been chronically depressed for years and a longtime alcoholic. Over time, I interpreted how Marsha tried to convince me he was fine, despite her own stories of his drunken behavior, his near suicidal depressions, and his periods of slurred speech and sleeping during the day. Also, I interpreted how she tried to convince me of how ok or good this marriage was, despite her own stories of how he no longer slept in the same bedroom, how he ignored her physically and emotionally, and how rarely they did anything as a couple. Along the way, I certainly would get bogged down in the counter-transference and act out some of her projective identification elements. As a result, I would occasionally find myself either saying that she seemed quite angry and judgmental or I would press upon her how "sick" her husband was. So, I acted out her own aggression toward herself and the resentment she felt toward her objects.

Over the course of her analytic treatment, now into the second year, I interpreted that she felt she was failing to please me. This was based on the interpersonal and interactional ways Marsha related to me. When I brought these transference moments up, Marsha was able to share how she felt pressured to "take action" and "do something to change the marriage" or to "stop talking about it and finally leave her husband." She felt I was "probably sick and tired of how she was always complaining but never taking action." I interpreted that she must not be familiar with having someone be patient and curious about how she feels and curious about what might be getting in the way of her making changes. I interpreted that she put her judgment and her demanding expectations, her control, into me and then felt she had better hurry up and please me or face a disappointed and frustrated object. I interpreted that these were in fact her own rigid and controlling ways that she was revealing in our relationship.

Marsha told me, "That must be what Jack means when he says I am so controlling and nagging all the time." After she went on for awhile, I interpreted, "I think he could be right about how you can be controlling. But, here with me, you are going on about it in a very blaming way so that all we get to focus on is how much it is your fault. Maybe that is easier than to look at why you need to be controlling." At that point, she backed away from her masochistic stance and began to explore her feelings a bit more.

Of course, in the counter-transference, through projective identification, I did indeed end up sometimes feeling these emotions and holding those ideas. By the way Marsha presented herself in a sadomasochistic fashion, I was nudged toward telling her to either grin and bear it or get out of the marriage. I was pushed into being an object that ignored her pain and dismissed her anxiety over making changes. Also, the urge to act out the controlling feelings she projected eliminated my ability to be curious about why she needed or wanted to be so powerful, controlling, and judgmental. So, I did my best to notice these counter-transference urges and to function as a container (Cartwright 2010) for them and eventually translate and interpret them to her rather than act out in response. Of course, enactment is inevitable in all analytic treatments so one tries to notice it as quickly as possible when it does occur and then try to learn from each element or aspect of it to better understand the patient's unconscious defensive and offensive methods of relating to themselves and their objects.

In this process of analyzing the transference and the projective identification based aspects of it (Waska 2010a), I realized Marsha was very anxious and scattered when we began to talk about her phantasies of me wanting her to leave Jack. I gradually explored this and found Marsha to be constantly frightened of being alone and becoming sick or demented with no one to care for her.

When at one point I interpreted how she was gradually having to acknowledge how separate and unfulfilled she was in her marriage, I said, "You are facing the death of your marriage, realizing it has been dead for a long time. This must be very difficult." Marsha replied, "Well, I think I want to live with a corpse because I don't want to live alone and end up being alone with no one to take care of me." She said this in a very concrete way that showed how strong her phantasies were and how not only reluctant she was to consider change but that change was really not a consideration given the nature of these emotional threats she lived with about being alone and uncared for. So, I interpreted her need to constantly be managing and controlling this corpse and to try and constantly resurrect, heal, tolerate, and prop up this lifeless object. She has to be stationed in the graveyard, guarding and controlling the gravesite. Sometimes, she is convinced he will rise up and walk among the living but most of the time she tries to seek a modicum of comfort from his place of resting.

In response to my interpretations, Marsha associated to memories of her childhood. She explained how because of her father's chronic job problems, the family had to move every few years. She said, "It was really hard. I could never make any friends and I was convinced no one would ever like me anyway. Why would they? So, every new school I went to, I decided to take on some kind of leadership role so that people would have to pay attention to me and talk with me. They might not like me but they would have to interact with me. So, I ended up being the controlling leader of some kind of club, team, or school drive and I was the one who told everyone what to do. I always volunteered for all the special positions. I was smart and dedicated so I quickly became the team captain, the class president or representative, lab monitor, and so on. Others had to pay attention to me because I was in charge. It was my way of making sure I would not be forgotten."

Discussion

Marsha was a patient who struggled with savage combinations of depressive (Klein 1935, 1940) and paranoid (1946) anxieties that left her feeling cornered, experiencing growth and change as potentially dangerous to self and object. Patients with the type of internal conflicts Marsha displayed tend to live in a stagnant, anti-life, anti-change zone in which self and object are kept in a self-induced coma, still alive but marginally functional. This is a variation of what Betty Joseph (1982) has termed the addition to near-death. She describes a sadomasochistic relationship to despair and misery. I believe this is an unconscious attachment to a dead or dying object that has to be guarded, controlled, and under strict and constant vigil. Joseph (1982) notes how these patients, through projective identification, will induce despair in the analyst and get him to either collude with their despair or to become harsh, sadistic, and critical.

Marsha frequently pushed me towards feeling commanding, controlling, and judgmental. I sometimes felt like telling her off and telling her to get rid of her lousy husband. Also, I sometimes felt like telling her to stop complaining and get on with things and get a life of her own. Other times, I felt like giving up along with her, just accepting this stagnant, hopeless way of being and accepting or ignoring the corpse in the corner of the room.

At the same time, Marsha projected her unwanted guilt ridden and primitive depressive urge for life and independence into me. I was then the one that felt active and motivated while she was passive and hopeless. As Joseph (1982) recommends, I had to be aware of this process so as to not push my interests or motives or anger into her. Instead, I gradually interpreted it as part of her transference and projections of unwanted aspects of her own self and her own internal conflict.

CASE MATERIAL

Don has been in analytic treatment, on the couch, for five years now. He has not worked for most of that time. For the first few years, he was overwhelmed with various somatic problems and chronic physical pains that we gradually traced to an intense sense of powerlessness, passivity, and masochism. After he felt better physically, he still felt so under-confident, so massively depressed, and fragmented emotionally and mentally that he only went out for walks, drive to our appointments, or drive to visit his ailing elderly parents.

For much of the time, we have explored how Don continues to challenge his mother to switch from "being a useless martyr bitch who plays at being helpless and stupid" to someone who "should use their brain and be an adult who can take care of herself." I have interpreted that this image of a decrepit, damaged, dying object that he spends his life trying to restart, heal, or resurrect is a parallel of the way he lives his life.

In the transference, Don has duplicated this dynamic in that he is the "brain dead" mother and I, in my counter-transference moments, sometimes feel like trying desperately or aggressively to revive him, wake him up, or at least maintain him in his coma-like state. On occasion, this results in my trying to become his coach, cheering him into life and agency but of course when he refused to immediately transform himself I felt angry, desperate, and sad. This, I realized, was a sharp taste of what Don felt all the time with his objects.

Don has described his childhood as "a parasitic-like relationship in which my mother would not allow me to have my own identity. I was there to care for her and hold her hand. She made me feel like my independence was wrong and that my growing up would kill her. For me to grow up and be independent was to pull the plug on her, to kill her. So, I had to sit by her emotional bedside and watch my life slip away!" I have interpreted that Don also accepts this role as a way to escape the anxiety and risk of having to grow up and the danger to himself and others he will unleash if he became an assertive and powerful man.

Bit by bit, over the years in treatment, Don has resisted change but has also allowed significant progress in his life. Recently, he said, "My life has never been worse. But, it is the first time I am not thinking of suicide." This was a watershed moment for Don in his internal experience and his ability to step out of the graveyard vigil he kept for himself and for his objects. I interpreted that he was talking about having some hope and the fact that he was choosing to share it with me was very different than the usual way he presented himself. In response, Don began to weep, a very rare occurrence. After a moment, he said it felt like there "was indeed some hope. This is very, very different."

We went on to discuss how he seems to not know how to move forward in his life. He talked about "feeling stuck in glass, with no way to move and no sense of what direction to take." He said, "I can only get angry with my mother. I have no feelings of my own." I felt he was genuinely conveying how lost he felt internally but I also felt he was digging in his heels to avoid a variety of anxieties about himself and his objects. I interpreted that he was actively resistant to expanding his life and it is easier to feel there is something "out there" that is preventing him or threatening him from growing up. So, I was highlighting the inner source of his anxieties and the fact that a part of himself was threatening him and holding him back, not something scary "out there."

Don replied, "I am never aware of my own part. I never realize I might be doing anything that affects my own experience. It always feels like something external. It is hard for me to really imagine that." I said, "It seems difficult to imagine any part of you that could have agency or power, whether it be for good or for bad." Don agreed and said he felt "like a robot that just goes on its pre-programmed way." I said, "Except you want to return to the factory and kill the scientist that made you." Don laughed and said, "I feel that way all the time!"

At the end of the session, Don was quiet for a moment and then he began to roll around on the analytic couch and make loud grunting noises of frustration. Finally, he blurted out, "I am really trying to bury myself. I am trying to shut off my brain, kill off my thinking." I replied, "Like I said, it is something active inside of you, not out there. It is you trying to kill off the strong, thinking, independent side of you and bury it right next to your unthinking, dependent mother." Don said, "Oh shit! I don't want to be like her! But, I see what you mean. I have to have this parasitic, mutual brain-dead relationship with her. How do I stop that? I certainly don't want that!" Here, he was consciously wanting to be different but also was relating in a passive, helpless manner that left him "brain-dead" and dependent.

In a recent session, Don was talking at great length with great intensity about his hatred for his mother. He told me he realizes he gets into fights with her "with the sole purpose to make her talk sense." After a bit, I interpreted that he was trying to rebuild her into a reliable mother who talks sense that he could depend on and look up to. But, because he sees her as senseless he must try and forcibly rebuild her into a new and better model. Don said, "I have spent my life trying to do that and she won't budge." Here, we were exploring his unconscious desire to take this fallen, dead object and breathe life into it or rebuild it into a new and better functioning object. He wanted to be able to rely on and project into a safe, secure, and strong mother object and have his projections make sense inside of her.

Don continued to talk about how he "just couldn't stop trying to make her make sense and stop acting so weak and out of it." I interpreted that he could use this battle as an easier, safer way to exist than to risk having to face the world on his own and become separate and independent. Don replied, "I am starting to try and be more independent. I have been considering doing some volunteer work lately. I looked into this one place that needs people to help out with the restoration of an old city building. It is a historical icon they are starting to rebuild and spruce up. They need people for a number of things. They told me I could help bring out all the old debris from the earthquake retrofit and help to put in the Dumpsters. It sounds pretty simple. You take your time, work as hard as you want, and they give you a T-shirt that identifies you as a city worker."

In the counter-transference, I felt pulled to be judgmental about how passive and meager his approach to the position sounded and I also felt pulled to cheer him on, in a controlling parental way, to achieve greater things and march to victory. I was fortunate to notice these feelings fast enough to simply say and do nothing.

Don paused for a few moments and continued, but in a different direction. He said, "Or, I could help give small talks to whoever stops in and tell them about the history of the place and what the city is going to do with it. I thought I might be good at that and it would be more in the spotlight, educating people about the significance of the building and its historical value." I was listening and noticing his reactions. First, he felt less anxious and more freed up by my interpretation regarding his struggle with independence which leads him to discuss the idea of getting out in the world and volunteering. So, initially he introduced the idea in a rather passive or timid manner, thinking about simply helping with the debris and not having many responsibilities. Then, he shifted to thinking about something more assertive and independent, the idea of being a docent who educates people about the building. They would depend on him for information and his ability to think, know, and communicate.

Now, abruptly, Don's direction of association changed. Suddenly, he told me that he had been "pretty sick all last week and yesterday he had blood drawn for an upcoming physical exam. I hope they don't find anything bad." I said, "You say that with a pretty ominous tone, like it could be something pretty bad or even lethal. I wonder if you noticed yourself out there in the world as a volunteer who thinks and educates. You were sharing yourself with me as assertive and able. I wonder if you are now reacting to that by slapping yourself down and predicting a scary blood test result. No volunteering for you, you are on your deathbed!"

Don replied, "How can I stop being angry with her? I want to but I don't know how." He repeated this question a few times in a way that seemed to pull on me to give him a practical way to still be with his mother but not be so angry. In other words, he was turning his back on the idea of being an independent, grown-up man, a thinking volunteer, and instead wanting the magical formula of how to stay attached to his mother in the same old way but simply without wanting to kill her. I interpreted this and he sighed and said, "So, you are saying I simply don't need to always go and see her. I need to strike out on my own and that is a way of not being so angry all the time." I said, "Right." He said, "This is so hard!"

Discussion

Don is certainly an example of the type of patients Riviere (1936) spoke of in regard to the negative therapeutic reaction. She noted how these patients are convinced that change and growth are lethal to their objects and to the analyst so they remain camped out in the graveyard of their injured or failed objects trying to either heal them or at least do no more damage to them. One way of achieving this is to join them in the grave for an eternal fusion of lifelessness and neutrality. Don was considering this when he said he was trying to bury himself. This is what Riviere (1936) called the status quo. It is the most these patients can bear or tolerate and, in phantasy, the most their objects can bear or tolerate. I use the terms bear and tolerate because I think these patients are convinced that they and their object's are victims who must bear this lifelessness but that self and object are also barely tolerating this situation and could become vengeful and persecutory at any moment. Therefore, the underlying anxiety pushes the patient to reinforce the lifeless status quo even more.

Grotstein (1983) has commented on the great difficulty more disturbed patients have with the depressive position anxieties of separation and individuation. He notes how patients, dealing with conflicts similar to Don's, feel there will be an overwhelming debt to pay, an emotional ransom due for the perceived sins of growing up, being separate, and creating one's own identity.

This concept is similar to Grinberg's (1964) notion of persecutory guilt and the paranoid aspects of guilt that emerge from immature ego phantasies of wanting to either devour the breast/mother or attack and reject the breast/mother. Don was unable to feel he could safely navigate these intense feelings and phantasy convictions. The guilt he felt was so intense and without forgiveness and the object was seen as so injured and so prone to seeking retribution that he felt he had blood on his hands for even considering his own life. Because of that emotional slavery, he wanted to either kill off his greedy, dominating, non-thinking parasitic mother or to force her into being a new vibrant thinking mother who could finally take care of him instead of the other way around. Through projective identification, in the counter-transference I sometimes felt like giving up on Don and having to camp out for eternity at his gravesite and other times I wanted to "make him" hurry up and grow up into a better breathing and thinking adult man. So, I ended up with a taste of how he felt towards his mother through his projective identification based transference interactions.

Malin and Grotstein (1966) have noted the dual and interdependent aspects of projective identification which the infant must hold a positive image of a receptive object to which he is projecting and the object must be aware and receptive to the infant's projective efforts. Don consistently described his lack of any internal image of a receptive object he could trust with aspects of self and when he did try to share himself with his mother, he felt she was unavailable or completely rejecting. Don felt his projection of his alive, independent self was never accepted or received by his mother so he had to settle for either being the emotional sponge for her hostile and deformed projections into him or to force her to become a shiny new receptacle willing to take in, tolerate, and encourage his projections of a breathing, thinking adult. But, up to now, Don has only internalized a barren void in which he feels lost and empty and in danger should he try and project an assertive, growing self into. This is his experience of being independent and moving out into the world. It is dangerous and unwelcoming.

Since Don is constantly trying to engage his mother by putting parts of himself into her and hoping she will accept them and understand them, he is always scattering himself into this unwelcoming void. As many of the Kleinian school have described (Joseph 1987), in using projective identification processes, the ego feels a sense of relatedness, connection, and attachment. However, when used excessively, the ego feels emptied, impoverished, and gutted as so much of itself has been pushed, jettisoned, or fired into the object for either defensive or offensive motives. So, when Don angrily projected himself into his mother over and over again, he felt a temporary sense of relatedness and comfort only to be quickly met with a horrible sense of emptiness, betrayal, and rejection.

CASE MATERIAL

At this point, I have only seen Dawn for fifteen sessions, on the couch, for analytic treatment. However, she has quickly demonstrated several complex transference states and an intense internal phantasy world that leaves her anxious and fragmented. Dawn came to see me after feeling extremely depressed and angry over the collapse of her relationship to her "life partner." She had met her boyfriend while traveling out of state for business. They "hit it off" and began a long-distance relationship. During the course of many phone calls and occasional visits in the year and a half long-distance part of the relationship, they had drifted apart for a few months and agreed to "see other people." When Dawn suspected him of being with another woman, he denied it but after they got back together he admitted to sleeping with another girl when he was drunk at a party. Dawn felt this was a sign he might "be a liar" or "someone I couldn't trust" but she also tried to give him the benefit of the doubt and they continued forward. At that point, Dawn suggested he move to be with her. He was reluctant at first but eventually said yes.

When he moved, he did not move in with Dawn. He told her he felt that "was too soon and he needed his space." Over the course of the next six months, their relationship became more and more rocky. Dawn said she knew he had a drinking problem when she met him, but hoped that he was going to get better. However, he never did. Also, he was trying to build up a new career once he arrived so when Dawn wanted to spend time together, he was often busy. She also worried he might be seeing someone else but "tried to keep those feelings under check."

In describing the unstable nature of their relationship, Dawn told me she often would "lose her temper" but "it seemed justified because he was always pulling away from her and ignoring her." From what she told me, Dawn would easily take something he said or did as a personal rejection and then feel extremely upset and angry. When listening to the stories, I noticed myself sometimes thinking she had a point, that this man seemed uncommitted to her and not very reliable. At the same time, I was struck with how intense she became over the slightest hint of rejection and began demanding love. In fact, her friends would frequently have to tell her to "chill out, relax, and don't take it so personal." In the counter-transference, I would feel pulled in that same direction, wanting to tell Dawn to slow down and not get so worked up over nothing. At the same time, I felt she was, from her description, dating someone who was an unreliable alcoholic who might indeed be cheating on her.

The other rather strong counter-transference feeling I noticed was a sense of "of course you have trouble with men, you are a big turnoff." This judgmental, rejecting feeling arose from quite a few different interpersonal aspects of the transference. From the very beginning, Dawn created a noisy, obnoxious persona that irritated me. For example, I could always tell when Dawn was walking up the stairs into the waiting room because she seemed to stomp on each stair as she walked. Then, when she opened the hallway door to go to the bathroom, she swung the door open so hard that the doorknob smashed into the wall making a small hole. This hole grew bigger each week. I wondered how to bring this up without sounding harsh and realized I felt I was being held victim. I didn't want to hurt her but this effort was also what kept me resentful and silent, under her thumb.

So, there was this counter-transference experience of just wondering how to relate without causing trouble, but feeling angry that I wasn't being respected or cared for properly. When Dawn came into my office, it seemed like it took her forever to take off her jacket and find her checkbook. Also, at the end of each session, there was an eternity for her to put her jacket back on, gather her purse and belongings and slowly make her way out of my office, and down the hall to slam the door once again. So, I noticed how I was being pushed by these external and interactive circumstances into not liking her, dreading her appearance, and judging or rejecting her.

On the other hand, I noticed that even though she was quite overweight, Dawn had a pleasing figure and a pretty face. She kept her hair in a classic and attractive manner. Also, Dawn was smart. She could engage me in an articulate, curious, and insightful way that showed she wanted to learn and had a wise head on her shoulders. So, I noted how scattered and in opposition my counter-transference feelings could be and wondered about the level of transference splintering that projective identification was causing with these split-off fragments of herself being bounced around.

This back-and-forth transference dynamic also appeared in the way Dawn felt about the treatment and about her progress. At first, she was desperate for my help. She was motivated and eager to learn about herself and what led her to "always pick the liars and the losers." But, very soon, this shifted to more of a desperation to have her panic, anxiety, and sadness go away. When her boyfriend broke it off with her and said he was "sick of all the fighting," Dawn was devastated. She told me in tears, "I am going to really need to see you. This has really left me in pieces."

But, a week later, she told me, "I have moved on and feel I am ok about it now. I am not sure what to talk about. Maybe we need to meet less." I interpreted that she was reacting to her feelings in a way that may show us how much of an emotional storm she goes through. I interpreted that she was shifting so rapidly in how she felt about herself and about others that she was unable to know what will emerge next. This must leave her very confused and anxious. These interpretations were based on my projective identification based counter-transference feelings and I was able to utilize them to begin to offer more of a stable container for Dawn than this erratic puzzle she lived in. I suggested we try and create a stable relationship that would allow us to learn and create change in ways that would be more lasting.

As I learned more about Dawn's past, I wondered if she was recreating certain object experiences in the transference. Growing up was a time of turmoil for Dawn. Her parents fought with each other much of the time and when Dawn was ten years old, her father left the family. She was told he had been cheating on Dawn's mother and that now he decided he would leave for good. The next few years were very difficult on the family as Dawn's mother barely could pay the bills. Over the course of her adolescence, Dawn grew used to hearing her mother talk about how cruel her father was for abandoning them in that way. Dawn's father never contacted Dawn on his own, without her practically begging for a visit.

When Dawn was in her twenties, she decided to search for her father. She found him and asked to meet and visit with her. This scenario occurred three times over the course of several years. Each time, her father seemed to enjoy spending time with her and suggested that "they make sure to do this more often." But, after the visit, he never contacted Dawn. She felt furious, devastated, and betrayed. She told me, "He is a liar. I just want to know why he doesn't want me. What is wrong with me, what have I done?" She also told me how each time they visited and the few times they spoke on the phone over the years, they would get into a fight. Dawn would bring up how she felt he was always lying about his lack of money. Apparently, he always failed to give the family money after he left them so Dawn grew up for several years in very difficult circumstances until her mother remarried.

As an adult, her father mentioned wanting to help her through college and to buy an apartment and a car. But, he never followed through and whenever she asked about it, he said he was "in between jobs and couldn't swing it right now." But, Dawn told him she was aware of the nice home he lived in, the nice cars he owned, and the fancy dinners he always went to with his girlfriends. So, when they talked, Dawn would inevitably bring this up and they would have a fight. When she described this, my impression was that her father was a very difficult if not cruel man but that Dawn was quick to start a fight with him as well, leading to the father's quick exit and Dawn's feeling of abandonment. So, there seemed to be a way she quickly participated in this phantasy of conflict, betrayal, and rejection.

This sad and disappointing relationship with her father seemed to follow her into many of her adult relationships. She was furious with her coworker for appearing to flirt with her boyfriend at a company party. She told me this was the same coworker who told her, "everyone cheats on each other and no one is ever faithful. That is just how people are." Not only did this make Dawn angry and suspicious of her coworker, but it also made her want to convince the coworker otherwise. She told me, "I just want to find out why she thinks that way and how on earth she could believe that. Why does she think that way? I always try and see the best in someone and I am shocked when I find out they are not trustworthy. I go out of my way to show the good side of humanity."

I said, "You sound like you make it your job to be the beacon of light in a world of darkness, trying to shine some light on those who live in the dark?" She said, "That is pretty much right. But, what is wrong with that?" I said, "Maybe it feels uncomfortable to have to live with such flawed, disappointing people so you keep trying to change them and make them better." She said, "I wish they were just good people to begin with."

Here, I was interpreting Dawn's vision of the object as essentially corrupted and fundamentally flawed. In response, Dawn seemed to want to attack and devalue the object and/or restore it and transform it into a better, more positive force. So, she either felt controlled by a broken, flawed object or tried to control and rebuild this disappointing object.

Another person on Dawn's list of fallen idols was a prior boyfriend she had been with for four years. She told me she "knew something was wrong from the start but tried to look the other way. I felt he was not really in love with me and that something else was going on but when I asked, he always said he was fine and really happy. But, it turned out that he had a thing for prostitutes and had been seeing them all along. I finally found out in the fourth year of being with him when I came down with an STD. He lied about the prostitutes but I found evidence on his cell phone and finally confronted him. When I came back from work the next day, he had taken all his stuff and left. I never heard from him again!" So, Dawn felt like she was living with an imposter and a liar but always tried to believe things were ok. She lived in the graveyard but didn't want to see that her best friends and lovers were corpses. So, she either pretended everyone was alive and well or did what she could to reanimate them. When all this denial and idealization fell apart, she was angry and depressed.

During a recent session, Dawn told me she had figured out a way to track her most recent boyfriend's email account, the boyfriend who had just left her. She told me she was able to see that he was communicating with "some other woman and I am going to test him by asking about it." When she did, he denied the whole thing. For awhile, Dawn tried to figure out "why on earth would he lie to me? Why won't he just tell the truth about being with someone else?" This was a mystery she felt she had to solve. It seemed it was more important to find out why a man was broken or lying than to find one who was whole and honest. Dawn seemed to need to find a way to understand the flaw and then she could either fix it or have some way of contextualizing and justifying what took place. I made this interpretation and linked it to her wanting to understand why her father needed to be so disappointing and unavailable. Dawn simply agreed with me and said, "I want to know that. Is that too much to ask?"

As it turned out, through her detective work, Dawn found out that her boyfriend was still drinking heavily and was now seeing another woman. Also, he had been in contact with this other woman the whole time he was seeing Dawn. Dawn was upset and could "see intellectually that the relationship was definitely over but couldn't stop thinking about how it might be different." She contemplated moving out of state to get a job in the city where he was in the hopes that things might work out. I was then put in the place of having to tell her she should wake up and realize her object was useless or dead and to go ahead and throw the dirt on the grave and move on. I made this interpretation and she told me, "Yes. But, it is so hard for me to move on. I want to know why it couldn't work out. Why can't he be my life partner? I want someone to be there for me that way." I pointed out how she said "someone" and that her desperate desire and need to own a loving object meant anyone would do but that also left her constantly wondering why someone with a face, with a personal love, wouldn't want her.

There was a transference situation that arose during one session that showed some of the ways in which Dawn tried to control her objects but as a result of excessive projective identification, this backfired and she often felt controlled and deserted. At the end of a fairly intense session in which she had been sobbing and lamenting the loss of her boyfriend and her unhappiness in general, she announced that she was thinking "she would cut back to only once a week since she had other things that she wanted to be doing and that coming so often was creating tension in her schedule." I said, "Well, it is up to you but I notice you are not asking me what I think about it. You want to work on some things and it may be harder to do so with less time. So, I think you would get the most out of this if you continue coming as we have it set up." She said, "I am the one calling the shots here. I want to come less and if I want to, that is what I will do. Are you saying you won't see me if I come less?" I replied, "You are not asking me what I recommend to be in your best interest. You are suddenly making the decision without including me. So, now I have to tell you what I think and you are seeing it as a debate, a fight, or a threat. Hopefully, we will have time to talk more about this next time."

Dawn brought it up at the start of the following session. She said, "I felt like you were saying you will stop seeing me if I decide to come less. Is that true?" I said, "I want to find out how you came to such a dramatic moment. How are you picturing me so demanding?" She said, "Well, you said you don't recommend I come less and that if I want your help I will need to keep our current schedule." I replied, "Well, that is not exactly what I said. I do want to help you but I need to have the time to do that. So, I am concerned you are not going to give us the best opportunity to make the changes you want. I do want our schedule to remain the same but I also notice you have a hard time picturing us talking about this together and working something out together. Either you call the shots as you put it or I call the shots. So, you were hearing me being controlling and then you also became controlling and told me you were the one calling the shots. Maybe it is hard to see us as working together for the common good?"

Dawn said, "My father told me, the last time we visited, either you do it my way or I will not ever see you again." After a moment of silence, I said, "Now your anxiety and your anger make a lot of sense. You heard me saying the exact same thing. I didn't say that and I don't mean that, but that is what you think is happening so of course you would be very upset. You are asking me if I will abandon you and get rid of you if you don't do it my way. What a horrible place to be." Dawn sobbed and said, "So are you saying that?" I said, "I will not abandon you. I want us to have the proper time to work together but I will not get rid of you for not doing it my way." She was visibly relieved as she had taken it all very concretely. So, the threat with me had passed. Now, we discussed this specter of her relationship with her father always hanging by a thread, depending on if she did his bidding or not. Love was completely conditional and never stable.

This transference situation helped me understand how Dawn was constantly struggling with finding or creating an honorable ideal object that she could always count on but her quest was so tainted by aggression, resentment, and a conviction of failure that she was left with having to always quickly presume the best but then turn around and find the worst. She wants to always control the object, know what is going on, have the answers, and know what to expect. When that doesn't happen, she feels betrayed and is furious and rebels in anger or shrinks in despair. She takes an object and decides it is optimal but is very suspicious if anything happens she isn't expecting. If anything out of her realm of prediction occurs, Dawn then reads that as failure, attack, or abandonment.

But, when these moments of collapse occur, she alternates between seeing it as her fault or as the object's fault. Dawn tells me, "I must be too sensitive or too honest." But, then she will lash out and blame the object for being so dishonest and insensitive to her. Next, she tries to either make the object turn around and be different and better. She seeks the resurrection of the dead, bad object, wanting it to wake up as a fresh, alive good object. If she can't accomplish that she wants to force the bad object to explain itself and reveal the reason behind its flawed badness. "Surely there must be a reason why you left me" is the interpretation I have given regarding her phantasies of her father and his chronic rejection of her. In other words, she hopes there is some legitimate reason that would justify her devastation, instead of the overwhelming sense of outright rejection, betrayal, and deliberate abandonment she envisions.

So, it seems Dawn is always picking men from the graveyard of broken ideals. She spends her time trying to rebuild them, trying to find out why they are broken, and feeling furious if they refuse to provide her the love and support she needs. The moments in which she feels these men are providing what she wants and living up to her ideal are moments of bliss that she then feels are tragically stolen when her father announces he will not be seeing her again, her boyfriend moves out on her, or she realizes another boyfriend is a womanizing alcoholic. I have been interpreting that her own struggle with these phantasies of graveyard zombies, resurrected corpses, and broken ideals in search of her magic mending power blind her to the actual failings of her objects.

In other words, she is so concerned with finding flaws in her objects that she fails to see the actual flaws they have. At the same time, she is ignoring the actual flaws in order to promote her wish for an ideal, resurrected object that has successfully risen from the grave and leads her out of misery to the land of commitment, love, and trust. So, there is a vicious cycle of projective identification that blurs and switches external and internal, outside and inside. I have interpreted that this leads her to not pay attention to critical clues about a man, such as his drinking, his lack of commitment, and so on but to instead end up focusing on the minor day to day mistakes or flaws he may show and Dawn seizes upon those and projects her rage into those. Then, she demands explanations and redress for those without ever having to look at the underlying feelings of anxiety, mistrust, or betrayal she feels overall.

Even though we have only worked together for a short period, by concentrating the work in the transference, the projective identification processes, and Dawn's conflicted phantasy world, there has been some progress. Recently, at the end of a session, Dawn asked me, "The session we have tonight is right after my class so I end up rushing here. In the future, if it is possible, could we meet later or on a different day?" I responded that I couldn't meet later but I thought I could meet her on a different day and we could discuss it next time. After she left the office, it hit me that she was asking about the same thing she had before but in a dramatically different manner. When she had provoked a power struggle with me about meeting less and how she "called the shots," it was over this same session and how she "had better things to do that day." So, the actual concrete external issue was still a concern but it no longer was infused with these paranoid, aggressive, either/or strands of dominance, betrayal, and defiance.

Now, she trusted me to be someone who might actually listen, understand, and consider her needs and we could discuss the situation as equals. This was such a profound shift in her transference that I didn't realize it was the same situation for a minute. In fact, I felt I had spoken with someone else, not the Dawn of a few weeks prior. So, I believe our transference work had helped reduce her anxiety and her reliance on destructive projective identification patterns that had kept us in the graveyard, two dueling corpses with no chance to ever rest in peace. Now, we were, in her phantasy, two objects that were much more whole and alive and who could coexist without having to be vampires feeding on each other or have our trusted object suddenly turn into a rotting zombie. We could be together and gain from it.

This hopeful change and evidence of analytic progress brought us to more insight as well. In exploring her thoughts about men and her relationship to me, her ex-boyfriend, and her father, she began to have some important associations. Dawn told me, "I seem to love to be around people who are falling apart, who are just in pieces. I am not used to or actually I think I am not attracted to people who seem to have it together and who are calm. I think I am addicted to broken people who are crumbling and I try and ignore it or I try and put them back together." I interpreted, "you sound confused about the differences between love and despair." She said, "Yes! I think so. I think I can't tell the difference between drama, chaos, and trauma and trust and love. So, I end up chasing a ghost, not a live breathing person but a ghost" I said, "You spend all your time in the graveyard with the ghosts, lonely and empty. We are working on why you prefer the sad and dramatic graveyard with your ghosts instead of the colorful real world where you could love the living."

So, we have only just begun our journey out of Dawn's emotional graveyard and her self-imposed imprisonment with her ghosts. But, we have made a start and she is motivated to learn more and to at least consider how to change this lifelong pattern.

Discussion

O'Shaughnessy (1964) notes that some patients experience a great hatred for the absent or unavailable object and this hatred or resentment makes it difficult or impossible to benefit or appreciate the good soothing and nourishment that already took place and already exists. In optimal development, the frustrating or absent object will help bring reality to bear, exposing vulnerability, differences, and dependency. Once exposed, gradual tolerance and acceptance can occur. This process appears to have been corrupted and broken down for Dawn. O'Schaughnessy (1964) notes that in normal healthy development, the absent object becomes a good object that is needed or pinned for. Instead of the experience of hateful loss and permanent collapse of the ideal object, this absent object is a good or potentially good object that can be found even if one has to wait for it and search it out.

O'Shaughnessy states that in healthy growth, the mature experience of the absent unreachable object is tolerated and the object is allowed to have its own identity, needs, and interests even if separate and different than the self. However, in more regressed or primitive patients such as Dawn, the absent or non-ideal object is simply a bad, persecutory object. So, in forcing her wish for her boyfriend to be the ideal "life partner" she yearned for, Dawn avoided allowing him his own identity. If she had, she would have seen flaws and traits that she may have avoided, confronted, or walked away from and thus not been hurt or surprised.

So, internalization can produce a union with a living, evolving, and complex object in more mature patients who allow the object to be a separate entity. But, in more difficult and regressed patients, there is an internalization and identification of a dead, hollow, decaying, and unfaithful object. This was the sad case with Dawn and her struggle with what she called "the ghosts" who were broken and betraying and in constant need of her attention without ever giving back much.

The cases presented in this chapter represent a group of patients who are all experiencing a lack of whole object integration and the lack of security available in healthy depressive position functioning. In fact, they tend to exhibit a combination of paranoid-schizoid (Klein 1946) and depressive (Klein 1935, 1940) pathology which leads them to find primitive methods of emotional shelter. I (Waska 2010a, 2010b, 2010c) have written about the breakdown of what Steiner (1987) has referred to as psychic retreats in which such patients seeks an internal refuge from both paranoid and depressive anxieties but then end up facing the worst of both chaotic internal experiences. Steiner notes how these patients show a significant lack of insight and resistance to change, both in themselves and in their objects. Healthy integration of the depressive position includes relinquishing control over the object, including no longer needing to protect, fix, or rebuild the less than ideal object and giving up the need to deny any flaw or difference. Instead, one can welcome a loving but human and sometimes absent or hurtful figure.

Joseph (1959) noted that certain patients cannot bear the dependence they feel for their object due to their early aggression that has in phantasy left their objects damaged or deadened. They are so full of anger, envy, and anxiety over wanting to be wanted but then so sure of rejection and disappointment that they resort to massive control, denial, and doubt regarding their objects. This leaves them with empty zombies they can only hope to revitalize into robots who work for them or to wait for the magical day the object somehow heals itself and comes to their rescue. This was the case in all the patients presented. They were sure they somehow had infected or broken their objects but were desperate and angry that they couldn't find anything better and were destined to remain as eternal caretakers and controlling wardens of their fallen ideal.

Joseph (1959) also points out that through projective identification, this type of patient put their own broken, damaged, and rejected selves into the object so as to not have to live with and manage this toxic and overwhelming internal void. But, then they feel surrounded by broken objects unwilling and unable to nourish them. So, the death instinct is a large part of these patients' dynamic in which they avoid life and growth and tend to link up with deadened objects that they can control and try and reanimate in their own blueprint rather than pursue life and the risk of being left by a living and loving object. So, rather than being able to fully love or be loved, the death instinct and pathological cycles of projective identification create a world of withholding, brittle trust, and false love. This gets back to the idea of not accepting the love and joy that does exist and that has occurred in a relationship, so that all bonds appear empty and suspicious and there is little way to tell if one's relationship is viable but needs work or is poisonous and needs to be terminated.

Gold (1983) notes how patient's like the ones presented rely so much on projective identification and splitting that they negate what goodness exists in the therapeutic relationship. Controlling a corpse that constantly disappoints is easier than risking the vulnerability that comes with true love and equal partnership. As Klein (1950) has stated, only once the patient feels able and willing to withdraw these hostile and desperate projections can their objects shift from persecutory and dead or ideal and eternal to good objects that can be counted on.

And, once the projective fog has cleared, some of those objects will have to be acknowledged for what they are, truly not enough and truly disappointing, leading to painful but healthy rejection and mourning. This in turn leaves the patient open to bring new objects, better objects, into their life and the opportunity to find a more stable and sustaining link to objects who can be loved and depended on for who and what they truly are.

Chapter Four

The Dark Side of the Depressive Position: Severe Struggles with Guilt, Persecutory Loss, and Excessive Reliance on Projective Identification

The case material presented in this chapter involves a patient who was convinced others were always in need and that she was obligated to always serve and protect them. To achieve this, she had to have a hidden or justified way of controlling others. Making sure others were always cared for and watched out for usually meant she had to be the willing victim who paid the price. This masochistic bargain included always giving others the benefit of the doubt instead of expressing a more assertive or aggressive doubt of the object. Behind these patterns of slave-like caretaking and guilty pleasing was a desperate wish for others to one day provide her with the same nourishing, loving care and protection.

By attempting to teach others by example, by showing us all the "right way" to behave, my patient hoped to one day gain her long lost sense of value and meaning from a caring, parenting object. But, in the meantime, she had to maintain a ruthless sadomasochistic relationship with her objects and use the analyst as a vehicle for her unwanted and forbidden desires, both libidinal and destructive.

This patient represents a group of individuals we often meet in psychoanalytic practice. These patients appear to struggle with caring for their objects, not wanting to cause trouble or conflict, and always hoping to find a way to "do the right thing." They feel pressured to accommodate to the object's needs or demands, an internal obligation, and they fear rejection if they don't. Indeed, they feel very guilty if they fail their needy object. This type of patient finds many flaws in themselves and is quick to be self critical, but underneath they see the object as extremely flawed and inferior, in need of constant mending. This leads to desperate and frantic restoration efforts to heal the sickly object as well as an ongoing sense of bitter resentment and envy over how their objects have it so easy at the patient's expense.

In the transference, the patient makes numerous efforts to rid themselves of any evidence of negative thoughts or feelings toward the object. Even more hidden are the patient's envious desires for a turn at being the one getting taken care of. Yet, as soon as this anger is pointed out, the patient quickly denies it and blames themselves or blames the analyst for incorrectly or maliciously pointing it out. Indeed, the patient often is on the trail of the analyst who is acting out in the counter-transference in response to the patient's projective identification efforts. The analyst may end up correctly but also reactively pointing out how and why the patient must be angry at their object. Overall, this type of patient feels burdened by their perceived need to always serve the object but feels they must meet that need as the object is either so demanding or so brittle and sickly. Indeed, the patient may emphasize their humanitarian desires to heal and save the object, always being forgiving and justifying to the object. These patients usually have a history of neglect, of being controlled or emotionally confined, and are very fearful of conflict as it brings on phantasies of damage to others but also reprisal and dire consequences to the self. This anxiety over potential conflict is usually a primary focus of the treatment, an integral aspect of the transference and resistance, and often one of the main reasons they enter treatment to begin with.

However, this also serves as a shield against facing raw dependence, desire, and a desperate wish to be taken care of once and for all. Yet, the guilt and anxiety around this phantasy create a defensive projective identification process of treating others by example. In essence, the patient is training others how to love and care by his actions but never reaps the rewards.

Indeed, the original traumatic bond and sense of persecutory abandonment these patients seem to have suffered internally and externally makes for a crippling sense of loss and emotional hunger. Through the excessive defensive use of projective identification, these feelings are moved into the patient's objects and, with the transference, into the analyst for multiple aims including communication, defense, aggression, evacuation, and narcissistic control.

CASE MATERIAL

J was a thirty-six-year-old bank manager who came to see me in a state of desperation. She was extremely anxious and depressed. Sometimes, J could not sleep at all, so she would drink large amounts of alcohol and take sleeping pills to try and "deal with the overwhelming anxiety." Other times, she would sleep so much, she would miss work on a regular basis. Often, J went out to the bars with her boyfriend, drinking in a reckless manner and then sheepishly telling me about her blackouts. I noticed immediately how this seemed to be an invitation to criticize her and lecture her about the dangers of alcoholism.

J had been in a six-year relationship with a man ten years her junior who had died in a fiery car crash right in front of their home some six months prior to seeing me. J saw the accident right after it happened and watched the fireman extract her boyfriend's dead body. Within a month of his death, she had moved in with her current boyfriend, a man she knew from her work. J now lived with W, a twenty-five-year-old nursing student with a pattern of excessive drinking. J began a three- to four-times-per-week, on the couch, analytic treatment.

During the first few months, J talked a great deal about her physical ailments, her intense anxiety, and the voices she heard from time to time. Initially, she was frightened by these voices but over time "just got used to it." She explained it was usually the voice of her dead boyfriend calling her. In the last few months, it was also the voice of her current boyfriend calling her. After two months of seeing me, my voice was also calling her on occasion. I asked for details. Apparently, there was no real demand to the voice or any other emotional inflection. It was simply a voice calling out to J, saying her name.

Based on how emotionally guarded J was with me most of the time, using intellectualization to dull any expression of feelings, I interpreted the neutral voices as her own neutralized self, stripped of any feelings so as to keep everything controlled and ok. I interpreted that she wanted to call out to me with strong feelings but felt she had better keep it all sterilized and managed because she was unsure of my reaction. J told me she was uncertain what I might think of her and worried I might see her as "all messed up." This "messed up" was partly a reference to how she wanted me to "provide her with a psychiatric diagnosis so we could proceed with the cure" but she also worried about the severity of what I might diagnosis her as. I interpreted that this constant worrying about what I thought of her was part of her constant search to find out how I "assessed her" and whether I might choose to care for her or would I not like her altogether. On one hand, she was able to respond with a few words about not wanting to "be misunderstood or labeled" but then she also went back to the "normal need to have a medical diagnosis so we could get on with the proper treatment."

I also interpreted that the neutral voices might reflect her own defended view, feelings, or opinion of her boyfriends and her analyst. She seemed to neutralize or soften anything other than positive feelings toward almost everyone in her life. J told me that she did have some negative feelings about her dead boyfriend but "mostly she just felt sorry for him. He was such a great man with so much potential. I just wish I had helped him more." In the counter-transference, I felt this was a combination of genuine remorse, a sign of superiority and control on J's part, and a screen against her more aggressive feelings. I made this interpretation and she told me that she had gotten so much negative feedback from so many people about how she should have left him, she never felt anyone would give her a moment to listen to how much she loved him as well. She said this was a problem in her current relationship. I said, "You are worried I am just going to be another person who bad-mouths him. You want me to step back for a moment and try and understand how even though you may have had negative feelings or resentments, you also loved him very much and miss him." J started to cry and said yes.

As we proceeded with the analytic treatment, I noticed how much J avoided herself and avoided sharing herself with me. Instead, the focus was often on some third object or topic. In the transference, she became very concrete and questioning, to the point of being demanding. Also, J quickly engaged me with numerous questions about how I diagnosed her, what my assessment was of her, and how did I treat people with her diagnosis. This went on for the first few months. This escalated when she went to a psychiatrist for medications to deal with her insomnia, her oversleeping, her depression, her extreme anxiety and panic attacks that brought on diarrhea and uncontrollable shaking, and the voices she heard. The psychiatrist put her on a number of medications and told J she was "probably suffering from PTSD, borderline personality disorder with psychotic features, and an anxiety disorder.

Now, J would insist on "knowing how the analytic process worked," "what exactly is my diagnosis," "am I a borderline personality disorder," "how long does this process take," "how good is my prognosis and how long will it take," "what type of homework should I do," and "what do you think about my problems?" All these questions were delivered in a manner that felt controlling, intellectually removed, intrusive, impatient, and demanding but all packaged as if she was simply being politely curious.

I interpreted that J seemed anxious and needed to "know" everything right away but in a way that kept her out of the equation, safe, but in control. I suggested that she wanted to change us into a mechanical vending machine where she just needed to be assigned a certain category for a certain length of time and then everything would be ok. But, it seemed to make her very uncomfortable to just be with me as we together tried to learn about her and how she related to herself and to me. I said that all her questions would be answered by simply learning what unfolds over time between us but that made her uncomfortable, perhaps not in charge and very unsure of what would happen to her. J replied that she is used to taking charge and managing things, which is her role at work. I said, "We are not a work project. We are humans who have to be unsure as we figure out what is going on. That unknown feeling cannot be managed like a commodity but can be gradually changed with both of us understanding the ways you do want change but also try hard to remain the same."

J said, "I don't often think of us that way. I don't even think of an us." I replied, "Perhaps it is safer to objectify us. When you do that, it looks like you take a superior, interested consumer approach to your treatment rather than be in touch with yourself. Making me into a vending machine and you trying to find the right coin to put into the vending machine leaves us out of touch with each other and out of touch with what is really hurting you on the inside." J said, "I see what you mean. I approach most of life that way, I think."

I interpreted that all these questions and lines of inquiry were serving the purpose of neutralizing any feelings J had about anything and instead she was steering us toward an intellectualized study of mental conditions and their treatments. More so, she was creating this third entity, her "condition," that we could focus on, speak about, and intellectually speculate about without ever going near J. At best, we were talking about J instead of talking with each other and her sharing herself with me. I interpreted that J had put herself in the middle of me and "the condition" and now could hide out safely without having to reveal anything about herself or have any expression of self that would stand out in any way.

During the first six months of treatment, it was not unusual for J to spend ten minutes in a given session asking me if I thought she "was a borderline" and how I went about treating such a condition. I would say, "Whether you are a borderline or not, right now you are not being yourself with me and not engaging with me. Instead, this is an intellectual exercise about some condition you may or may not have and is nothing about how you are feeling or thinking right now. I want to know you but you only want me to think about the textbooks I read on borderline conditions. Maybe, you are anxious about me getting to know what is really inside you and who you really are."

These types of interpretations seemed to relax J. They allowed her to stop and reown herself, a moment to look at herself instead of away from herself. She began to consider what was inside instead of deflecting everything outside. Of course, as soon as she started to do this, it brought her in touch with phantasies that made her very confused, anxious, guilty, and unsure. So, J would then return to the more concrete and controlling questions about my practice, her conditions, and so forth.

Certainly, the gravity of J's symptoms, her past traumatic experiences, her chaotic behaviors, and her drug and alcoholic use over the years did lead me to think she was suffering from PTSD, borderline personality with psychotic features, anxiety disorders, and depression. But, from an analytic perspective, the overriding element seemed to be the way she wanted me to focus on something external to her and to me that she could control, even if in a masochistic manner, rather than have her own identity, express her feelings, and risk me knowing her and being affected by her.

When I brought up that J was hiding some of her feelings about her objects from me in order to protect me and them and in order to not have me react in some way, she was able to open up a bit. She explored some of these internal conflicts for a brief period before retreating back into her pathological organizations (Steiner 1993) and primitive depressive phantasies. She agreed she "had many mixed feelings about my dead boyfriend but I thought it wasn't right to bring them up." I asked her for details and J explained that "throughout the relationship with him most of her friends told her she should dump him because he was an abusive loser." But, J loved him and felt people just didn't understand him. She felt he "had great potential in life and just needed someone on his side." I interpreted that perhaps this was exactly what J wanted from someone, a caring understanding person who was on her side. This was an interpretation of her projective identification process and based on some of her traumatic experiences as a child.

Growing up, J was subjected to periods of great stress. After her parents divorced when she was five years old, she was put into a foster home. It is still unclear why neither parent took care of J, but J says she thinks they both "were so into their drinking, their violent lifestyles, and their self-absorbed chaos, they didn't have the capacity to be parents." After being at the foster home for almost a year, J's grandparents took custody of her. Apparently, this was after the grandparents found out that J was being sexually abused. She is still unclear about what happened but it is obvious from her memories of being taken by the foster parent into a bedroom and then she "felt everything go blank" that she was probably sexually abused over the months she was there. When talking about her childhood, J is quick to tell me she "doesn't have parents." She has written them off and feels she never had the experience of a mother and father but credits her grandparents as her parents. However, she felt "so sick and tired of her grandparents' constant loud arguments and their miserable way of living that she did whatever it took to leave home at seventeen and put them behind her."

Interestingly, J now pays all their bills for the nursing home they live in. She alternates between telling me how great she feels to be able to help them and "be there for them" and then other times telling me how they take her help for granted and seem to simply be using her.

After she moved out of her grandparents' home, J had a boyfriend in his twenties that she moved in with and lived with the next few years. After that relationship dissolved, she met her now-dead boyfriend. That relationship started off very well according to J. She felt they had much in common regardless of the age difference. But, very soon, he began to be very controlling and very jealous. He was constantly accusing J of cheating on her and would not allow her to do many things because he suspected she was "going behind his back." J was restricted in how she spent money even though he would spend lavishly on himself.

J told me she would have to sneak out to have a coffee because she "wasn't allowed to buy one, only make one at home." Emotionally, he was abusive and on a few occasions he hit her. Listening to J describe the relationship, she indeed sounded like a victim and an abused wife. But, she also sounded like she was involved in a complicated sadomasochistic dynamic with this man. I interpreted that she would tell me details that really showed how nasty this man could get. But, as soon as I made any comment about J's description of him as nasty, she would quickly defend him and clean it all up. In other words, I interpreted that J was showing her unhappiness but as soon as I gave it life by acknowledging it in some way, she took it back and blamed me for misunderstanding this good man.

So, she was the only one allowed to badmouth him and at the same time she expelled her guilt-ridden aggression into me and then distanced herself from it. In addition, this projective identification based transference pattern created a situation where we were busy sizing this man up as either good or bad and ignoring what was going on inside of J. Again, a third object was used to free J from being noticed or from claiming ownership of her feelings and thoughts about herself and most definitely her feelings about her objects.

As her boyfriend became more depressed, drank more, worked less, and became more abusive and controlling, J felt guilty for "not finding a way to help him through his troubles and get to the other side." Again, she told me he "had such great potential and just needed support and patience." I interpreted that in saying that to me, she was trying to communicate the great struggle she had and still has over not having patience and sometimes feeling fed up with him. J was silent for a bit and then said she agreed.

J said, "I feel so bad admitting that. But, I did feel angry with him for constantly blowing it and for wasting his life. But, again, I feel like it was my fault for not being more of a partner and helping him out." I interpreted how she had momentarily revealed something that felt aggressive or wrong to me and then hastily retreated back to self blame. She agreed and said, "I just don't want you to think he was only a bad person." I said, "You worry that your negative feelings will cancel out all of the love and care you have for him. That we will only hate him and not be able to love him too." J cried and nodded yes. Here, I was interpreting her splitting and projection of all her aggression into me and her fear of coloring him as an all-bad person with no value.

So, as J's boyfriend sank into deeper depression and alcoholism, J tried to help him feel better. When he said he was sick of his job, J told him to quit working and just "try to find out what made him happy." So, he immediately quit his job and left J to pay all the bills while he just sat at home drinking. When he told her he had decided to not look for any other sort of work because he didn't feel like it, she supported his decision and justified it as "a period where he needed to have some space to collect himself."

Indeed, in the transference, J told me these events in a manner that pulled and provoked me into feeling judgmental and outraged. Here, this was an interpersonal aspect of the total transference situation (Joseph 1985) in which the patient's subtle or not so subtle interaction with the analyst elicits certain counter-transference responses that match or counter-balance the patient's various unconscious object relational conflicts.

In these moments, the patient evokes intense projective identification dynamics in which various internal conflicts and aspects of both self and object are projected into the analyst. There can be a strong interpersonal push and pull that creates potential enactments (Steiner 2006) from the analyst. My patient J would present her stories of woe about both her dead boyfriend and her current boyfriend in a manner that pulled me to take sides. It was the type of details she shared, the tone of her voice, and the nature of the story she told that all pulled and pushed me to feel a certain way toward either J or her object.

So, initially in the analytic treatment and still sometimes now, I find myself feeling judgmental of J's dead boyfriend and how he took advantage of J. Also, I notice myself feeling angry at her current boyfriend and occasionally making interpretations that clearly have that flavor to them. But, when I catch myself starting to blame the boyfriend or question what the boyfriend had said or done, according to J, I am able to regain my analytic balance and see that J was comfortably on the sidelines of this conflict, not having to cast a vote and could plead innocent. She could simply and innocently defend her boyfriend from her judgmental analyst. So, over time, I have interpreted that she is so uncomfortable with her own feelings about herself and others that she is utilizing me to be a vessel or vehicle to hold and speak what she could not or did not want to say or feel.

In other words, I began interpreting the various ways J would use projective identification to create a diversion in which we focused on a third object, often in an attacking or critical manner. In this defensive strategy, J never had to claim her own identity, feelings, or differences. This kept her safe and in control, but also neutralized her self worth and internal sense of meaning. She was left formless and without definition. I interpreted that this in turn caused great anxiety and that this pathological organization was fragile and prone to breakdown. I interpreted that part of J's difficult grieving process with her dead boyfriend had to do with these unacceptable feelings breaking through and becoming known. To avoid all of this, J drank to the point of blacking out fairly frequently. I also interpreted that since her dead boyfriend and her current boyfriend seemed to both be alcoholics, she may feel compelled to drink just as destructively or risk being separate and different, which could led to conflct, difference, hurt, and loss.

Right now, since she drinks too much too often, J can't be critical about anyone's drinking without feeling she is being hypercritical and unfair. In other words, drinking destructively keeps her safe from that potential difference and conflict. J agreed with my interpretation and told me she doesn't want to drink so much but has got "into the habit with her boyfriends." She has actually suggested that they both drink less but then would get drunk with them "on special occasions," which occurred fairly often. However, as we explored these ways of acting out, we noticed how she was getting me to set limits regarding her drinking as she wouldn't with their drinking. Also, she was trying to ensure the love and acceptance of her objects by going along with whatever they wanted. As we came to understand these ways of relating, J's behavior with alcohol gradually shifted.

Over the last six months, J gradually drank less although she still would report black-out episodes and sometimes came to session smelling of booze. When I asked about this, she told me she "needed it to help with the intense anxiety." At those times, I interpreted she was worried to show her true feelings to me so she needed a buffer. She would often say she didn't know what her feelings were, only that she felt very nervous. However, during a recent session, I was bringing up her drinking and how that was no doubt interfering with or creating bad side effects with the multiple medications she was on. I remarked how this might be a sign of her rebelliousness or outright anger emerging in this "I don't care" attitude and behavior.

After I said this, J froze up on the couch and was silent. Then, she said, "I am having this very intense odd feeling. I feel uncomfortable about how you keep bringing up my drinking." I said, "You sound angry, like you feel I am picking on you or nagging?" J was quick to say, "Well, no. It isn't anger. But, maybe it is some kind of mild irritation about you continuing to bring it up. I want to go on to discuss something else now but I wanted to report that feeling as it is so odd." I said, "Maybe it feels odd because you censor any negative feelings toward me or others and when you let yourself be more aware of them or share them with me, you are anxious about how I will react. Now, you want to quickly move away to another topic, a topic less volatile?" J said, "I see what you mean. It is very unusual for me to have that kind of a feeling. It feels very odd. My body is not used to that kind of sensation." I said, "Your mind is so uncomfortable with it that the feelings and thoughts end up in your body."

In the last few months, there has been other times when J would speak of her more negative feelings but always with a neutralizing or justifiable caveat that essentially took me or the other person off the hook and saved us from J's anger. I made this interpretation fairly frequently and also pointed out how she preferred to recruit me to be the angry, resentful, or judgmental one by giving me tales of her boyfriend's nasty behavior and abusive ways. Then, J would sit back and see what I do. A fairly constant theme in these stories was how J went out of her way to spend her money, time, and emotional energy to help her boyfriend out and others as well. I noticed how in these tales of martyrdom and ongoing sympathy for others, there was an air of superiority and pity.

One day, J told me she "felt bad for me when she found out how little the insurance company paid me to see her." I asked for details and J explained that it seemed "sad that I was paid so little." In discussing this over the next two sessions, several issues emerged. The more apparent transference element was the parallel to how J viewed both her former and her current boyfriend. Now, I, too, was another man who deserved more and while I did my best and had a good heart, life was being unfair to me. J wanted to help out or at least express her sympathy. So, she once again was trying to patch up her downtrodden object and pump me back up. In this scenario, she blamed herself for my condition, as it was her insurance that was doing the damage to me. She felt responsible to make it up to me somehow. In fact, she offered to do as much.

So, in the transference, I interpreted the same sort of guilt and remorse she felt in her other relationships. J felt she had somehow added to my burden and not helped me to obtain my full potential. I noticed myself feeling irritated, like it was none of her business in the first place and that she was trying to control me or take over. Not only did I feel controlled but I felt demeaned as well. I felt J was essentially looking down on me and feeling sorry for me in an arrogant manner. Actually, one of the first things J had told me about herself was that she was "an arrogant person amongst other things." So, I said she felt sorry for me and in that sense sees me as a poor little child she has to keep an eye on, protect, and nudge forward. In that experience, she is more the dominant one than the passive victim. I interpreted that she saw us all as the victims and she would have to step in and offer assistance to help us.

So, I was interpreting J's grandiosity that was camouflaged within her masochistic way of relating. This is similar to Cooper's (2010) notion of the underlying grandiosity in many patients' self-loathing stance. In response to my interpretations, J told me she "certainly didn't feel like she was looking down on us but if she were able to make someone's life better than it was she felt an obligation to do so." Noticing her sudden resistance, I choose to go at it from a different angle. All conflicts are encased within struggles with love, hate, and knowledge (Britton 1998) so when she pushed away the interpretation regarding her aggressive superiority and controlling stance, I took up her conflicts regarding love and need being utilized in a controlling manner though projective identification.

I interpreted that J might be doing for others what she wished had been done for her. She told me she would have really "benefited from a normal set of parents and a better experience in my early years but that is not what I got so I can't change that now." I said, "Maybe you are still trying to change that by the way you relate to me and others, still trying to have someone end up happier at the end of the day." J nodded and said she thinks "that is right on some level but it is hard to touch."

J felt sorry for me in other ways, such as thinking I must be tired because we had an evening appointment or feeling I was "bored with hearing about her same old problems again and again." Here, again, I made interpretations regarding her seeing me as somehow weak and small and that since she was bigger and stronger she needed to help me or save me. But, I also made interpretations regarding how she was wanting to help me and others who seemed so down and out and maybe this was a way to avoid the uncomfortable reality that she needed me to "feel sorry for her." In other words, I interpreted that she was avoiding having me take care of her sorrow, anxiety, and sense of inferiority so she projected that into me and took care of me instead. This line of interpretation seemed helpful, but only in combination with us exploring the more aggressive, superior, and controlling manner that she tried to use to help out all her ailing objects.

While I find it important and useful to move back and forth from a focus on one aspect of love-, hate-, or knowledge-based phantasies when the patient is too sensitive, anxious, aggressive, resistant, or fragmented, ultimately we must bring all three levels of psychic functioning into the integrative process of our interpretation efforts.

J eventually started standing up to her boyfriend when various situations arose. But, when J would tell me the story in detail, I noticed that often she stood up for herself in ways that were flimsy and false. There was a pattern of her pushing back but then collapsing emotionally, letting him have his way after all. I noticed that the transference mode was such that J pulled me to potentially step in and make some sort of judgment call. So, after telling me a story of how she was upset he was spending money again on something frivolous, she would go on to the next topic of how she was going to "reward" him with a expensive surprise.

During one session, J had spent twenty minutes telling me how she had "expressed her discomfort and irritation at him for wanting to buy another motorcycle." She said she had "drawn the line" with him about it. Shortly after we finished discussing it, she told me he had been asking her to write him a check so he could buy a new leather jacket. And she "decided to let him have it since it meant so much to him." This seemed aimed at making me say something punitive such as, "How dare you go back on your word? Why can't you hold the line with this freeloader?" I would then interpret that she couldn't stay firm and felt guilty for demanding he respect her needs and as a result caved in and tried to appease him. I added that she had me take over the role of the "heavy." Over time, these type of interpretations seemed to help J to take back these aspects of herself and begin to work with the anxiety of having likes and dislikes toward the same person without having to disavow or jettison them in some destructive projection.

Another example of this ongoing transference dynamic had to do with J telling me about how her boyfriend "really enjoyed" playing golf once a week at the high-end resort club that charged $150 each time. There were plenty of golf courses in the area that charged $30–$100 but he insisted that the resort club was "special and really made him feel good. He enjoyed looking forward to it." J told me she "knew how down he had been this year so if I can do something to make him enjoy life more, I really want to make it happen." Temporarily off balance in the counter-transference, I pointed out how even though J made sure to pay for expensive golf every week, there were times when she couldn't pay her copay of $15 to me. As we went along, I noticed how not only was this a way she tried to say she was "just being a nice person, giving him this special treat that he loved so much and deserved" but J was also showing off how understanding and giving she was.

In other words, this was also a thinly shielded pompous method of bragging and showing off how she could easily afford such luxury. Indeed, she eventually justified this expense by telling me how much she made, how she was the highest paid in her department, and how many thousands of dollars she was expecting in bonus money. I had to point out that while in the past she was often claiming to be a victim to his greedy and controlling ways, now I was the victim to her greedy and controlling ways of having to manage her object in whatever way she wanted without regard to the fallout in our relationship. Again, these types of interpretations were at first met with resistance. J took them as punitive advice on how to better live her life.

Or, when I was more neutral and less caught up in my enactments, she would take what I presented in the emotional realm and turned it into concrete advice that I gave her and that she should carry out as an external exercise, thus avoiding having to expore the internal meaning of my interpretations. But, overall, as I tried to relay a more benign curiosity on how and why she needed to manage me and her boyfriend in these ways, J gradually allowed herself to think about these matters and consequently make some changes over time.

My sense of J's loss with the death of her first boyfriend was that she was truly missing a person she pictured she could count on but the "count on" feeling was guaranteed by him having to be around at all times to be taken care of. Indeed, with both boyfriends, J seemed to feel she had found a solid foundation but had to do whatever she could to ensure that foundation was going to stay around. This meant a great deal of self-serving masochism. By keeping them as her little first-aid projects, she had someone to always look after and be with, an emotional kidnap victim of sorts, without whom she would feel very lost indeed.

This was similar to how J had several people staying over at her house because they were without jobs or in-between jobs. They often drank up her booze and slept long into the afternoon. J told me she felt she was "being a good friend but also thought it was important that they feel like they were pulling their weight." So, J had them start doing house choirs or errands and in turn paid them. She felt sorry for them and provided for them, but it was all in a manner that sounded like she was ignorant of how she was being taken advantage of while at the same time ignorant of how she was taking advantage of them to serve as yet another emotional nanny.

As mentioned, as we proceeded along in the analytic treatment, J would make statements that were challenging, condescending, and devaluing of me and the treatment. But, as with other matters in the transference, it was often actualized though a projective identification process. J would bring in a third object, such as her boyfriend, her psychiatrist, a friend, or others and tell me how they had questioned her treatment or said something disparaging about me. I would interpret that J was bringing in barbs and jabs to my office and then claiming she was just the messenger. I pointed out how she was quick to avoid ownership of these so-called outside questions and critiques.

In response, J would tell me that she was "just wanting to convey some concerns others have had and to clarify the type of approach being used." She would quickly retreat into intellectual control and tell me, "I just want to make sure I am aware of the procedure and how to best participate in it. If there is something that we are not doing that I need for my problems, I would want to know that so I could go about correcting it." I interpreted this was a tightly managed devaluation and that she seemed to be worried about depending on me and not always knowing exactly everything about me or what was going on. J was able to reflect a bit on that and become more in touch with herself for awhile before drifting back into her more logical base of operation.

During a recent session, J came in and told me about sleeping for eleven hours, right through her first client meeting, and how frustrated she felt about it. After I asked for details, it turns out that she had taken two sleeping pills and a few cocktails on top of her regular psychiatric medications and then passed out. After a bit of questioning on my part, I noticed how she was being a naïve innocent and I was being a judgmental lecturing parent about how to never mix alcohol with sleeping pills and why was she acting so stupid. I made my next interpretation out of this counter-transference information. I said that she was not thinking for herself or about her behavior and in this way she was leaving it up to me to be the one to actually think and care. I was the one trying to sort out what was happening to her and how to understand things in her life while she was just left puzzled and frustrated about sleeping through her workday.

So, here again I noticed J taking herself out of the equation and leaving me to run the show. Through projective identification, she was enlisting me to be the thinker and she was in the resulting void. I asked her about this and wondered out loud if there was something that made her anxious about thinking *with* me about these things instead of it being so radically divided. I asked if it was uncomfortable to think with me about the big picture.

J said, "I never think about the big picture, I only react to the immediate panic I feel and try and get rid of it." I said, "So, I wonder if we have gotten lost in the panic? We are talking so much about the pills and the booze but not about what the big picture is?" J was silent for a bit and said, "What I think about all the time, what causes the panic, are my feelings about losing my boyfriend. I am often thinking of seeing him dead at the scene of the accident, I am starting to hate my job, the job I used to love, and seeing my new boyfriend go from someone I respected and admired to into someone always drinking and feeling so worthless. On top of all that, yesterday, I got a call from my uncle who I periodically send money to because he has never really gotten himself together in life, always just floating around in life quite aimlessly. He said he was getting evicted and asked me to give him some money. Of course I will do it but it felt like just one more thing raining down on me." I said, "Or just one more person that you feel compelled to save from drowning and hope you get there in time." J nodded and sighed. I said, "Maybe, you wish we would hurry up and notice you drowning and come to save you for a change." J said, "That feels right on target!"

In our most recent analytic sessions, we have been able to focus more directly on this sense of emotional drowning that J lives with. I have continued to interpret the ways J seems to want to take care of me and others in a controlling and guilt-ridden manner as a way of dealing with her lifelong sense of loss and neglect. I have interpreted, to a very positive response, that J is trying to show us all the proper way to take care of someone, always being understanding, forgiving, and loving. Never should a bad thing be said or done to the one in your care. So, using excessive reliance on projective identification, J is trying to show us all the right way to parent her instead of the abusive, painful experiences she had throughout her early years.

As we proceed and examine these transference dynamics, J seems to slowly be able to relinquish her grip on these rigid ways of relating to others and to herself. Now, she can begin to consider a life of her own in which she would have needs and desires and trust that others might be willing and able to meet them or at least care enough to make the effort.

Discussion

The sense of internal loss was extreme for J and seemed to encompass a paranoid-schizoid (Klein 1946) state of emptiness as well as a primitive depressive state (Klein 1935) with crippling persecutory guilt that was the result of her projection of loss and desire onto her important objects. She consistently evoked a third outside object to play this out with, allowing herself to hide in the middle and deflect any possible attention or conflict. This was such a regular feature of the transference that I would frequently be swept up in it without noticing it for awhile. Then, I would notice myself on the trail of whatever her most recent crisis was, exploring her subtle sense of superiority, examining a sudden panic state or severe depressive lapse, or analyzing some other aspect of her inner and outer life. But, as genuine and important as these areas of focus were and still are, I would finally realize that something was missing from the transference and from our immediate conversation. She was lost and that was the greatest loss that was created by her lifelong struggles with her feelings and the internal conflicts she felt with her objects.

A symbolic or external example of this internal void was evident in the reason J came to see me in the first place. This was her extremely disabling physical and mental symptoms, which seemed to have been triggered or reissued by the sudden death of her boyfriend. So, I would periodically notice that this topic was completely missing from our relationship. I would have to realign myself in the counter-transference to this missing aspect of J's life which I think symbolized a lifetime of loss, suffering, and trauma. So, I would have to stop what we were pursuing or discussing and interpret that J had become lost and forgotten, excerpted by her tales of pity for others, her concern about my needs, her sense of obligation to save others, and so forth. I had to bring the focus of concern onto J. I would say, "I think we are forgetting your needs and how much you still miss your boyfriend."

In response, J would always pause and after a period of silence, she seemed to become less anxious as she started to talk about her feelings. She would begin to tell me how much she missed her boyfriend and how "regardless of how he treated me and how others saw him, he was a good guy. I loved him and we had many special years together. I go through every day thinking about him. I try and not bring it up because I know my current boyfriend doesn't think much of him." I said, "So, you have to keep your sorrow and grief to yourself, not wanting us to be irritated or judgmental of you." J said, "Yes, I try and not think about it." I said, "You want to think about everyone else's needs instead. That is a way of getting your needs met in a controlled, safe way but ultimately it leaves you empty and probably angry." J said, "I think I know what you mean. Everyone else seems to always be asking me for something."

So, to deal with the unwanted conflicts regarding self expression, identity, independence, difference, and aggression or need, patients like J employ powerful projective identification dynamics to manage their phantasies regarding love, hate, knowledge, and the relational aspects of these emotional states. In the transference, they utilize the analyst as a place to deposit unwanted, toxic feelings toward the object and if the analyst tries to interpret these feelings, the patient will completely deny ownership of those feelings and instead enjoy the safety of someone else sorting out these precarious states of mind. So, in a spectrum of neurotic to borderline and narcissistic cases, these patients disparage and defend their objects, acting as victim, aggressor, martyr, and assassin. Some of these patients will become more in touch with their aggression, envy, and sense of superiority and feel entitled to lash out at others, including the analyst. To find the way to a more balanced sense of self-appraisal and object perspective can feel vulnerable and like an unfair loss and surrender. For others, it can also feel like a scary admittance of hatred and grievance that brings on a sense of primitive or persecutory guilt and emptiness.

However, with steady interpretive focus on the patient's phantasies of weak and broken objects that need repair and rescue, the patient can come to accept that it is them, through projective identification, that actually desires and craves to be found and rescued by the object. In owning this hunger to be rescued from emptiness, betrayal, and inner collapse, these difficult patients can finally discover themselves and learn to love themselves as well as their objects in a healthy and integrated manner.

As Mitchell (1995) explains, modern Kleinian analysts view projective identification as an expectable and regular aspect of most analytic treatments. In addition, the interpersonal and intra-actional aspects of projective identification are usually present, especially with the more active, action prone patient. This dynamic pulls on the analyst in a variety of ways. The case material showed the analyst being recruited into a few ongoing patterns such as judge, advisor, and holder of all things aggressive.

These projective identification patterns were the outgrowth of the patient's phantasy world and the resulting conflicts and anxieties. As Spillius (2001) states, phantasy creates creativity and destructiveness in all of us, giving meaning to the external world and providing a richness or gothic darkness to the inner world. Internal phantasy casts a shadow on external events and people as do external events and people shape and shift the internal climate. For my patient, J was constantly bringing internal desires, conflicts, and anxieties to bear with her objects and then fortifying these phantasies with her actual experiences with the external world.

In a panel report (2004), Hinshelwood reported the three central elements of current Kleinian technique to be the interpretive process aimed at modification of anxiety, the analyst being drawn into playing certain roles or parts of the patient's phantasies and gradually becoming conscious of it so as to then interpret it, and how all of this is part of the goal of bringing new knowledge to the patient's mind and helping him allow, accept, and integrate that new knowledge of self and object.

Joseph (1987) has explored how Melanie Klein thought the aims of projective identification to include getting rid of unwanted parts of the self that cause anxiety or pain, projecting the self or parts of the self into an object to dominate and control it and thus avoid any feelings of being separate, getting into an object to take over its capacities and make them its own, and invading in order to damage or destroy the object. Since that time, Kleinians have expanded the possible aims to other unconscious goals including the core of J's phantasy, that of having the lost child be found by the good mother. But, the patient who goes on using such mechanisms can avoid any awareness of separateness, dependence, need, or its resulting sense of loss, anger, envy, and so on. But, Joseph (1987) notes that it sets up anxieties of a persecutory or claustrophobic type panic as well as other forms of anxiety.

She goes on to state that if the analyst who is subjected to the reoccurring projective identification process is really open to what is going on and is able to be aware of what he is experiencing, this can be a powerful method of gaining understanding into the patient's transference and underlying phantasy conflicts. A good deal of the current Kleinian clinical use of counter-transference comes from that understanding as well as realizing the accompanying enactments that can result. This was all a part of J's treatment and many examples were provided in the case report.

Andresen (1996) talks about the cultivation of imagination and the ability to reflect on the self as a result of healthy container/contained experiences between infant and caretaker, with images of an I and a you that can exist in harmony both independently and dependently. This was definitely not the early experience for J and as an adult she continued to struggle with problems of containment and conflicts regarding independence, dependence, need, and loss of a nourishing object that could provide its own container as well as offer J one that could be trusted and relied on.

Instead, the container was always broken, collapsing, or turning into a constricting prison. Marilyn (2001) has written about the confusion between being held and being controlled. For J, this continues to be an issue in which she is prone to controlling the object while thinking she is holding and containing them in a protective manner. This is one aspect of her deep conflict regarding desire, loss, guilt, and persecution. She wants to help the object but feels guilty about her desire to lash out or drop the object and demand her own nourishment and holding.

But, J is also anxious that if she were to risk this longed for containment and holding, it would turn into a traumatic betrayal, a loss of hope and trust, and a breakdown and collapse of her internal world, a repeat or resurgence of the early agony of childhood onward. We continue to slowly find our way to and through this treacherous experience.

Part Two

Kleinian Work within the Narcissistic Realm

Chapter Five

The Difficulties of Working with Thick-Skinned Narcissists: Envy, Projective Identification, and the Internal Void

Herbert Rosenfeld (1987) has made groundbreaking discoveries about the nature of narcissism and the method of working analytically with what he terms thick-skinned narcissists. These are the patients who disavow any need and refuse to depend on others. Envy, power, and control are hallmarks of their presentation and projective identification, devaluation, and splitting is usually overly relied upon.

Feldman (2008) reviews some of Rosenfeld's earlier work on the narcissistic parts of the patient's personality that battle with the analyst for control over the dependent and vulnerable aspects of the patient's personality. Feldman believes the narcissistic attacks and destructive neutralization of the value of self and object are always the consequences of overwhelming envy. Clinically, I think it is helpful how Feldman details the patient's envy, the following destructive narcissistic attacks, the manic triumph, and then the resulting internalization of damaged, useless, or devalued objects. This fusion with such feeble victims is a significant area of struggle in the treatment that brings about further defensive reactions that often are confusing and difficult for the analyst. The patient presented in this paper's case material seemed to view his objects as so neutral, concrete, or without depth that he could never feel fed by them or ever nourished by their value, security, and understanding. For him, objects were simply flimsy flotation devices that barely keep him afloat in the sea of chaos and eternal nothingness that ruled his internal life. For a moment, he could feel safe and in control, only to then sink back under.

Feldman makes a helpful point in stating how hard it is for narcissistic patients to take in our interpretations because it puts them in touch with the unbearable reality of feeling limited, in need, without knowledge, and powerless versus an analyst who apparently, given his interpretations and interest, must have knowledge and thus have power and control over the patient. Therefore, in this vicious cycle of projective identification, the patient becomes even more envious and prone to neutralizing or outright attacking the treatment and any link between analyst and patient or between the self and any doubts, fears, and uncertainties. This will be illustrated with the case material that shows the constant difficulty and frustration the analyst must endure in the counter-transference with such patients.

Regarding the operation of the counter-transference, Ogden (1997) has explored the issue of using reverie in the aid of understanding the patient. I see this reverie as a conscious byproduct of counter-transference, similar to the interpersonal aspects of the patient's unconscious transference state. Like the clues the patient's interpersonal patterns of relating provide, our counter-transference reverie is a gateway to understanding our internal constellation of love, hate, and knowledge that has been put into play by the patient's projective identification processes. A symbolic and creative counter-transference play unfolds in the mind of the analyst which with examination can provide valuable information to the nature of the patient's phantasy struggles.

With more narcissistic patients, the transference includes a concrete attack on the symbolic and tends to dismantle or block this rich reverie state. Bass (1997) examines this concreteness as a defense against separation and difference. So, individuality is muted, even in the counter-transference ability to mentally roam about and muss.

Rosenfeld (1987) has emphasized the importance of being firm and direct with narcissistic patients, using confrontation as part of interpretive observations. Rosenfeld stated that with such patients the analyst must avoid merely accepting what is given interpersonally or psychologically in the transference and instead attempt to properly contain the material. Hamilton (1990) has summarized this Kleinian notion of the analyst internalizing the patient's projective identification process, transforming it by giving it meaning and after a period of containment, returning it to the patient via interpretation.

Steiner (1996) has examined this process in great detail and highlighted the difference between understanding and being understood. He notes that the first phase of containment is when the analyst is able to tolerate, manage, translate, and return the patient's material via an interpretation that ideally includes a reference to the transference and the patient's core anxiety and phantasy conflicts. This allows the patient to feel understood. For the narcissistic patient, they will use this as a source of information with which they can find a concrete and immediate fix to their symptoms and anxiety state so as they can return to their previous narcissistic identity. They take the understanding as a patch and the containing analyst as a faceless repairman they can use for a moment or two.

Steiner (1996) states that the second phase of containment is much more difficult and I would say often unbearable for the thick-skinned narcissist. In this phase the patient must realize his dependence on the analyst for understanding. They must gradually work through the mourning of their attachment to the containing analyst until through the grieving process they begin to view and understand the world in a more independent fashion. This is the genuine, depressive position (Klein 1935, 1940) development and healthy internalization of the containing function. While existing within the paranoid-schizoid position (Klein 1946), all this is experienced as dangerous, foreign, and insulting to the narcissistic patient who at best will attempt a false independence and claim to have always understood, preferring to think only for themselves. This ongoing clinical struggle with the narcissistic patient can make for hurtful and confusing counter-transference states of mind.

A similar notion is expressed by Billow (2000). He discusses the necessary pain and passion of the counter-transference and the containment process. Billow states that the analyst must not evade the love, hate, and curiosity that emerge within the counter-transference. With narcissistic patients, this may include a premature separation and mourning experience in the counter-transference when we are forced to drift from feeling understood by ourselves via an empathic reverie in which we imagine the patient's internal life through our feeling and reactions. We are forced away from this place to a more solitary, lonely sense of having to accept that we cannot always understand or even that we may never understand such a patient. However, the struggle is to remain in touch with the love, hate, and curiosity we feel and not shut off ourselves from the object we can't understand, killing it off with envious feelings, casting it aside, or using narcissistic indifference as a defense in the same way our patient does.

CASE MATERIAL

B came to me after his wife found out he had been frequenting a "Gentleman's Club" and an "After Hours Club," where he would get drunk and watch girls strip. Sometimes, B would "go along" with their efforts to charge him extra for them to masturbate him in the back room. B described himself in a very passive manner. According to his stories, he was usually very drunk and sounded like a submissive, naïve tourist who wondered in to the club and suddenly was being masturbated. I interpreted this manner of relating the story to me in the transference and B told me that he did feel it was a very passive experience but certainly one he enjoyed. I said, "So, you are saying they called the shots and you went along for the ride." He said, "Yes. I think so, but I am not proud of it."

In fact, for the first month, B told me he had just sat and watched the strippers. It was only when his wife confronted him on the "services" offered at these places and threw him out for a few days screaming at him for being a liar did he confess to me that he also had sexual encounters with the women. He said he was too embarrassed to tell both of us. I interpreted that he seemed ashamed but also seemed to not want to get caught by me or his wife so he was keeping a dirty secret from us. In that sense, he was in control. So, while B did seem to practically be the victim of these women by the way he described it, after awhile I was struck by how he had actively and callously told his wife he was "going to the gym to relax for awhile" and instead set out to the sex club.

In this way B was active and seemed to not ever think about how he was affecting his wife. She was just somebody to put on hold while he took care of his pleasures. However, over time, I also had the sense from his stories that his wife was volatile, prone to severe anger, and very much ran the show and called the shots at home. So, there was this passive little boy who got pushed around by all the big women and a cold, do-as-he-pleases narcissistic man who didn't ever think about the feelings of his partner. This polarized set of relational patterns also colored the transference.

On one hand, I felt B was my little kid who was the poor victim of all these pushy women and needed my help in navigating himself into adulthood. I should tell him how to be a better man and how to fix his problems because I had the answers and he needed them. But, it also seemed he was the sly, manipulating man who was treating me and others like disposable children who should wash his windshield and then get out of the way. Just as he related to me as so powerless but also seemed to look down on me from his place of power, I also ended up feeling my own lack of power in the counter-transference when I made my interpretations and he brushed them aside with a brief concrete nod. Here, I was after his mutual collaboration in the treatment, a working together potential that he seemed to keep from me. In fact, I felt he had spoiled that desired state and left us in a barren place in which everything was a one-way street with me servicing him or him being the malleable victim to my special and dominant knowledge.

B was also an alcoholic and had been drinking a great deal on the weekends for at least ten years. It was only when his wife found a calling card from one of the women in B's jacket that things started to unravel. She demanded to know the truth and all the details. She also confronted him on his drinking and threatened divorce if he didn't seek help immediately. That is when he came to see me.

B was a manager at a local restaurant. He said he enjoyed the fact that he "really ran the show and called the shots for years. I made most of the decisions and could pretty much decide the direction of the place. So, I felt engaged and motivated." About three years ago, because of the collapsed economy, the owner of the restaurant elected to start being on site every day and "began to micro-manage everything." B said, "I felt terrible every day and I dreaded going to work. My drinking really took off at that point and I think I started to go to the clubs way more often. I couldn't sleep at all for that first year. Finally, last year the owner sold the business and the new owner didn't want to be there so now things are back to where they used to be. I run the place for the most part. But, I think I am still getting over that hellish period."

B had stopped drinking two weeks before he came to see me and I told him it would be a priority to remain sober so we could slowly get to the bottom of what was really going on. I began to see B three to four times a week on the analytic couch. Right off the bat, I noticed certain ways B related to me in the transference. Like I said, there was a mix of passive willingness and active demand. He wanted to know what he should be doing to prevent any reoccurrence of his drinking and his "cheating" behavior and was "ready to do whatever it takes." This was all said in a way that felt like he was passively throwing himself at the mercy of the court. He was ready to make me the leader, teacher, and commander and would follow my instructions. This seemed part of a very mechanical, intellectualized approach B had in which he wanted to know the cause of the problem, the solution to the problem, and how to obtain maximum benefit as quickly as possible. So, his intention seemed good and he seemed motivated, even if it was because of his fear of his wife's rage and by a masochistic stance with me. But, his motivation also seemed false in the sense that he was treating me as a pill to fix his problems and he was wanting to know what medication to take, what dosage, and how long to take the pill without really being involved in the process himself.

On a more active side, B seemed to have a way of demanding things from me and putting me on the spot, turning the tables so he was in charge. He kept telling me about the latest books on sexual addiction, troubled marriages, and gender power games that he had just read, quotes from so-called experts in the field about what the more modern cutting-edge treatments were. This was done in a way that gave me the message, "you must not have what I want because you haven't given me what I want yet" and the ominous feeling of "these other people obviously know the answers so I must be wasting my time with you."

B also brought in all the latest research he found online as well as various articles touting the immediate progress shown when certain medications were used. I felt dismissed, insulted, and told how to do my job. I wanted to lash out but the sheer intensity of this counter-transference (Grinberg 1962) and the striking lack of affect in what he said to me actually helped to stabilize me.

I was able to realize I was in the crosshairs of his unrelenting demands, devaluations. He wanted something the other therapists allegedly had but I seemed to be lacking. I noticed myself feeling this oedipal threat of being left for someone else who has something better to offer, initially making me want to hop to it and try to prove my worth. I was able to realize this projective identification envious assault was taking place and gradually make some interpretations. I interpreted that B was talking about the positive attributes of all these other people and approaches so he must not be able to take in the work we are doing. I said he must not know how to slow down, trust me, and feel comfortable working together, which might help him feel more hopeful about what we are doing and what we have discovered so far. Here, I was interpreting the psychological fallout of envy and projective identification.

I also interpreted his wanting an instant cure and therefore the fact that we had met for only three or four weeks must feel like way too long. I wondered if it wasn't instant then maybe he would have to stop and notice the feelings inside of him that he normally dismisses and tries to drink away or deal with via the sex clubs. Here, I was interpreting the underlying anxiety of the thick-skinned narcissist and the fear of internal emptiness and relational chaos. Loss, difference, separation, and overwhelming anxiety were all looming but B was working hard to prevent this by his rigid, controlling, and concrete defenses.

B told me he could see what I meant and would try and be more patient but then sarcastically added that he was only trying to be an "informed consumer" and wanted to fix whatever the problem was as soon as possible for the sake of the marriage. I said, "You want to fix it so fast but it is unclear what 'it' is." He agreed and slowed down for a moment. But, it wasn't long before B was bringing other objects into the room who always had something sweeter and better than what I had to offer. When I interpreted this, he told me, "don't take it personal Doc, I just want to find the best remedy for what ails me and the longer it takes the more my wife will be angry. She wants to know what the issues are and what I am doing about it." I pointed out that suddenly he was putting himself in the middle of his wife and I and feeling pressured to perform. As a result, he was passing on the pressure to me and telling me I needed to hurry up, so now I was in the middle of him and his wife. These are interpretations of very primitive paranoid schizoid phantasies of oedipal calamities where issues of envy and persecution rule.

A similar situation occurred when B told me that he wanted me to talk with his couples therapist. He had started couples therapy with his wife and had been telling me that this therapist didn't seem to understand much about alcoholism. B wanted me to call him up and "talk to him about it." This was said in a very matter of fact, plain sort of way. I asked him more about it and he explained that he was sure it "was standard procedure" for therapists to be in touch with each other. In fact, he cited how his wife's therapist was talking with the couple's therapist so it seemed only "normal medical protocol" to do the same. The more he talked about it, the more I noticed my counter-transference feelings about it and that helped me understand the transference.

I felt B was being a very pushy, demanding, and devaluing baby who felt misunderstood by this other object and wanted me to step in and rescue him. He wanted me to call this guy up and set the record straight. Essentially, B wanted me to call the other therapist up and say, "Hey, you obviously don't know much about alcoholics. Here is what you need to know and now you will treat B better and give him a break. Stop being so hard on him and hurry up and learn the ropes, buddy."

So, it seemed like B felt powerless and picked on by this therapist, much as he described his relationship with his wife. He wanted me to step in on his behalf and set this bully straight. In the process, he was putting this therapist down as ignorant and off track, needing someone in the know to educate him on the basics.

But, the way he was laying this all out also was to put me down as he took up the power and passively demanded I call the therapist and if I didn't I would be ignoring "normal protocol" and "standard procedure." Indeed, he was also putting me down for not having done all that already. So, B was acting out a triangular oedipal situation in which there were frequent role changes, power struggles, and envious attacks. There was someone being picked on and neglected, there were irresponsible neglectful parents, and there were objects who could rescue and protect. But, B had to orchestrate all of this. He was the victim yet held the orchestra leader's baton. Everyone else had something B needed and was withholding or he felt it in reverse, everyone was demanding something from him that he didn't have. Envy and greed, fueled by projective identification and desperation created an emotional kidnap and ransom situation that always ended badly.

I interpreted all of this over the course of several sessions. As with much of the way he reacted to my input, B took it in a very concrete manner. He told me I was correct about most of what I said but he thought I should simply "make the call" to the other therapist. When I tried to explore his feelings in the moment he was reluctant to share much, saying he just thought "that was normal procedure." He did say he understood and "kind of saw what I meant" when I emphasized the way he had placed himself in the middle of two objects, myself and the other therapist, just as he felt in the middle of myself and his wife who was demanding results and answers. But, instead of trying to expand on this, B just waited for my next question.

I interpreted that this was in fact part of the problem, the reason he may end up feeling so empty and without any personal definition. B seemed interested and we talked a bit more about it. But, by and large, B devalued my comments, neutralizing them with intellect and preventing any emotional link to me or my interpretations. When I then made that interpretation, B would make somewhat of a shift for a moment, but swiftly return to more concrete ways of seeing the issues. So, he would not spend much time or even for the most part allow any discussion or acknowledgment of the dynamic I was interpreting because it made him have to look at the ways he tried to control things and manipulate others as well as having to look at how powerless and dependent he felt in this vicious cycle of narcissism, loss, and envy.

To avoid all that, B choose to stick with viewing things as concrete problems with quick, logical concrete solutions, with no emotional exposure in the process, and no self-reflection needed. When he did start to focus on himself, it was limited to a harsh, critical attack of "how could I have screwed up so much in my life," "how could I be such a lousy human being," and "I can't believe I would do this to my wife." There was only severe self-blame and the threat of an emotional firing squad. There was never any room for understanding, learning, or forgiveness. I interpreted this and B calmed down for a few moments but then returned to the whip rather quickly. As Rosenfeld (1987) has noted, the analyst must maintain ongoing firm and direct confrontive observations with thick-skinned narcissists and use these as a base from which to interpret the underlying core anxieties and desires. It may be a very long time before any progress is seen and in some cases it may never be seen. However, one of the most helpful therapeutic strategies the analyst can take is to remain steady and faithful in this direction.

The moments of transference in which B showed a touch of closeness or yearning were difficult to access or explore as he kept them boxed in a controlling, sadistic sphere. Several times as we began a session, he would say something like, "I sure could spend my time doing something else more enjoyable," "here we go again," or Oh, it's you again." I would enquire about the feelings he had and the meaning of these barbs and B would always tell me, "it is a sign of affection. I only put down those I like." I tried to pursue this with him but it seemed to go down a dead end. However, I certainly had the sense that he felt compelled to maintain distance and control by means of this sadistic way of showing affection.

On one hand, I thought it was a good sign and perhaps an indication that he was having some connection to me and some investment to the treatment process. But, the slightly aloof manner in which B delivered these friendly barbs and the way he wouldn't explore them in connection to me, his wife, or others was part of the overall brick wall he presented to me. B might give a bit but then back to the concrete we went. Sometimes, it was two steps backwards as if we needed to be punished for going too far. The security system had been broken so new security measures had to be applied with double strength just in case. When I made those interpretations, B listened silently, but didn't say much in reply. I felt he was taking it in but didn't want to admit it or show it by responding.

This manner of occasionally being close or needing me but in a very controlling defended way was combined with B's narcissistic method of reducing relationships to things and stripping feelings out of the equation. When I told B I would be out of town for a week, he initially said "fine" and when I told him we could certainly be in touch over the phone if need be, he said, "OK." But, a few days before I was leaving, he announced that "I will be seeing another therapist since you won't be available." B meant he would see someone else in my place and the manner he said it seemed to be a threat that he may or may not return to seeing me. The way this was delivered was curt and cold, very intellectual, and simply factual. It was an announcement.

In the counter-transference, I had to take a moment to get through the initial feeling of being stunned, hurt, angry, and outraged. I felt like a completely replaceable part, a lightbulb that had burned out and was now being replaced with a new one. One thing that really stuck out to me was how B was announcing his method of dealing with his lack of me without saying anything about missing me, needing me, or now feeling left without me. So, I interpreted that it must be very difficult to talk with me about needing me and now feeling completely on his own. I said he must feel angry, abandoned, or scared but maybe was too anxious or uncomfortable having to share that with me so it was easier to just replace me. To myself, I also was considering his envy of me being off with my vacation, separate from him and out of his control. He would not own me anymore and therefore would feel abandoned, powerless, and without his supply of answers. So, he had to spoil me, reject me, and replace me with a new piece of property he could count on.

B told me that he "needed someone to talk to and someone to get the answers to his problems from so that if I was not available he needed to find someone else." I interpreted that he must see me as not very concerned about him and not very accessible because he never thought of bringing up these issues for us to talk about and see if we could figure something out. He asked me what I meant. I said that if it would help, I certainly was willing to talk to him by phone whenever he needed during my time away. He seemed happy to hear that, but in an "I guess that meets my needs" sort of way. He felt he was without his proper medication and now he had found a new pharmacist.

This was not the first time I felt expendable with B, but certainly the strongest experience of him cutting off our relational connection and instead making it a mechanical requirement. He was like an engine. He needed gasoline and if my gas station was closed for business he would simply go across the street. When I tried to explore these issues with B, he seemed to understand me for a few moments and allow some dialogue for a bit, but quickly moved back to a neutralized, emotionless state in which he seemed both to be a little boy needing me to take over and make it all better without him participating and a cold machine in for repairs before going back out in the world to fit in as best as possible without too much conflict. In both accounts, he seemed very empty and lost. When I made that comment, B was very fast to agree and I felt this was one of the few times he was genuinely present in the room. But, he agreed in a way that pulled us back to him being the helpless little boy or the demanding machine. We had no way to work together. We had to be apart. I made this interpretation but it drifted past the little boy and the cold machine.

Without much surprise but an understandable amount of frustration, self-doubt, and curiosity on my part, B quit treatment in an abrupt manner. Many of our more difficult patients, usually narcissistic or borderline, will enter treatment for a short and chaotic ride and then suddenly jump ship midstream. It is a difficult aspect of our chosen career but one that must always be scrutinized and learned from. After I came back from vacation, B left me a message telling me he had a fight with his wife and had felt very depressed. From what he had read on the Internet, he decided he needed antidepressant medications and so he made an appointment with a psychiatrist who promptly told him he needed medications and that instead of seeing me several times a week, he should be seeing that psychiatrist a couple of times a week for cognitive therapy. In his message, B told me how "this form of treatment sounded like a much better match and promised to help him more directly and quickly to find solutions to his problems." He thanked me and hung up. That was the end of it. I was taken off the list and someone else was added to it.

Discussion

Narcissistic patients seem to work overtime to neutralize or psychically assassinate the potential for growth and change in themselves and have constricted, contaminated, or cauterized their connection of life in the process.

A hatred of love based on chronic envy is common with narcissistic patients who subsequently create an anti-life transference (Ignes Sodre 2008). Klein (1975) posited the ideal bountiful breast and the harsh reality of not ever being fully satiated at the breast as a primitive and early triangular conflict. In other words, in the internal phantasy, mother is in private unity with the perfect breast but baby cannot be part of that all the time or sometimes never. Envious and greedy attacks follow, now making the ideal perfect breast the bad object.

When overwhelmed by frustration and need, the baby may imagine their prior experience of being with the breast as another baby who has what they want so now there is competition and a reason to attack both the other baby and the mother of betrayal. Sodre notes this is a vicious cycle because the more envious one feels and the more one attacks the source of love, the more excluded and starved one feels, creating even more hunger, anger, and envy. Such patients want an immediate fix or cure and therefore see the analyst as withholding and keeping the breast/answers to himself.

The case of B seems to illustrate this principle over and over. In action, he wanted to be with the father breast but kept his mind vacant of any such feelings so as to not feel envious, powerless, or deprived. This in turn prevented him from ever being able to create or allow the very loving and gratifying feelings he was so starved for.

Sodre describes the dreadful phantasy of the breast "that was mine or should have been mine and has instead been given to another" or "that mother has kept for herself." This creates envy, rage, and persecution. Sodre points to this and other possible experiences of the breast being part of a triangle that leaves the patient/infant envious of the third element of this triangle. While at times a problematic or pathological oedipal triangle, this is often more of a paranoid-schizoid phantasy of self, object, and third object in which self is left to suffer without the benefits of the couple's union.

B described not only his father in that way, but imagined himself as a third entity, one with potential, drive, and purpose that the other B could never find, obtain, or get to. He could never learn or partake in that union with the hoped for self.

Sodre describes how in treatment this results in attacks by the patient on the parental couple or on the nursing baby and breast with the patient devaluing the moments of genuine analytic contact and the moments when a helpful interpretation is given. The patient sees these moments as that which the patient wants but never been given and therefore cannot tolerate now having to depend on the analyst and reveal his helplessness. So, he neutralizes these therapeutic moments and ends up asking, "So, what do I do?" or "OK. But, if that is the case so what?" or "What do you suggest for my problems? I want to know how to make them go away as fast as possible."

Learning is considered a cruel and unnecessary task. Knowledge should be given over, not earned. Manic defenses and entitlement are used to shield oneself from the despair and sense of deprivation that is at the core. The death instinct is a force that then pervades the treatment with the patient claiming to want to change but killing off any invitation by the analyst towards genuine growth that would highlights differences, vulnerability, need, mutual reflection, and dependency.

So, B not only viewed himself as an unobtainable source of goodness and potential but also viewed his analyst that way. He envied what he could have, should have, and never had from himself and from his analyst. He felt deprived from his father's love and interest which now shaped his view of self and other in his adult life.

B constantly reduced the life blood of the analytic relationship to pre-programmed questions of what to *do* "next" instead of having to *feel* and *think* "now."

B demonstrates how thick-skinned narcissistic individuals systematically attempt to neutralize the entire treatment. The death instinct is mobilized through projective identification mechanisms to subtly neutralize any sense of need and replace it with a general demand for answers and concrete solutions. Feelings are voided and buried, difficult to locate and not prized. This ongoing climate of demand for a "fix" handed over from the analyst turns a serious emotional situation into something like a parent applying a Band-Aid to a child's knee and then the child goes running out the door to play again. Envy can create a detachment, a neutralization, and a choking denial of affect that eliminates vulnerability or need except as a commodity to be used or traded when necessary. The counter-transference is difficult to bear in such clinical situations.

Bion (1959) made the pivotal discovery of how envy attacks links between self and other and therefore is extremely dangerous to the pursuit of life affirming activities, to creative outlets, and to the ability to think and grow mentally.

Caper (2008) makes an excellent point in exploring how envy does attack these basic links between relationships and between thought and thinker, but it is often more of a defensive move than an outright destructive act. Caper believes envy serves as a preemptive strike designed to avoid those situations that might evoke envy. But, in the process, the defensive devaluation of all objects and any need or dependence on linking is what becomes most destructive to the pursuit of life and creativity. Caper reminds us that in Klein's original paper on envy, she lists a number of defenses against the experience of envy, including devaluation of self and other, turning away from the primary object to another, denial of love or need, narcissistic identification, and acting out. I would add the defense of intense neutralization of self and object so there can no longer be any good or bad to envy or be judged by.

B illustrated this by his eradication of feelings. This attack on internal life created the resulting internal void and emotional numbness which protected him but also left him lost, depressed, and out of touch with others. Since B was now safe from judgment he seemed to have no conscious and cared little for the well-being of others. But, as we met and explored his life, this broke down and a sense of severe self-judgment emerged.

Regarding envy and narcissism, Caper (2008) states that projective identification is a common narcissistic mechanism used to obliterate the recognition of needing others or wanting what other's have. The consequences of this primitive defense are severe (Waska 2004), eliminating the distinctions between good and bad and neutralizing the love and desire one has for one's objects. However, the narcissist relies on projective identification to feel that one does possess what the other has by feeling there are no differences between self and the loved or needed object. By creating a sense of fusion, a land of no differences or conflict, there is no need to feel envy or deprivation.

Caper states that the real emergence from narcissism and the positive step into the depressive position (Klein 1935, 1940) involves giving up this delusion of control and admitting and acknowledging that one's life and happiness depends on others whom we never have any real control over. So, we have to accept this complete loss of control and vulnerable dependence which can be so overwhelming for the narcissistic patient that they cannot in turn realize that they too are able to provide love and care to others who need them. When one is more in touch with this reciprocal state of mutual dependence among differences, it leads to a faith that being open to showing need can and will work out most of the time and when it doesn't, survival is still possible.

For B, this was still felt as very dangerous and he could not imagine how his wife would ever forgive him. Part of this may have been his wife's actual angry and unforgiving ways. According to B, she had a history of anger problems and was prone to "throwing things and screaming." But, part of it was B's lack of faith and trust in the object's ability or desire to understand and forgive him if he was honest and open with his feelings and thoughts. This was true in the treatment and outside of the treatment setting.

Alessandra Lemma (2008) has explored the clinical vicissitudes of those patients who are tied to others by grievance, hate, and envy. They feel locked into an eternal dispute for what is owed but was never given. I would extend her thinking to the large group of narcissistic patients who seem to be emotionally drowning in the more chronic sense of loss and eternal rage for the breast that never was or the milk that turned sour. Their sense of conflict, the back and forth and memory of moments that could have been good or were but quickly vanished seem to create incredible pain and a determination to not allow connection to the object again.

Of course, to feel this pain is like having what they want but can't have pushed in their face over and over. So, the complete elimination of envy through massive projective identification and splitting is necessary. However, it will show its frightening face again and again in the transference.

Contemporary Kleinian thinking includes the idea of always trying to sort out how the patient sees the analyst in the immediate transference situation. Are we an available breast to others but never to the patient, are we a difficult to engage breast, are we a dried up frustration, or are we a source of nourishment? While Klein's notion of deprivation, greed, and persecutory anxiety was mostly in regards to the mother's breast, I would add that the patient can also have these experiences in relationship to the father object. So, while B felt completely empty and unwary of these conflicts, they emerged in the transference situation.

Lemma (2008) states that Klein helps us master the confusions around how love is always painful and how we attempt to eliminate the anxieties encountered and the dependency we have for each other. She goes on to say that feeling forgiven by the object for our destructiveness is essential for healthy loving and helps us internalize a generous object that can tolerate knowing the good and the bad within us. We can then mirror this balanced, understanding, and tolerant object. Early troubles in object relations during infancy capsize this opportunity and lead to the various narcissistic difficulties so often met with in treatment.

I would add that one of the more significant clinical difficulties in working with narcissistic patients is that they resist the acknowledgment, let alone the internalization, of such a forgiving and understanding object as it makes them feel weak, needy, and wrong. In the working through process of psychoanalytic treatment, they have to accept responsibility for how they impact others and allow themselves to learn about internal states of mind, both of which always involve a lack of control, separation, loss, and uncertainty. So, it is not unusual for a patient to tell us, "I just need to know what to do to change these problems. Sure I am sorry and sure I need to forgive myself, but what do I need to do to change so I don't have this problem anymore?" This is the typical reaction of someone envious of an ideal other who has no problems and doesn't need anyone's help. Also, it is evidence of the struggle such a patient has with genuine reparation. The idea of feeling sorry and wanting to make restitution, all of which might take time and leave an ugly scar, feels unbearable to this type of patient. Instead, they want to know how to eradicate evidence of the crime ever occurring, pay the fine, and move on. In this conflicted world, gratitude is a limited if not unreachable reward because love is like a strategic chess game instead of an evolving, uncharted work of art, unfolding as it goes.

Guignard (2008) outlines some of the serious psychological consequences envy has on the individual. These include an increase in persecutory guilt and an excessive and pathological reliance on projective identification to rid one's self of need and fault. There is also a pattern of severe splitting, pulling apart of links between self and other, and refusal of basic identification and introjective processes. This is usually to avoid being linked with dreaded and envied object but leads to a corruption of basic thinking, symbolization, and creativity. Guignard points out that one variation is the patient who refuses to accept or allow the creative analytic couple of patient and analyst to exist, thereby preventing communication, growth, and exploration or curiosity. This was certainly evident with B.

Steiner (2008) points out that while some patients are extremely violent in their envious destruction, if the patient has isolated himself within a narcissistic organization, the destructiveness becomes more chronic but more hidden and subtle. Instead of trying to completely destroy the object, the objective seems to shift to stripping it of its creativity, value, and meaning. This more ongoing chipping away at the essence of the object is also focused on the self, leading to chronic depressive states and empty as-if states of mind and personality. Again, this was also the case with B.

Steiner states that envy is often the result of a patient being overwhelmed by the seeing the growth of something new or different in himself as a result of the treatment. I think that even the potential of growth can stir such envy and threat that it must be canceled out before it can be born. So, creativity, curiosity, and change cannot even emerge within the linked bond of analyst and patient. One way to prevent this threat is to make sure the link is neutralized, denied, or destroyed. This hatred of desire or direction also triggers the original hatred and anxiety of deprivation, loss, and lack of containment that was part of an original envy and greed with the primary object.

In discussing some of Klein's ideas on splitting, projective identification, and envy, Heinz Weib (2008) mention's Rosenfeld's (1971) notion that projective identification is often triggered by unconscious envy and intolerable separateness. As long as the patient can find a way to see the analyst as an extension of himself, fused and identical or at least serving to provide exactly what the patient wants, then this envious state can be avoided. He notes how Rosenfeld found some patients to pathologically fuse life and death instincts in an effort to claim a pleasant goal of harmony and peace, where everyone is on the same path and needing the same results. This "smile on your face and dagger under your coat" way of relating can be overlooked with patients who seem so willing to go along with the work of treatment but are really finding a way of narcissistically ruling over it.

Contrary to what most people (including analysts) wish for, simple encouragement, sensitivity, and attunement are not enough to help someone through their difficulties. In fact, as Fonagy (2008) notes, that approach will actually foster and breed contempt, envy, hatred, and resistance because the subject feels pushed to face his differences, limits, needs, and weaknesses and this triggers envy, greed, and jealousy.

I think this is one of the best ways to understand the mistake of trying to provide "supportive therapy" to patients, to whom we give advice, support, and encouragement instead of using psychoanalytic technique to slowly help the patient work through all of their painful internal conflicts. Even though the patient demands an immediate fix to their conflicts, we must realize this is a narcissistic level of control to override the more immediate anxiety they are overwhelmed by and need to work through. The fix they demand or beg for is not a method of facing, understanding, and transforming internal states, it is a magical denial that lets them feel back in control and without any disturbance in how they view themselves.

So, at times I felt dramatically pulled to tell B how to work on his marriage, how to improve his self esteem, and how to best get his boss, wife, or couples therapist off his back. Of course, in the process I would be turning away from our relationship and the immediate anxiety B was experiencing about himself and his internal objects. If I had acted out some of this counter-transference pressure to provide "supportive therapy," I think that would have made B feel even more hopeless, helpless, and needy. This out-of-control state would in turn only fuel his sense of envy, deprivation, anger, and fear. Perhaps, B would have become more masochistic and passively taken on my "supportive" lead, but ultimately, I would have been controlling him, creating a pathological dependency, and not honoring his potential for growth, independence, and emotional creativity which the analytic method promotes.

With B, to push past this projective identification pull to sidestep the analytic process and provide meaningful interpretations was always difficult because of his transference reaction to my interpretations (Racker 1960). He would either dismiss my interpretations with neutralized indifference or act eager to passively swallow whatever I said if he thought it gave him the immediate solution to his problems and made his wife stop yelling at him.

Moser-Ha (2001) notes the importance of not just interpreting the destructive aspects of the narcissist's envy but the libidinal as well. As illustrated in the case of B, I routinely did so, but unless I consistently confronted him on the manipulative, controlling, or neutralizing ways he treated himself and others, it was more of a counter-transference enactment of his sadomasochistic transference to only interpret the libidinal aspects. But, I certainly did do both as I felt it vital to try and reach him and establish analytic contact (Waska 2007).

This is a similar technique to what Spillius (1993) describes as the conscious sense of grievance and resentment with an apparent absence of guilt. She goes on to describe how this defends against a massive sense of loss, guilt, and a fear of total collapse should one fully feel the lack of the needed object, the phantasy of having always been denied that object, and the realization of never being able to ever reach that object and its desired love and supplies. Very parallel to this and in line with B's pathology, Joseph (1989) thinks one should assess if the patient's masochistic stance has to do with anger turned inward due to neglect and trauma or as an aggressive maneuver to defeat the analyst and destroy the analyst's capacity to effectively interpret and heal. I think it is often a combination of both and certainly this seemed to be the case with B.

I think B indeed had suffered enormous neglect and loss in his formative years and was taking out his rage on himself through his drinking, lack of direction, and psychological numbness. His activities at the strip clubs, the drinking, and his narcissistic manner of treating others was a flimsy attempt at finding respite from the grip of these overwhelming feelings of psychological fragmentation. As Segal (1982) states, the transference is not a duplicate of the patient's childhood but a dynamic, evolving relational state that hopefully will gradually evolve and change in healthy and integrative ways. However, with B, he seemed to bring to bear a self-hatred that was self inflicted or formed through his pattern of sadomasochistic relating combined with a desire to control, neutralize, and destroy any link to the object and the love and direction the object could provide.

Chapter Six

Striving Toward Useful Interpretations with Narcissistic Patients: Managing Counter-Transference Enactments with a Thick-Skinned Narcissist

Some patients enter psychoanalytic treatment and quickly create a difficult, confusing, and often frustrating experience for the analyst. Although doing our best to help these patients locate the nature of their core conflicts and help them begin to think and feel in a new way, we are met with a rigid and concrete method of non-relating. The essence of this narcissistic pathology is complex. However, there are some common and even predictable transference issues, including a destructive stance against feeling or relating. Envy, projective identification, and devaluation usually define their object relational style. There is an adherence to concrete thinking with an associated avoidance of more abstract or symbolic relating. Talking about feelings is met with puzzlement and a lack of interest. It will be tolerated if told that it will lead to "answers or solutions" but it is ignored as otherwise without value. Often, these patients are unable to access their feelings because they have systematically dismantled, destroyed, or discarded them in favor of a controlled, intellectual approach in which everything can be organized and managed in a predicable fashion.

The patient presented in this paper represents the clinical profile Rosenfeld (1987) termed the thick-skinned narcissist. Rosenfeld states, "There are many narcissistic patients whose narcissistic structure provides them with such a 'thick skin' that they have become insensitive to deeper feelings. To avoid impasse these patients have to be treated in analysis very firmly and have to be confronted with their narcissistic attitude and their envy particularly as their envy causes devaluation of the analyst and the analysis and of any need for help. With these patients the frequent repetition of interpretation and confrontation seems to be unavoidable, even if for a long time these repetitions do not seem to make any impact on the patient. When interpretations at last manage to touch them they are relieved, even if it is painful to them" (p. 274).

Narcissistic patients often have certain early experiences of deprivation in common. With this said, I still take what I hear of their childhood experiences as a blend of reality and the conflicts between love, hate, and knowledge being played out in the internal object relational field. These patients frequently report a history with one or both parents never providing, allowing for, or demonstrating a loving bond, a tolerance for differences, a containment and support of feelings, or the encouragement of self expression as a positive creative act.

Instead, the primary object(s) were withdrawn, critical, rigid, and often completely lost in their own world without showing much sense of value for others. The patients recall their own feelings being constricted, restricted, or voided when emerging, by either themselves and/or their objects. It appears there was a locked emotional door that prevented the patient from ever reaching the warmth of mutuality where giving and receiving and forgiveness and understanding were possible. In fact, not only was there a locked door but it seems unclear if there was ever such a treasure behind the door to begin with. Abstract or creative thinking was a victim and feelings are nowhere to be found in most of these cases. This makes interpretation particularly challenging and exploration of the transference can be a barren and frustrating experience, mirroring the patient's own experiences of banging on the locked door of parental interest and love.

Normal oedipal and pre-oedipal phantasies of coupling with the primary object to produce something together, such as love, ideas, hopes, and understanding of each other internal dynamics is distorted or absent. The phantasy of a baby who is separate but the result of a union is not part of these patients' experiences.

So, in treatment, these patients do not respond to the analytic invitation to create together, through thoughtful intercourse, a new product of understanding and a working through process that comes from the mutual vulnerability, the dependence, and faith that over time, a gestation period of sorts, something new will be formed. Of course, the currency of such a coupling is feelings and the experience and sharing of them. Due to their early experience of the parental refusal to give and receive and the patient's sense that those good things are what others have but not I, they attack and destroy, prevent, pervert, and devalue their own authentic birth within the treatment process.

Instead, there is a perverse demand for an artificial solution. The patient demands a third entity that is either borrowed, desperately adopted, kidnapped, or mechanically engineered as an immediate fix without having to get their emotional hands dirty or feel any persecutory (Klein 1946) or depressive (Klein 1935, 1940) anxiety. This creates the familiar situation in which these patients bring up what someone else said, what they read about how their problem should be treated, how medication might be the answer, and other methods that are inherently better than what the analyst has to offer. The Internet seems infinitely smarter than the analyst. The Immaculate Conception baby is safe and lets them stay in control without having to risk the messy coupling that could leave them rejected, powerless, needy, or without their desperate sense of self-sufficiency.

Often, these narcissistic patients will have a "designated devotee." Even though these patients seem unable to bond with anyone and truly express their underlying feelings in a dependent manner that engages another enough to built an authentic relationship, they will often have a designated person whom they will allow themselves to feel for, depend on, and love. This is a person of their choosing and in that way can and often does change at a moment's notice. However, this sudden shift is more typical of borderline patients. The narcissistic individual will keep their devotee for long periods. This might mean years of marriage with a wife or the love of a child over the period of their development. But, upon close examination, the relationship is fairly circumscribed yet does allow the patient to feel dependent. However, these positions of loyalty and dependency are often quite controlling and if not devoid of feelings they are expressed in ways that are at their core masochistic and show an underbelly of more abrasive narcissistic defenses. Or, this special relationship can be expressed in a very neutral, unfeeling form in which the patient is mechanically watering their favorite plant but it is still a possession even though one they depend on.

As will be shown in the case material, this designated devote may be the creation of the patient's massive evacuative projection, so the patient can feel sorry for the object but never have to feel sad themselves, either for themselves or about themselves.

Some patients, including the one about to be presented, who felt shut out from the ability to bond and emotionally couple with their primary object, who have felt that the object denied them basic attention, value, and understanding, now seem unable and unwilling to seek out a relationship with the world. They identity with the cold, cutoff object and have eliminated or ignored, attacked, and denied all their feelings except for passive anxiety and helplessness when out of their usual element of control and comfort.

Anti-life attacks on any linking between self and object and between self and one's own feelings are common as it is an extension of envy of what the withholding object must have but keeps to him/herself. It is the object and the object's potential capacity to love that is the envied relationship since the patient cannot find a way to break into this private relationship.

CASE MATERIAL

My patient G told me how he was "sorting out the best strategy for deciding what to tell his wife in order to get her to go along with things for a few more years, so as to avoid a messy and costly divorce." I interpreted, "You seem to see everyone, myself, your wife, and your friends, as all just moveable pieces in a puzzle designed to get what you want, when you want it. You don't seem to care about the impact you have on others in the process." Here, I was making what I call a confrontive and therapeutic interpretive observation. It is the use of one's counter-transference to guide a firm observation that brings a connection between reality, self, and object. The apparent lack of feelings or dismissal of feelings in self or object is usually part of what is addressed in this analytic confrontation and observation. After this more firm observation, the patient's core anxiety can then be interpreted more easily, examining both the destructive and libidinal aspects of the phantasy conflicts regarding self and object.

G replied, "That is absolutely correct. But, I don't see what is wrong with it and why you are bringing it up. If I think about it, it might be because the work culture at my company promotes treating everyone like dirt. But, I think I have been that way long before I ever worked there." On one hand, G seemed to be reflecting on himself and the possible source of his actions. However, at the same time he was simply stating a fact, "Yes, I treat people like dirt and I always have." Here, he was stepping away from any creative, symbolic thinking or feeling state and resorting to his narcissistic stance of cold hard facts and logic.

I interpreted, "you seem surprised that I even bring it up as an issue. Perhaps you are not used to relating to me or others with any feeling. Maybe, you are very out of touch with your own feelings so you don't have a way of knowing that I, your wife, or your friends would have feelings too." Here, I was interpreting G's possible reliance on projective identification that left him vacant and barren inside and then left him surrounded by empty objects with no value. G replied, "I pay you to tell me what is wrong and how to fix it. I am waiting for that to happen. I am waiting for you to tell me the procedure to turn things around and when that happens we will be done. What is strange about that?" Here, I was struck by how he was being robot-like without any sign of feeling or understanding of self or others. He merely felt I had a commodity that he lacked and wanted me to hand it over. At the same time, I thought he was being manipulative and controlling, putting me in my place as a vending machine, his personal vending machine.

During another session with G, he was surprised at his wife's reaction when he told her he had not loved her in the ten years they have been together. He was "shocked and taken back" at her reaction of devastation and tears to hearing he never loved her. G said he didn't really understand it but "guesses she would be upset if she thought I loved her for all that time."

G went on to talk about how he had never thought out the actual consequences of getting divorced and after consulting a lawyer he "experienced the lowest day of his life when he realized how much of his money she would keep." He said he was devastated about the idea of losing his money if they divorced but when I asked G said he had no feelings about the loss of his marriage. Equally, G had absolutely no empathy when his wife was shocked and began sobbing after she heard he was dating someone else even though G and his wife had started couples therapy to allegedly work things out.

G told me he was shocked to hear his wife wanted him to remain faithful while he moved out and they tried to work it out in couples therapy. He said, "I am expected to just sit around all by myself and not able to date whoever I want! I have to wait around to see if things work out? What is in it for me? Nothing!

After they had a big fight over these matters and G did have to move out temporarily, he told me he felt "devastated and lost having to walk away from my home, the foundation I had for ten years." When I asked if he was sorry to walk away from his wife and family, he said, "Sort of, but mostly my home, since it represents my foundation that I have been used to for so long."

I noticed that since G's arrogance is not usually directed at me, I don't feel devalued and don't have the urge to directly retaliate. But, I also noticed how in order to feel some degree of empathy for G, I have to imagine him as a robot from another planet, the planet of "ME." In other words, I had to struggle to understand and explore his way of seeing everyone and everything as simply an extension of himself and how he is shocked to find out otherwise. If others have different opinions, different needs, or different agendas than him, it is a surprise.

O'Shaughnessy (2008) highlights Klein's notion that envy is extremely dangerous because it interferes with the creation of a useful link to internal and external good objects. Likewise, gratitude is extremely important in development as it creates a bridge to the good object and is the blueprint for appreciation of goodness in self and others. O'Shaughnessy notes that Klein firmly believed life is punctuated by the constant gaining, losing, and regaining of the good object. Envy can pose a poisonous threat to this healthy pattern while gratitude offers a strong transitional faith in those natural times of uncertainty. This is in contrast to those narcissistic patients who take their objects for granted instead of with gratitude.

In working with G, I had constant opportunities to reflect on the clinical difficulty of this narcissistic omnipotence and denial of need or connection. I think that if love or gratitude are simply gratuitous concrete items that are exchanged when demanded or expected, they only have the value of commodities being shopped around for, like the obligation of buying a present for someone you don't really care for. The other aspect of narcissistic devaluation of gratitude is that one is only good or valuable until the next best thing comes around, so you are always at risk of being dispersed. This holds true for how the narcissist treats their objects but also how the narcissist feels about themselves.

This creates a paranoid core that must be defended and bolsters a vicious cycle of entitlement, neutralization of feelings, and an everyman for himself mentality. Gratitude becomes false and something to use to impress, convince, or defend. Imperfection cannot be tolerated and control becomes more important than understanding, compassion, and forgiveness. To have gratitude is to admit need and weakness or vulnerability. So, envy can be of the idealized self-sufficient object or self as well as of the openly needy and vulnerable object who doesn't seem to be frightened of the consequences.

At the start of another session, I asked G, "What are you feeling right now?" He responds, "Not a lot has happened since I last saw you." I replied, "So, you fill yourself up with what is out there, things that happen around you. I wonder what has happened to what is inside of you." He was silent for awhile and then told me he "is truly stumped. I don't look inside. I never have. I don't think I know what that is."

G went on to discuss his uncertainty about "what to do" with his marriage. I interpreted that in his "what to do" approach he sees his marriage as a work project. He seems to never share his feelings with me, but instead conferences with me about his latest work project strategy. G said that he sees the world as "a place of either rational organization or emotional chaos." He says he pictures "Losing control and everything going to pieces" if he lives his life based on emotion so he "takes the predictable, logical path of rational thought where things are known and quantifiable."

Here, G was describing the narcissistic anxiety of total emptiness. Britton (2000) has elaborated on how the thick-skinned narcissist fears total emptiness and chaos. There is a deep fear of endlessness, confusion, and lack of control. As a result, they push for constant agreement between self and object with no differences allowed. I would add that this rigid demand for no difference creates an envy of others who can be flexible enough to reflect, think creatively, and feel. To prevent the suffering of envy, the narcissistic individual makes sure to never drift into thinking reflectively or examining their feelings and subsequent conflicts since it would produce this dreaded lack of control. Then, they would face the underlying empty void, stripped of all feelings and connections due to their massive reliance on projective identification.

Bit by bit, through our analytic work, G is working through some of this frightening anxiety and as a result is able to think more about the link between self and object. He is noticing that his way of being, wanting what he wants and assuming others are on board with that, is not matching up to reality so he is trying to start to make "some adjustments." Although he is starting to risk self-reflection and consider differences between self and other, he is still extremely quick to feel the envy of difference and separation and then react defensively.

Therefore, I interpreted that these "adjustments" are to prevent trouble, fallout on self or others, but not really changes he wants to make. I said, "It looks like you are telling me and your wife what we want to hear but deep down you still want something quite different." G explained, "Yes. I feel like I am trying to go along with the cultural and societal demands of what I should want and do. I should want to work on my marriage. But, you are right. If it was solely up to me, I would take off and go fishing on an island for the rest of my life. I would walk away from my family. However, I would still want to stay in touch with my son. I wish my wife would want to just be friends and let me do things my way. Unfortunately, she says she is in love with me so that makes it very complicated." Once again, G's matter-of-fact, coldly factual manner created counter-transference turbulence.

One reason I was able to generally contain my counter-transference with G, most of the time, was that his narcissistic ways of dealing with the world were shocking and detestable but he did not direct it at me in such an obvious manner. However, my counter-transference was still tested with G because he treated me without any emotional value. I was just there to provide an oil change to his vehicle or to perform a diagnostic test and provide him with the results and a recommendation for what to do. He did not consider, for a moment, that I was a human being with whom he was in a relationship with. But, this narcissistic treatment was not as sadistic or overly dismissive as my experience with certain other narcissistic patients.

When narcissistic patients treat us with the same level of indifference, envy, contempt, and devaluation as they do all their other objects, in an attacking manner that is in our face and obvious, it can be very difficult to avoid counter-transference acting out. But, G tended to neutralize his feelings so much that I felt more a part of a lifeless mechanical procedure than outright attacked and used.

During the second month of G's twice a week, on the couch, psychoanalytic treatment, he was talking about his life and his struggles with his marriage in a way that seemed so flat and business like that I told him he once again seemed to be describing his latest work project. I added that he seemed to being trying to find the best way to manage the pieces of the deal, avoid any hidden costs, and end up with a profitable deal for himself by carefully strategizing and controlling all the players. I said he was being the ultimate manager of a business project yet this was his life and his marriage we were talking about.

I said, "Therefore, perhaps it is very uncomfortable to show me any feelings behind the business armor." G told me it "is always a dreadful moment when anyone asks him about his feelings." He said, "I don't have any. I don't know what I feel. Actually, I feel nothing most of the time. There is nothing inside of me."

From this genuine and disturbing revelation, G shifted back to the more controlled, devaluing defensive stance he normally took. He told me that he agreed with me that he sees life as a project that he can manage. G said, "I do very well with an assigned project that I can manage and then when the end point is reached, I walk away. I am done. So, I think you are right. I never thought about it like that, but why not? My marriage is like a project that I want to manage and now I am done with the project and am ready to walk away and find my next project. But, as you know, it is problematic to leave right now so I think I will stay until I can figure a better exit strategy." So, G went from momentarily revealing this bleak, void of nothingness inside himself to flipping it all around to a difficult business project with no easy exit strategy.

I said, "In the meantime, you are presenting yourself to your wife as interested in resolving things and working on the love and the commitment. She thinks you are motivated and still in love with her while you are telling me you would be gone yesterday if you had no kids and she couldn't take half your money. So, it seems you have built a damaging façade and falsehood. But, you are so used to having your world divided and kept apart by erasing your feelings that I think you don't think twice about the twists and turns of what you are telling me." Here, I was interpreting the massive denial and splitting that G used and the adverse side effects of pathological projective identification. I added, "I think you want me to hold on to the feeling part of you and make sense out of this divided land so you don't have to deal with how overwhelming it is to you." Here, I was interpreting the projective identification aspect of the transference (Grotstein 2010a, 2010b).

G replied, "I don't want to have to deal with what feels like a total collapse. I picture being out of the house without my family and I don't know what I would do with myself. I would miss everything. That is my house!" I said, "You sound devastated but also sound like you are losing your property, not someone you love." He said, "Well, I see what you mean. I do love my son and I don't want to have to have the disruption of joint custody. It doesn't sound great to anyone and I don't want him to be affected by all this." I said, "You picture he would never see or feel the troubles in the marriage if you stayed together?" G said, "I don't think he has any clue." I felt a pang of sadness for this child and wondered about G's own childhood and the transference projection of that onto me and onto his son. I thought he so wanted to erase his own feelings and have a safe, sterile, in control status that he had to picture, by extension, his son as equally in control and without impact. Otherwise, the difference would force G to wake up and see himself and his world crumbling.

So, I asked, "When you were growing up, did you think your parents were having a perfect marriage?" G replied, "What I remember was a perfect textbook marriage but without any feelings or affection. I have not one memory of them holding hands, hugging, or showing any demonstration of love and affection. Our house never had feelings in it. That was something that did not exist. And since they didn't live that way, expressing feelings, they didn't relate to me that way either. It was like one big happy blank-stare family."

During another session, G said he hoped his wife would agree to "just let him be, even if he doesn't love her, until their child is grown and gone." G said if she would just agree to go along with things as is he would "hopefully be able to find plenty of distractions between now and then and not have to deal with his feelings or have to try and love her." He said he hoped his wife would find her own distractions as well so she won't be bothered by his lack of love and "then everyone would be just fine."

In the counter-transference, I feel outraged. I couldn't believe how cold and manipulative G was. I wanted to be angry and to tell him to wake up. I wanted to make some sort of judgment cloaked in therapeutic advice to start living in a more healthy and caring manner. After sitting in this state for a bit, I realized I was mostly just stupefied and overwhelmed at how lacking in feelings he seemed to be, apparently oblivious of how callous he was to himself and others. I was drawn back to what he said about his upbringing. I thought he was still lost in this land of no affection, no feelings, and no connection. Here, I think that by containing my own counter-transference state, I was gradually able to come to some sort of understanding about it.

G went on to say that it would be sad to live without his family and that he didn't want to give up his house. After listening to him describe this for awhile, I noticed myself being drawn to be critical again about his lack of empathy because he seemed to be talking about his upset over losing his property rather than any mention of his feelings about losing connection with his wife and child. I said, "You seem to be talking about giving up the house and not living with the family in a way that makes it sound like you would be without your favorite toy, your favorite piece of property." Even though I had been exposed to his concrete narcissistic void of feelings many times by now, I was once again taken back when he said, "Yes. That is what it is like."

G went on to tell me of his upcoming lunch date with his secret girlfriend as an entirely separate topic and event from when he just told me how he is planning to tell his wife that they should continue to work it out and continue couples therapy. I felt quite confounded in the counter-transference and wanted to scold him and judge him. What helped me was to picture him as operating within a dream or that he was now relating his dream to me. In doing so, I was more able to be curious and want to find out more about it rather than judge it. Therefore, I was able to focus more on the severe splitting and the intense projective identification in which he deposited most of his internal sense of self and feeling state into me. All conflict and guilt was now somewhere else so he had no problem keeping things so separate. I felt he was unwilling, out of guilt, anxiety, and envy, to show me the two as joined together. So, I interpreted that G was unable to think about the two women and the two states of mind together, that he was telling his wife about how they can work it out while he was cheating on her with his girlfriend.

G replied, "You are right. I don't know how to figure that one out." Then, he went on to tell me how his wife and him have had no sex for the last three years, so he "no longer considers her that way." I interpreted, "You somehow have ignored this serious red flag in your relationship and just gone along for those three years pretending everything is OK. You have taken her off the list of the women you see as desirable. If it is a list and you just cross her off, then you don't have to feel anything about it." G agreed in his usual concrete manner. I added, "You seem to have taken yourself off the list as well, not letting yourself have any feelings about missing that part of the marriage." G said he had "started to realize that and started to miss it recently, which is why he had started to look toward other women that way. I never found my wife terribly sexy but didn't have any desire for other women. But, now I do or at least I am thinking I might."

So, at this point, I am concentrating on interpreting G's paranoid-schizoid phantasy state and anxiety level at exactly the point he is existing in currently rather than trying to push him into more of depressive state via interpretations that forced his splitting to come together. That said, I am definitely offering interpretations that address the dread and anxiety G must feel when contemplating the two states joining together in his mind.

On one hand, I am confronting him about his denial and making him look at the reality of his actions. However, I am not pushing my ideas of his core guilt, suffering, loss, envy, or aggression onto him at this point. Sometimes, when overwhelmed by my counter-transference and inability to properly contain my inner reactions, I have made comments in this direction in order to ease my counter-transference envy, outrage, or loneliness. But, otherwise, I have simply followed him along at his current level of phantasy functioning just making analytic observations about it. This is a fine line between the necessary firm and direct confrontive interpretations that help narcissistic patients (Waska 2010) versus the attacking and heavy handed counter-transference based advice and judgment these patients bring out so easily.

During a recent session, G asked me to talk with his couples therapist "Since she does that with all the couples she sees and she has already talked with my wife's therapist." I asked him about what he was thinking and he said, "Not much. She asked me to ask you so I thought it would probably help things. What do you mean?" I told G that I thought there were two issues. First, I didn't see any clinical reason at this point to talk to anyone else about his confidential treatment and I didn't see how it would help his couples therapy. But, I said, the second and more important issue was for us to notice how he hadn't given any thought to what this would really mean. I said, "You seem to have blocked your mind from realizing that if I call this therapist, I would have to tell her that you have been lying to her and to your wife. You have been telling them you are still in love and want to work on everything so the family stays together. I would have to tell her you really want to leave immediately but feel stuck because of your child and the threat of paying alimony."

Here, I had to be confrontive, direct, and firm about the reality of his splitting and how he was trying so hard to keep things neutral and separated that he had lost contact with the reality of the sum of the pieces. I interpreted that he never thought of the consequences because he had left all his feelings with me, the wife, and the other therapist. I held the guilt, aggression, and the self-judgment while his wife and couples therapist held the hope and trust. I also interpreted that he was creating an oedipal situation in which he wanted me to protect him from the others finding out and hating him. I had to protect his secret.

G replied, "I see what you mean. I hadn't thought about it in those ways but I think the couples therapist is onto me as well. She really came down on me when she sort of detected my false optimism and called me on that. She said I seemed to be trying to paint it all rosy but didn't seem to genuinely feel that way. I guess, like you said, I have different feelings that I try and hide."

G went on to tell me he was looking at a place to move into and had started negotiating with the landlord but he "dreaded all the little details." He told me about "what a hassle it will be to have to go through all the stupid details of moving furniture, signing a lease, turning on utilities, and so forth. It will be a big headache." I interpreted that he was telling me about the "hassle" of logistical details so that he could not have to feel or share the painful sense of separation and loss that was about to happen.

G then went on to imagine how after he leaves, his wife would have to go "through the incredible pain and sadness of standing there looking at a piece of art or something in the kitchen that I had bought and realizing I was now gone. She would be devastated. I don't want her to have to go through that!" At that point, G began sobbing uncontrollably. After a few minutes, he said, "I haven't cried in many years. Wow! I don't know why I feel so sad for her but I do!" Here, I believe my prior more direct and confrontive interpretations had allowed G to be more in touch with himself so he could talk a bit about himself, even if it was in this thinly disguised displacement about the "hassle of details." Then, when I made my interpretations about that defensive system, I believe he felt a lull in his overall dread and anxiety long enough to allow the intensity of his internal conflicts to emerge via this projection of sadness and loss onto his wife.

So, I now interpreted, "it must be so hard to face your own feelings of loss and sadness that it is easier to feel sorry for her. You want to make sure she is ok but maybe it is very foreign or uncomfortable to have me know your feelings and be here for you as you go through them." G said, "I have never felt I had someone there for me like that. But, I also never shared those kinds of feelings with anyone, so it would be very new."

Discussion

Caper (2008) makes important clinical points regarding envy and the destructive instincts, the death instincts. He discusses how the destructive aim is to attack and eliminate all links to internal and external objects, which then provides a controlled and secure distance from any connection to oneself or others. As Caper says, a mind cut off from itself and others is a dead mind. I would add that feelings are, of course, an additional casualty. Carnivorous projective identification attacks involve the subject taking on the persona or imagined goods of the object. "I am you, therefore I am not bothered by what you have or your differences. I don't need you because we are identical. I don't have to give or concede, we are always in agreement. We are one" is the nature of this defensive posture.

Caper notes that the actual object is devalued or ignored because it is now considered non-self. This produces the well-known narcissistic profile of apparently being completely oblivious to others. Empathy is forbidden as it triggers recognition of internal emptiness and lack of internalized goodness as well as painful separateness. However, feeling sorry for the object like G did for his wife is OK because there doesn't have to be an identification with it. It can be something or someone else that one is looking down on in a pitiful way. This was the case with G's sadness for his wife when he imagined her grieving for him. As his designated devotee, he was able to have some sense of connection and caring but in this controlled and managed way.

In studying the pathologically envious individual, Ronald Britton (2008) notes that conventional Kleinian theory places greed as libidinal and places envy as both destructive and an expression of the death instinct. Britton points out that not only does envy make one an aggressive spoiler of others but a spoiler of one's own potentials. He states that this compassionate and sympathetic attitude is part of Melanie Klein's (1975) view of such pathology. I would add that this attitude helps when we are confronted in the counter-transference with these patients' often vexing ways of relating, non-relating, or un-relating.

Especially for patient G, he was never able to feel any direction for his life, any passion or meaning. In fact, at first G had many stories of the way he wanted to sail away on a yacht to a wonderful island and leave everyone and everything behind. He also had plenty of ideas about retiring in the south of France and spending his time working at his own vineyard, free to do as he pleased. In fact, the free to do as he pleased without having to deal with anyone or anything, completely independent and above it all was the main theme of all of his fantasies.

But, as the treatment went on and we made some progress finding out what actually was going on inside of him, the stories changed. Bit by bit, he had to face reality and seemed to try to weave some reality into his getaway fantasies. So, G started to talk about "knowing that he couldn't afford to just drop everything and move to France" or that he could "now see that it was a bit improbable that his wife would let him stay married but sail off by himself and date other women." He started to consider "more balanced goals that took his family into account but also let him pursue some of his pleasures." This was a very promising sign and a gradual shift into more depressive functioning, at least in certain moments.

John Steiner (2008b) recalls Bion's (1959) idea of the patient's hatred of being linked to objects and how that linkage provoked envy. To be linked to a good object and receive that goodness is the same as being needy and weak. So, the envious self instead appropriates the goodness, calls it his own, and rations it out when he deems fit. Britton discusses this hatred of being receptive and the powerlessness, lack of control, and humiliation that can occur with it for the narcissistic patient.

Steiner notes how some of these ideas are parallel to Betty Joseph's (1959) ideas about envy being a reaction to being dependent on the analyst which triggers the possibility of love and value, something the patient has grown to hate since it brings up envy of the internal object that withholds or is completely unavailable and apparently fine without the patient. Steiner (2008b) examines how the defenses to ward off these anxieties involve pathological reliance on splitting, projective identification, and cannibalistic introjections. These often blend into a narcissistic organization that denies separation or difference and thereby circumvents envy. Any goodness or needed supplies are felt to now be owned and to be part of the self, so dependency on others is unnecessary. G was often exhibiting such defensive acting out in the transference and in his personal relationships.

Steiner (2008b) reminds us that when we notice ourselves being frustrated at not finding any redeeming qualities in such a patient, it is helpful to remember that the patient is worried about our predatory and envious nature should we notice such a glimmer of goodness. This dynamic is readily seen in depressed patients, narcissistic patients, and borderline patients. Steiner's recommendation helps us with those patients who are consistently hiding any success or goodness and instead always emphasizing their faults and failures. Some patients have had experiences of primary objects being angry or disapproving of their basic feelings, especially sadness, autonomy, or anger as it signals difference and separation. As a result, the patient has felt in danger if they didn't immediately seal off, destroy, deny, or dispute their own feelings. So, when the analyst attempts to revive that lost and split off aspect of the patient, all types of transference resistances are common.

This traumatic early experience with primary objects can include not just objects that disapprove of one's feelings through active judgment or attack but also by a complete lack of response altogether. For G, he repeatedly reported an upbringing without internal life, without feeling in his parents or in himself. He observed his parents in a lifeless relationship. He described them "going through the motions with no sign of affection or attachment for each other" and he felt no encouragement or recognition from them for his own feelings or thoughts. Everything in his external world seemed toneless and neutral and his internal world mirrored that void.

For some patients like G, this early trauma seems to produce the repetition of no emotional response to others in his adult life. In the treatment, this emerged in how he would completely ignore any interpretation of the transference. There is no acknowledgment of the link between patient and analyst. Often, this type of patient sees the therapeutic interaction as a mere exchange, money for answers, a transfer of knowledge, or an application of a bandage onto a wound. It appears these patients strive to make sure the relationship has no meaning or value. There is no relational significance.

Peter Fonagy (2008) has written about patients who are envious of envy and gratitude. He discusses defenses against envy including idealization and devaluation which protect against the pain of envious attacks on the object. These defenses place the object out of reach or make it unworthy of any effort altogether. Either way, the subject doesn't have to face their painful connection to the object. Fonagy makes the point that it is more often helpful to interpret the direct destructive desire for the object, the envy, than to interpret the defensive attacks of devaluation or sadistic idealization. The patient will feel more understood as the core phantasy and anxiety are being addressed rather than pointing out how he is wronging others with his defensive behaviors. Also, Fonagy points out that it is often the defenses against envy that do the most damage to the patient's relationships. Therefore, centering on the core feelings of envy and the reactions to it can help to mitigate that pathological method of relating.

This is related to Rosenfeld's (1987) recommendation of being therapeutically firm and using confrontive observations as part of the interpretive process with thick-skinned narcissists. As discussed previously, the thick-skinned narcissist is struggling with anxieties and phantasies regarding such overwhelming powerlessness and lack of control that for them there seems to only be two solutions. Either the object is destroyed by envious attacks and taken out of the equation or the needy envious self is attacked and neutralized. This is very similar to how Segal (1993) defines the workings of the death instinct. The life, difference, and creativity of either self or object must be voided. Thus, we have certain patients who seem so sadistic and controlling of others while other patients seem so bent on allowing no life within themselves.

Fonagy reminds us the desire to control the object is always part of the desire for attachment, nourishment, and security with the object. So, feeling no ability to control the object equals loss, rejection, and the anxiety of not having the nourishment needed. A power struggle over control can mask the core desperation for connection. This was why I interpreted G's use of "the hassle of all the details of divorce" as a shield against his massive sense of loss, failure, and collapse. Ultimately, in this situation, I am working toward making more interpretations of his envy of his wife's ability to love and to grieve. For now, G has to use projective identification to attack, deny, and erase any evidence of that in himself. So, he ends up sterile and lonely but masks that with a stance of control and logical concreteness.

Steiner (1993) has explored the dynamics of patients who feel resentful about being rejected by their objects or angry at not being able to access the attention, validation, or nourishment they wish their objects had but seem to either lack or purposely deny them. They feel deprived and isolated which leaves them fragmented, lost, and revengeful. The attitude is "if they are going to be so selfish than I will be too." But, out of great fear, guilt, and hopelessness, they retreat into a much more hidden, subtle, and disguised form of grievance. The envy they feel becomes a silent backdrop, smuggled into the transference through projective identification mechanisms (Grotstein 2010a, 2010b).

Part of the way these intense, lifelong unconscious conflicts are disguised is the constant redirection of transference feelings into external extra-transference figures. So, much of the patient's material will be about everyone and everything except the analyst or the analytic relationship. This was certainly the case with G, as he mostly told me about his marriage, his child, his dealings with the couples therapist, and his work situations. I was the one who had to bring the focus back to us. In the total transference situation (Joseph 1985), I was the excluded, unimportant bystander who had to raise my hand for his attention.

Joseph (1989) and Steiner (2006) are among those Kleinian thinkers who examine how the patient's unconscious conflicts pull the analyst into various forms of interpersonal and psychological acting out of the patient's unspoken phantasies regarding self and object. Steiner (2008a) has discussed how when patients such as G focus all their love, hate, and desire to know into others, excluding the analyst, the analyst's counter-transference state will be effected. With G, I felt I was simply the observing listener, excluded from his reports, sterile as they were. They were all about everyone else and him but never about us. As Steiner notes, this pushes the analyst to either act out to regain the place of importance as primary object or to seek revenge by becoming the outside judge of all I hear G report.

With G, I found myself mostly struggling with not judging him personally and also about his cold controlling approach to his wife and family. The more I could tolerate and manage my feelings of envy, loss, and aloneness in the counter-transference, the more I could understand that these were exactly the core feelings G was so mired in. I also felt on my toes at all times with him because of how agreeable G could be while the more hidden feels of envy, grievance, and control emerged in his lying and manipulation. He was often sounding so agreeable and ready to take in my next interpretation without any fuss that I felt on guard against him being a complaint container for me. This is what Lamanno-Adamo (2006) has considered with the patient who prevents any differences, contradictions, or disputes, thus controlling the object and forcing a fusion of smiles, agreeableness, and pseudo progress while really having a much more complicated world going on underneath.

At this point, G's twice a week analytic treatment continues with all the slippery twists and turns I have described. However, I remain hopeful that we are making progress toward some stable sense of analytic contact (Waska 2007) and may slowly find our way to further change and psychic transformation.

Chapter Seven

Patients Who Avoid the Threat of Persecutory Mourning by Means of Entitlement, Devaluation, and a Demand for Action

Some developmentally more mature neurotic patients are able to realize they are special in many ways but also confined by the mutuality of the world, their dependence on others, and the pain of not always having the object be available in the way they want it or when they want it. These depressive position (Klein 1935, 1940) patients struggle with loss, guilt, and control but are still able to tolerate the loss of divine specialness and the disappointment of not being catered to or rescued by the adoring object.

One such patient was B, a woman I had seen for several years and we had worked on the trauma of her rejecting, cold, and belittling mother who in B's mind had very obviously favored her sister and turned her back on B whenever she needed to be comforted. She would tell B to "just deal with it and stop whining." During the course of her analytic treatment, B's husband was diagnosed with cancer and after several years of decline finally died. This left my patient alone after a thirty year marriage to a man she dearly loved. Six months after his death, my patient was describing a terrible, lonely day when she was sick with a painful stomach flu. She said, "I was sick the other day and wished either my husband or my mother could step in to take care of me. But, then I had to face the harsh reality that my husband is dead and that not only is my mother dead but that she never took care of me when I was a child so she certainly wouldn't have taken care of me now. I was sad and upset but I got up, took a blanket, curled up with my dog, and drank some tea. I tried to soothe myself. I am also glad to be here today to talk to you." So, she was able to work through some of those painful moments of loss and loneliness, see herself, her dog, and me as a resource, and make her way past that difficult place.

Other more paranoid schizoid (Klein 1946) patients are not so able. They want to be taken care of. They are angry, they collapse, and they wait for their caretaker to arrive. Some feel entitled to receive special gifts, love, and status without having to work for them or they never feel safe enough to reach for anything and instead stay quiet while waiting for their ship to sail in. Other patients struggling within this same pathological transition between the paranoid and depressive position outright demand that their ship hurry up and gift them the love, supplies, and knowledge they deserve.

Using one difficult case that terminated prematurely as an illustration, this chapter concentrates on a certain group of patients who as Freud (1914) noted, try to repeat their early conflicts, trauma, and internal catastrophes (Bion 1966) rather than remember them, acknowledge them, and work with them towards some type of acceptance and mourning. These patients demand we immediately fix their crippled self and help them reach what they see as their owed, privileged, or special destiny. This is usually in the form of special recognition, love, attention, or success but can also be in the form of something less direct, flamboyant, or aggressive.

For some of these patients, they have internalized a crippled or inferior object (Horner 1987) which they want repaired immediately. For others, it is more of a resistance to giving up the phantasy of a king to be, a child to be loved finally, and a lost soul that will finally be found and brought to a heavenly bliss with the rescuing object. Therefore, much of the transference difficulty with these patients is that they insist on getting better in a perfect, exact sort of way. The road to feeling better is rigid and demanding and they will pause at nothing but perfection. So, even when faced with therapeutic progress, they will dismiss it if it doesn't fit with this phantasy of becoming someone special, being with someone special, or achieving something special. To give this sort of phantasy up is to face an unbearable type of primitive mourning. It is a state of los in which the patient must face the pain of never having the attachment they wanted or needed, to face the knowledge of being hurt and rejected by those they depended on, and the truth of being only human and cared for by someone who was only human and may have even acted less than human. This type of patient will attack their own emotional and mental links (Bion 1959) between self and other and between self and self to preserve the entitled desire of being special instead of having to be one of many in a world without guarantees or instant retribution and atonement for what one feels the self or object has done. The trauma or emotional crime that dependency seems to hold is felt as too much to accept (Grotstein 1987) so an independent, special identity is formed and maintained, but in need of constant fueling, feeding, and reassurance.

Bauer (1993) has written about the importance of using the here-and-now transference situation when exploring the patient's core conflicts.

With the patients I am presenting, that here-and-now focus is crucial as they constantly feel unfed and needy and are anxious about their object's status and condition in relation to them. Bauer (1993) notes how the patient may avoid dealing with the frustration that accompanies the realization that his or her secret longing might never be fulfilled. The type of patient I am highlighting almost violently refuses to face the knowledge of never having the object of their longing. They fend off the underlying agony of never finding it. This is a loss of a primitive order, often a bit more stable than a more raw psychotic experience but certainly not as integrated as the more mature, guilt ridden form of loss found in depressive functioning. This is more of a painful, torturous, persecutory mourning that leaves one lost and empty, feeling surrounded and suffocated by the lack of anything and the ripping apart and ripping away of the dream of specialness. "I no longer matter to you or myself, be it then, now, or forevermore" is the ever nearing catastrophic emotional threat to these patient's psyche.

In the transference, I find this type of patient is constantly enlisting me to deliver some form of reassurance. Or, they are asking me to map out just how to find, retrieve, resuscitate, or build from scratch the self that never was and/or the object that never was. Yet, the patient simultaneously clings to the repetition of destructive object relational patterns since, as Guntrip (1969) notes, a bad or dying object is better than no object. I would add that with these patients, a vision of greatness, the demand for directions to that greatness, and the constant desperate frustration at not yet reaching that special place is better than realizing there is no self or that the self is merely mortal and without the security and strength one wishes for. Indeed, to give up on this special place or position is to experience a descent into an objectless void, a terrible sense of loss with no safety net.

It is a persecutory mourning in that depressive mourning has the safety net of guilt but this more primitive loss and grief is not about harming others but about facing the lack of a soul, the lack of oxygen, the lack of a future, and the lack of meaning and love.

These patients both resist the awareness of the transference as well as the resolution of the transference, the two main transference resistances defined by Gill (1979). To examine the transference would be to give up the analyst as concrete fixer and gratifier. These patients want and demand love, advice, contentment, and direction and avoid stepping away from that concrete expectation of a customer/vendor relationship. Working with such patients is difficult because while they turn away from both acknowledgment of and working through of the transference, it is primarily within the transference work that their best bet for integration, resolution, and self confidence lies.

In regards to pathologies of both the paranoid (Klein 1946) and depressive (Klein 1935, 1940) positions, Betty Joseph's (1989) focus on the importance of the here-and-now transference work and the concept of the total transference (Joseph 1985) have provided the best technical approaches with the hard to reach patient, including those outlined here. Joseph has taken Klein's idea of the total transference (Klein 1952) and elaborated it into a highly thought out examination of how the patient relates to the analyst and the ways these internal and interpersonal patterns reveal core transference phantasy conflicts.

As mentioned before, I have paired this concept with my own approach of the complete counter-transference. Clinically, this is a parallel examination of how all aspects of the analyst's inner experience with the patient may contain vital information about the nature of the object relational climate within the patient that is being played out via projective identification and sometimes via the analyst's enactments.

Klein's original concept of the total transference was an elaboration of some of the fundamental ideas put forth by Freud (1925), Ferenczi (1925), and Heimann (1956) in which the analyst is encouraged to take every element of the patient's presentation as an expression of transference. Using this moment-to-moment here-and-now tracing of the transference and counter-transference can enable the analyst to gradually come to some understanding of these difficult patients who suffer with the conviction that to give in or give up their quest for specialness would result in an internal betrayal from which they would emerge an eternal orphan who is left alone, unable to escape their own desperation and unable to reach an object who seems safe, caring, or rewarding. The sorrow and anxiety of the past would swallow the present and future. This primitive irresolvable mourning would rule and torment forever.

The tragic nature of these patients is that their struggle to avoid this internal collapse is actually what now brings that despair alive in the present. Their defensive flight from the unbearable past creates a destructive present. For these particular patients, the sorrow of past loss, the intense persecutory mourning, and the pathological defenses against that loss leave them in the grips of their past phantasies, unable to find a foothold in the present and unable to have faith in the future.

Due to this primitive and unstable combination of conflict, despair, desperation, and anger, the type of interpretations offered such patients are important to consider. Although interpretations that focus on the transference and on the core anxiety of the patient's pathological phantasy state are crucial, the nuances of such interpretations is important as well. Alvarez (2010) has brought attention to the importance of making interpretations closer to the point of available psychic functioning. So, with patients that are operating more in the depressive mode, it makes sense to make interpretations that are, as Alvarez has defined them, more explanatory. These are the interpretations that tell the patient "you are feeling X" and then add an explanation of "because you feel Y." In other words, they are descriptions of internal conflict that help the patient become aware of a desire or internal phantasy involving self and object that then brings on some state of conflict, be it guilt, fear of punishment, envy, fear of loss, or competition. Then, the analyst might possibly add a description of the resulting strategy the patient takes or wishes to take to avoid, repair, or conquer the conflict. These types of interpretations often work fine with the patients I am examining however sometimes they are too complex, complicated, and too intellectual, providing a verbal defense for both patient and analyst to hide in.

For these patients, they do better in certain moments with what Alvarez (2010) calls the more descriptive interpretations. This is a clinical technique that combines careful and thoughtful containment with interpretations that simply state or describe the affect or phantasy the patient is struggling within at that moment, without adding much about the conflicts, the motives, or the strategies the patient may be contemplating to solve the conflict. It is a simple demonstration of understanding, a show that the analyst knows or is trying to know the core aspect of the immediate dread the patient is facing. Of course, as Steiner (1996) as noted, containment initially involves the keeping of something for the patient and the return of that to the patient. But, at some point, the patient must take over the containment we provided and accept and mourn the reality that the emotional conflicts to be within themselves. They must face that it is something they are now living with, working with, and having to find resolution to.

This last part is again the pivotal terror for these patients, who find mourning to be a paralyzing, terrifying, and fundamentally traumatizing experience of losing the only shred of security, be it false security, they have. Instead, they are left facing the reality of a past without special status or any status at all and the sense that this hollow despair is their current and future fate without choice. They feel a rapid, immediate slide from potentially special to permanently damned. So, in these moments an interpretation that is more rudimentary and close to the raw, one dimensional place the patient is in is more helpful.

Finally, Alvarez (2010) notes that when patients are in even a worse place of psychic collapse, they experience themselves and their objects as full of holes, without potential or hope, and that no meaning can be found in life, self, or others. She advocates simple but powerful interpretations that try to bring life to this dead world by placing some meaning and some attention to the patient's world and to the transference. The patients I am examining can easily slip into this chaos, this ultimate loss and alienation state and therefore also profit from this more spoon feeding of meaning, hope, and simple observation that interpretation can bring.

Alvarez (2010) also notes that the term "working through" is helpful in some situations but that the term "working towards" might be more helpful in describing the needs and state of progress more regressed and primitive patients must traverse. Her term signifies the adding of new internal objects and experiences to one's mind as older more negative or pathological ones are worked through, shed, let go of, and transformed. The patients I am describing dread the introduction of new objects and new object relational experiences as it means the mourning of what never was and the sense that now they are adding a sorrow, deep void, and persecutory loss into themselves without any method of coping with it. They are giving up their special vision, the promise of unique importance, for the grief of unimportance, lack of value, and inferiority. The way they demand, overly depend in a predatory manner, and impatiently push themselves or the analyst for the quick fix, the golden answers, and the best possible way to proceed all are ways of controlling the self and the object and avoiding this terrible sense of primitive loss instead of having to own it, face it, tame it, and accept it.

The Kleinian view of development includes the gradual, healthy coming together of good and bad images of self and other, leading to a firmer grip on reality and a more confident interaction with reality. Once the object is allowed presence in the mind as another with difference, needs, and identity, there is a dawning realization that this object could turn from friend to foe and could leave, abandon, or reject. Suddenly, loss is prevalent and threatening. This is the birth of the depressive position and it brings on such anxiety regarding the relationship of self to other. The safety of both that attachment and separateness suddenly are core elements of psychic life, bring up enormous anxiety. Some more mature defenses against this include manic denial of separation or excessive reparative efforts.

The patients I am examining are not so stable and resort to other mechanisms, such as rigid and intense projective identification dynamics, as well as splitting. Rather than denial of loss, there is a bitter or violent protest of it emerging as a demand to be special to avoid the danger of such loss. This protest fends off a state of impending loss that has little to do with guilt but much to do with persecutory grief. It is a chronic and chaotic inner panic that MY object, more like a security blanket, is gone. It is more about a possession one claims they should have had all along but was never given and now the potential of having this owed trophy is also snatched away. So, it is about loss of something that is mine, a piece of me, rather than a lament that the other person is gone and can't be found. At first, these patients do lament the loss of the other and long for the return of the other, but very quickly in their minds, the loss itself becomes larger than what is lost until they feel they themselves are fundamentally and fatally lost.

So, in elaborating and extending some of Alvarez's ideas from a more strictly Kleinian perspective, these patients tend to benefit from a careful mixture of interpretive and descriptive approaches. Certainly the more higher level explanatory interpretations are critical because they aim to help replace one meaning for another, to illuminate the unconscious workings of the mind over the defensive, acting out aspects of the conscious mind to help the patient regain ownership over what has been internally excavated through excessive reliance on projective identification. But, these sorts of difficult demanding patients also are best helped with interpretations that match their inability to tolerate or contain the stormy object relational chaos inside themselves for very long. So, we must provide interpretations that grow out of initial phases of containment, using a gradual and watchful method of re-introducing the patient's split off pieces of self back to them with simple comments or suggestions that leave them able to hopefully contemplate the return of their cast off self, the emergence of their orphaned self, without a violent reaction and rejection. Here, Alvarez emphasizes the need for empathic but amplifying comments that lend meaning to the patient's phantasy or transference stance but avoid the more two dimensional complexity included with the more explanatory styled interpretations discussed above. So, descriptive interpretations can help these patients feel understood at the more basic and primitive level they are operating from at that exact moment and provide some stabilizing meaning or connection to the terrible anxiety they are consumed by in that moment.

The sum of these interpretive guidelines are part of making analytic contact (Waska 2007) from the bottom up, siding with the most basic and destructive aspects of the patient's mind at that moment in the clinical encounter. At times, the patients I am investigating are quite removed from reality and overcome with anxiety, despair, and their defensive demand for special objects and special personal status. They are in the grip of their own pressure to be more. The constant controlling of others to meet their demands leaves them so overwhelmed and emotionally turned inside out that they cannot listen, think, or feel for periods of time.

Again, they are not so much concerned with who they lost as they themselves feel profoundly lost. It is as if they were a child going for a walk in the forest with their mother and suddenly they became separated and lost for days. In the beginning, they wish to be back with their mother. But, after awhile, they are more and more consumed with being lost and alone and strangled by the sense that they are the only thing alive against this terrible frightening and threatening forest all around them.

For this type of patient in this type of panic, the analyst must consider interpretations that address the patient's dreadful conviction that both the self and all of their objects are dying, lost forever, and so without value or specialness as to not matter at all. This sense of emptiness, death, uselessness, and lack of meaning creates such despair, grief, and mourning that for these patients there is a constant, desperate drive to find specialness, meaning, answers, knowledge (but only for the quick fix), and reassurance.

All these variations on how to interpret to such demanding and desperate patients operating in a very trapped trough between paranoid and depressive functioning, with more of a persecutory loss creating fragmentation at the core of their being, are organized in part by close attention to the analyst's complete counter-transference state, including any fleeting associations, bodily sensations, conscious fantasies, and so forth.

The following case material shows the clinical struggles of an unsuccessful treatment that was very volatile and only lasted a short time. It is not uncommon for patients with similar internal conflicts to terminate abruptly out of anger, impatience, disappointment, and overwhelming anxiety. This is very difficult for the analyst to bear and very difficult to not feel guilty or vindictive about. However, the nature of this group of patients is such that it is always very touch and go. Almost literally, we may manage to touch them with understanding and a moment of analytic contact before they bolt.

However, if we do our best to try and establish analytic contact throughout whatever time we can spend with them and work with these patients' constant, dire search and demand for specialness and some type of recompense or future reward for past crimes, we may help them to slowly mourn in a healthy manner. This, in turn, can lead to gradual acceptance of self and other resulting in a chance to feel hope for being special as a regular human with a unique past, present, and future experience. This will bring them to feel special to themselves and glad to be themselves, as is, without having to claw their way through life, combat the world, or always stare at the jaws of ultimate loss of self and other without a safety net.

CASE MATERIAL

Mary came to see me after feeling "depressed for a long time and determined to not end up stuck in another shitty relationship." She told me how she had spent the "last five years with a jerk, taking care of him and sacrificing myself for his needs in the hopes that one day he might return the favor." Mary explained that she "wanted her boyfriend to love her, understand her, and take care of her but he seemed selfish and self centered most of the time, demanding to be taken care of instead." So, she obliged in the hopes that one day he would realize how much she had done and start to take care of her.

But, after five years, Mary realized this was never going to happen so she broke it off. Now, she was angry and depressed because she "couldn't find any men out there that appreciated her for herself. They all seem to want some cardboard cutout model that fits some cultural stereotype and that is definitely not me. So, I am constantly disappointed in the quality of men out there and have practically given up. I think the problem is the type of men that are in this city. They are all shallow and stuck up. I am sick of their shitty ways and unappealing behavior!"

Mary saw herself as a creative artist, not a part of the mainstream. She was a writer and had published several books on poetry but never made much money at it. To pay the bills, she worked at a software development company and hated the "corporate system and the grinding and boring nine-to-five mentality. I feel stuck and definitely see no better place down the road. This job is just like my last relationship, a dead end and a place where I never get any gratitude or genuine appreciation. I just give and give but never feel like I am truly given back to or fulfilled in any way."

Over the course of a year in treatment, discussing her anger, frustrations, and anxieties about her job, Mary did begin to look into going back to school to change careers. But, when it came right down to signing up and taking classes, she never followed through. She didn't have "the conviction that it was the right thing." My sense was that she was scared and resentful at having to make such a change on her own and too upset about feeling she would have to start from scratch that way. Indeed, this was a thread that seemed to run through much of her life, in which Mary felt very angry that no one was there for her, helping her out and showing her the way or just giving it to her from the start.

One main way this came out countless times in the transference was her telling me about her mother and her brother. She was constantly furious that her brother made no effort to ever travel to see her. Mary said she had "made the effort before" and went to go see him several times over the years but that the effort was never returned. She said she thought his saying he was really busy with his job and his family "was bullshit" and that he "just didn't want to make the effort. He is self centered and never thanks me for the letters I write or the phone calls I make. He is only into his thing. It is so ironic. He likes to talk about how important family is and how important it is to always focus on the family first but God damn it, I am family. Why doesn't he ever make the effort to pick up the phone and call me? He was on a business trip last year and had to fly out here for a meeting. You would think he would call and see if we can get together, but no! Nothing at all! I told him I was really upset and disappointed in him afterwards and he actually got angry with me and told me I don't stop to think about the reality of everything going on around me. I couldn't believe it. Sure, he might be busy with meetings but he could certainly make time have lunch or something."

I said, "So, you end up feeling like you are not important to anyone. I wonder if you are so angry about never feeling important to anyone that you end up hopeless, stuck, and angry with everything and everybody. It seems you feel that way with your job, with boyfriends, and with our work together." My descriptive interpretation about the transference was a reference to what felt like countless times Mary had said she "wasn't' getting anything out of the therapy" and that "it would be more helpful to bitch and complain to my friends. At least they would offer some advice and I wouldn't have to spend my money and time for this disappointing experience." If I made the comment that she now included me in the bucket along with her disappointing brother and boyfriends, she would respond, "Absolutely!"

When I remarked about it this time, Mary responded, "I agree. That is indeed my problem. I know I am not an easy person. I can be difficult. But, you still haven't told me what to do about it! All I do is tell you my problems and you never do anything about it or tell me any techniques or direction to take. You are useless!" Whenever I tried to investigate her sense of "being difficult" and "not easy" and how that feeling of regret or guilt was in the transference, she would barely consider it, telling me, "I feel bad that I dump my anger on you but when I see that you don't give me anything or show me what to do, I feel I am completely justified in being as angry as I want to be." I would follow up with interpretations about her feeling I was ignoring her and not caring for her and neglecting her, but she simply agreed with me, unwilling and unable to work with the transference and instead clinging to it and raging against it.

In other words, there was this sense of constant rejection, a deep feeling of being unwanted that plagued Mary. She quickly mastered this by rejecting others and making them feel unwanted. When I interpreted this dynamic, she illustrated it by her usual reply of, "That is all fine and well, but what am I supposed to do about it!" before slipping into a long resentful and withholding silence. Over time, I would make the suggestion that Mary was trying to leap over looking at herself and rush to the "what to do about it" part so she could avoid the painful anxiety and disappointment that she was carrying around. Mary told me, "Of course I am disappointed. My family treats me like shit and I hate my career. But, again, this is not news to me. I want to move on and find something new, not dwell on all this crap that I have known for years!" This was an example of how Mary retaliated in much the same manner to both explanatory and descriptive forms of interpretations.

When it came to discussing her relationship with her mother, this caustic, bitter anger was almost always present. Mary always described her mother as someone who was "oblivious to other people's needs and only talks about herself, unless she has something critical to say to you." Most of Mary's angry rambling complaints about her mother were around how she had called her mother "again," since her mother "never takes the time or has the thought to call her own daughter. I have to make the effort to call her and you would think that she would realize that the next time it would be nice for her to be the one to call me. But, that never happens. Even when I am really upset she never calls me. I have called her crying and asking her to give me advice or at least listen to what I am saying and she has actually told me she was busy and needed to call me back! Other times, she has listened for a little bit and then turned it around to talk about some stupid problem she has or has had and then the whole conversation is about her! Whenever I try and share some of my frustrations with her, she always ends up blaming me somehow. For example, I was telling her how much I hate my job and how I want to figure out something else to do. Her way of being there for me as my mother was to tell me to not be so upset and be glad I have a job in this tough economy. I can't believe it!"

When I commented to Mary that she felt equally disappointed in me for not providing immediate advice or fixing her and making her feeling better, she simply told me, "You are right. You and my mother both fail to help me and don't do anything to really be there for me in the way I need. It feels just as useless to see you as to call her. So, what is your point?"

When Mary was attacking me in this way or when she complained about her mother, brother, or other people who disappointed her, she voice took on a very raspy, coarse, and nasal quality. She seemed to drone on and on until it felt like she was just literally whining without actually saying words. In the counter-transference, this was very irritating and I found myself wanting to walk out on her or ask her to leave. I took impulse to be a helpful clue of the projective identification process she utilized, an evacuative and suffocating drip, drip, drip of demanding, impatient, and disappointing feelings. I wondered if this protected her from some sort of terrible loss or mourning of an object that never was who she wanted or needed and that by constantly fighting for this debt owed to her or this entitlement of love, advice, and guidance, she could avoid the painful or even shattering and devastating experience of not having and never to have the phantasy of a good mother object.

When I made these descriptive and explanatory interpretations, there were moments when Mary seemed to slow down, calm down, and consider. But, she was not able to hold on to that moment of transition to more depressive functioning for very long and quickly shifted to telling me how I was letting her down. So, it seemed more comfortable for Mary to be actively engaged with a disappointing object that she could attack than to face being lost and alone without the object of her desire. So, mourning was avoided by persecutory means but this left her angry and empty. The defense against the original catastrophe was in fact an ongoing catastrophe.

As mentioned, it was easy to feel irritated with Mary from the way she behaved and acted toward me. Very quickly, I would feel, in the counter-transference, a sharp exasperation. I found her annoying, grating, and extremely self absorbed in certain moments. These were times when Mary began to complain about how someone was not providing her with what she wanted. So, she might spend most of a session complaining about her job and her boss, but it was in a manner that was caustic, whining, and full of grievance. As a result, it was hard to feel sorry for her. Indeed, it created more of a feeling of me wanting to tell her to go away and stop complaining. When I noticed this, I thought about how it might be a result of the projective identification process in which she was making me push her away like she pushed me and others away and that her caustic ways might be a narcissistic defense against feeling different, useless, and unlovable.

So, I interpreted that she was having difficulty showing me the more tender, hurt, or frustrated side of her feelings and perhaps she was unsure if she could trust me with such a vulnerable and raw aspect of herself so instead she tore things up and demanded others deliver what she wanted. This line of exploration seemed to help most of the time for a bit. Mary would talk about feeling unwanted in her family and in present situations or like "she just never fit in and no one seemed to give her the time of day." But, rather quickly, she would turn on me. So, at first she would talk about her fears of never finding anything better to do as a career, her sadness over not having more in her life to feel proud of and secure about, and her loneliness about not having someone to love. But, then the reasons Mary was upset began to grow and pretty soon there were countless angry grievances pouring out and the total absence of any hopeful or positive ideas or options. This was said in a way that was like she threw it all at me. Mary would say, "I am stuck in my life. That is why I am here!" I interpreted how in this way she was both demanding that I fix her and becoming this angry helpless child without proper guidance. I interpreted that showing me her vulnerable rejected side felt too overwhelming so she had to seal it over with anger and a demand for action. Predictably, she would tell me I might be right "but so what. That doesn't help me get a better job or a better family!"

I believe my line of interpretation, exploration of the transference, and ongoing efforts to establish analytic contact did have some positive effects. These changes appeared to mostly be external but external shifts are usually the result of some type of internal movement. So, I think we did manage to work some things out a bit. However, the conflict Mary had over allowing herself to mourn and move past her unavailable and disappointing object made her slip back into being more of an angry, demanding person with irresolvable grievances and no desire to change unless others offered her immediate redress and special attention.

So, Mary did begin to look for other types of jobs in careers that she felt more suited for and had more passion for. She went on several interviews which went well. But, after awhile, she lost interest and felt she "couldn't really tell what she might like or what area would actually feel fulfilling over time" so she stopped looking around and felt locked back into the job she felt to be "an endless grid with no reward."

Likewise, she started accepting some opportunities from coworkers to go out on dates with their friends and she had a good time with a few of these men. However, it quickly became rather black or white. The first one "turned out to be another needy bastard just like my last relationship." The next one was "great in bed and we really hit it off in that department, but otherwise he was completely unavailable emotionally. I need the whole package. I am not going to set myself up for failure again." On one hand, this was progress as she was looking out for herself. At the same time, she ran out of steam and stopped looking around for other dating possibilities. Ultimately, Mary decided "this town is a real dump for dating. There are no available men and I am giving up. They are all married, unavailable, or just too stuck up!"

When she shared her laments with her mother, her mother advised her to "put on some makeup, buy more attractive clothes, and don't be so picky or critical." This infuriated Mary and she told me at great length how "unheard, put down, and unsupported" she felt, telling me that she "is not about to change her natural way of being to make someone love her. Either they can see my positive attributes or they can't but I won't give in to some damned cultural stereotype of how women should dress and act to catch a man."

This sort of rage, defiance, and sense of being judged instead of loved came out in the transference as well. When I made interpretations that pointed to how she might be contributing to her upset and frustration both with me and others, she felt I was attacking her and "blaming her." I replied, "You seem to be using me as a pit stop where you can get a quick fix for your hunger and upset. When I don't fulfill that duty, you are angry with me. I think you feel very deprived and feel there is something that is owed to you sometimes."

Mary paused to think and then told me, "I do feel like I am owed something. I deserve to have a mother who listens to me and helps me out when I need it instead of always making everything about her! I should be able to call her up when I want to so I can talk about things and get her advice. Instead, she won't call me back for weeks and when she does she gets critical if I have anything I am unhappy about. And, if I go out with a man, I expect him to be intelligent enough to realize I am not a cookie-cutter woman but someone with a unique personality and a brain. I am not ready to just hang out in some goddamned bar and flirt like a school child so I can have a man on my arm. If that is all there is out there, then forget it! I would rather have none. And, as far as seeing you goes, I came here to get some answers to the problems in my life. If you don't have them or don't want to give them to me than I will go somewhere else!"

At this point in the counter-transference, I was well aware of being in a very familiar spot. Very quickly, Mary's voice had become shrill and obnoxious. I felt I was simply listening to a shrill monotone of high-pitched, high-volume complaints with no words but only pestering nuisance. I realized I felt like answering her, "fine, then go somewhere else!"

I took a quick account of all this and interpreted, "You start to share with me your feelings of being lost and rejected but then turn it into an attack on everyone who won't give you what you want right away. Maybe it is very difficult to stay with the feelings of not having and the suffering you have gone through. Maybe it is very hard to mourn the fact that you didn't have the mother, boyfriend, career, and therapist you wanted. We were and are all different than what you wanted and what you still want."

So, here I was directly interpreting her struggle with the mourning and loss of transitioning to the depressive position as well as her core phantasy of persecutory loss. "We are all less than you expected," I added. Mary was quiet for a few minutes and finally said, "That is exactly the problem. No one has been helpful or understanding. I have yet to find someone I really connect with. I don't think it is me. I think there are a lot of shitty people out there and I won't settle for that. I want something decent and if I can't have it then I will be fine by myself."

I felt like we were able to take a breath of fresh air for a moment before Mary felt it was somehow poisonous air and retreated back to the stale, suffocating darkness she lived in and felt somewhat in control of.

After several cycles of these volatile transference interactions with Mary, she told me, "I don't think we have a good connection. I don't think we are a good match. I am asking you for help and advice and you never give me anything. I find this a complete waste. I haven't gotten anything out of this. I don't think I will return." I asked her to at least give us time to explore these feelings, to better understand her needs, and to sort out just how I am failing her. I asked her to consider that I am now one more person that has failed her and fallen to the wayside. Perhaps it would help her to think more about this and talk more about it.

Mary said she had "wasted enough time" and left. I was not surprised but I was a bit sad that she had once again thrown out someone, deeming them as useless as she felt she was. This violent reliance on projective identification probably left Mary empty, anxious, and lonely once again, barely buoyed up by her angry narcissism but crumbling around the edges as she tries to find her way in a world that seems to always be much grimmer, grayer, and harsher than she hopes for.

Discussion

The case of Mary illustrates the dynamic found in patients who to varying degrees are chronically anxious and often quite depressed. As a rule, they are aggressively expecting more in their lives, demanding some immediate fix to their problems and fed up with "waiting for my ship to come in." Some are baffled about why their ship has never come in, some are shocked that it sank before ever arriving but quickly and defensively feel entitled to having it brought back from the depths and magically delivered. They demand to be placed on a cruise ship with all the benefits but do whatever they can to resist the acknowledgment that their original childhood vessel was in fact the *Titanic*.

They avoid the persecutory and emotionally shattering reality of primitive loss in which they are left alone and hopeless, useless and without. Some of these patients, such as the case of Mary, show extreme entitlement, impatience, demand, and a sense of being owed. They feel that there is an abusive or neglectful object that should and has to make restitution by becoming the good or ideal object it should have been all along.

Angry defenses of entitlement to avoid the paranoid-schizoid experience of ultimate loss and longing include a cry and demand for reparation and restitution in the form of "I won't do anything to better myself until you take care of me first. I refuse to have to be at your mercy and I demand to be at your care and comfort. These pathological internalized compromises, or internal bargains, contain a high psychological cost (I will wait for a savior, which means I do nothing for myself in the meantime). The progress, acceptance, mourning, and change that analytic treatment offers represent a cruel betrayal and the forced glance at emptiness and loss that seems unbearable and beyond repair. The search, the wait, and the entitled demand seem preferable, regardless of the concurrent anguish and frustration. To have to bang on the door to be let in is better than feeling there is no door, no home, and no object.

Chapter Eight

"I Thought I Was Special. If Not, I Am Nothing": The Treatment of Primitive Loss and the Defensive Search for Uniqueness

Some patients in psychoanalytic treatment do what they can to deny and avoid a terrifying sense of grief over early primary objects who failed them, objects who were less than ideal, and objects who treated them as useless or without potential. When the patient needed special attention, they were ignored. For some of these patients, the same neglectful or abusive parents gave them an additional contradictory message that they were destined for greatness. They gave their child a promise of uniqueness, directly or indirectly telling them they would eventually come to be very special and great.

Other times, these patients created their own grandiose phantasy of special destiny or an eventual reward of greatness in exchange for prior suffering. Analytic treatment can be difficult with such individuals as they are reluctant to give up these phantasies of entitlement. In fact, they do whatever they can to side step this intense and catastrophic sense of persecutory mourning.

The devastating unconscious feeling of never having a secure, safe, and affirming object who loved them as a special and unique being is disturbing and shattering. But, in addition, there is the sense that the object viewed them as inferior, unimportant, or useless. This leaves the patient feeling they are adrift forever, as a soulless, empty nothing, separated from their desired good object. As a defense and in retaliation, these patients aggressively search for their special status and refuse to give up their demand for reward or unique standing. They concentrate on what they deserve and have intense grievance about not having received it. They live within a torturous place of seeking out their long owed destiny but feeling constantly revoked and rejected. But, this feels better than to mourn the unbearable infinite suffering of never having and never to have any reliable source of emotional nourishment, support, or trusted object to rely on. To be special to no one is an internal experience that feels beyond tolerable. So, to insist on being given special status, in some form, is the method of avoiding unbearable primitive mourning. This phenomenon creates difficult transference standoffs.

Weintrobe (2004) has described patients who seemed fixated on a set of grievances against their objects. Like his description of such character conflicts, the patients I am examining feel their objects have fundamentally failed them and the anger and anguish is profound. Indeed, these patients are unable to consider understanding or forgiveness in any capacity except perhaps a fleeting intellectualized idea about their parents "doing the best they could." But, as Akhtar (2002) notes, certain patients, such as the ones I am exploring, do not easily grant forgiveness or accept forgiveness. Instead, there is often a clinging to grievance because it provides a defensive righteousness to stay afloat on rather than feel like they might sink and perish in the cold dark realization that they really did feel alone, unappreciated, and unprotected as a child and still feel that way.

These feelings are so intense as to create a sense of self-destruction should one give up on recompense and the arrival of one's special superior destiny. These patients fight for status above others to avoid a persecutory mourning of what has never been and the accompanying sensation of being below others and even invisible or without meaning to others. This primitive mourning is not about guilt or concern for the object. It is the loss of self-sustaining nourishment and the loss of essential and rudimentary importance in the object's mind and heart, leading to a sense of banishment, persecution, and rejection without recourse. As Weintrobe (2004) notes, nursing grievance can block this unbearable mourning and create hope to restore or finally locate the ideal object. Also, the maintenance of grievance propels an ongoing sense of entitlement that also guards one from this primitive and painful loss.

With these types of entitled patients who will not give up the search to be special and find their blessed destiny, the analyst's focus on transference as well as the analyst's ongoing interpretation of deep phantasy is essential. So, while the here-and-now manner of the total transference approach (Joseph 1985) is very important with these patients, the more holistic interpretive style of Segal (1973) is also very useful since much of the patient's phantasy conflict involves the past and external manifestations of internal chaos. Segal (1973) notes that a complete interpretive approach must include analysis of the patient's daily life, the transference, and the relationship between those two, as well as an understanding of early childhood experiences. Linking internal figures with external figures is also critical in making emotional and mental bridges for these patients and providing them a chance to survive their terrifying and looming grief and mourning.

As Steiner (1990) notes, most pathological defensive organizations are founded on the over reliance of projective identification as a method of coping, controlling, defending, and aggressing. This intensive focus creates a blur between self and object and distorts reality testing, leading to a sense of being overwhelmed by core phantasies and their accompanying anxieties.

Ogden (1990) notes that psychoanalysis is a method of treatment that helps the patient modify unconscious conflict as well as experience those conflicts differently. The core phantasies are not eradicated but tamed, owned, understood, and mourned. The pain remains but in forms and levels which are tolerable. The patients I am examining are not willing to make that shift. They do not want the pain, in any form. They just want it gone.

In fact, they do not believe it would be in a different level or tolerable. They picture the pain to be the same overwhelming, devastating catastrophe as when it first consumed them. So, there is no reason to turn toward it again. When they begin to face the grief and mourning of what was never available for them, they immediately retreat or lash out as they do not have any faith that it would be different or ever any less devastating. In this primitive mourning state, the patient believes there is never any lessening of pain, no forgiveness, and only an endless continuation of unbearable loss.

As Steiner (1990) notes, these "borderline position" patients fight off a fundamental sense of betrayal. It is as if they had been promised an ideal object. I would add that by identification with this phantasy, through projective identification, they believe in the promise of an ideal self. The sense of loss and disappointment is unbearable. Pathological mental organizations and internal bargains offer temporary respite and false hope that can easily break down.

Steiner (1990) sees mourning as a two-part process in which the self must first accept the loss of the object and all its goodness as well as accepting that the self has been and is still utterly dependent on the object. This leads to a persecutory sense of mourning in which all is lost and the internal world is shattered. All hope is gone and survival is uncertain. The only way to continue is to either deny any dependency, a move toward the death instinct, or deny the loss altogether, which is more the route these entitled patients take.

At this point, these patients usually shift to their phantasy of being special and simply wait for redemption and their ship of uniqueness to sail in. But, they are always feeling dangerously close to being cast into the inferno of meaninglessness.

The healthier neurotic or depressive patient gradually faces reality after the painful grief and mourning period. And, it is a period rather than an eternity. They face reality, their dependency, and the loss until gradually they start to build a new life separate from the object while still honoring the object in their heart and mind. The grief remains but alongside it is born a new relationship to the self and to life.

CASE MATERIAL

Paul initially came to see me for troubles at his workplace. He felt he was fairly happy for a few years in his management job but just when he was hoping to be asked to shift into a position he saw as "much more in line with my goals" and "something in which I could stand out and shine," he felt he was "pushed to the curb." Paul felt his opportunity for something special that he would really enjoy, "deserved," and had "waited and worked for," was replaced by something "regular, insignificant, and not helpful to my future." He felt it "wasn't done to me on purpose, but it feels like it in a way."

Within a few weeks, Paul was telling me more about feeling confined to something mundane instead of being able to move toward his desired goal. Now, he was sharing with me more intense and generalized feelings of seeing himself as "stuck." He told me he had a lifelong sense of being "held back and unable to reach the Promised Land." This way of viewing himself and the world was to be one of the themes of our ongoing investigation over the following year. Bit by bit, Paul revealed ways he has always felt special but also many ways he has felt tore away from that special status, unfairly and often in ways that left him "suspicious and even paranoid about what exactly is going on around me."

During one session, Paul told me, "I have always felt I have a special destiny, above the rest, but I feel that something went wrong and I am being pulled back into something very ordinary or very much less than special. When I was a child, I was in church one day and when everyone closed their eyes for a particular prayer, I opened mine. Suddenly, everyone was gone and in their place there was this wonderfully beautiful creature. I think it was a deer or a majestic bison of some sort. It looked magical and had glittering stars all around it. It walked very slowly through the church and toward me. I felt very good and at peace. I closed my eyes again and when I opened them everyone was back and the animal was gone."

After we talked about the dream for awhile, I interpreted that Paul seemed to want to exchange his family and others for this special sense of peace and majesty. I said that perhaps he wanted a special place to go to get away from the lack of peaceful feelings he had every day with people. Paul said things were "rarely peaceful, mostly unpredictable and certainly not majestic."

After a few months of psychoanalytic treatment, Paul seemed to be revealing himself to me in a much more vulnerable manner but as a result feeling more exposed and threatened at times. On numerous occasions, he has felt I am Satan and fears I will use what I know of his "weakness" and vulnerability to control and humiliate him. While Paul says he rationally understands this is not the case, he feels overwhelmed by the phantasy and the feeling of persecution. He tells me he sometimes sees others as agents of Satan as well and that we are all trying to stop him on his road to "his special destiny." I interpreted that he not only fears we are trying to keep him back from being special but also somehow make him look and feel less than special, either ordinary or less than ordinary. He said, "Yes! Why are you doing that?" Paul was laughing when he said this which meant he partly knew this was not so but also was feeling quite convinced it was so.

With Paul, it is very common for him to come into the office and immediately look very anxious and suspicious. He will then struggle to come up with "the right topic," "return to where we had left off," or simply have the "proper direction figured out so we can keep the therapeutic ball rolling." He will quickly freeze up as he realizes he doesn't have the perfect line for me or the ideal set of topics ready to go and prefigured out. I tell him, "you picture I want you to come in with your homework done perfectly and ready for me to inspect. You are worried that I will be upset if you just are yourself with me." This line of interpretation has gradually helped him become less anxious and he slowly struggles and risks coming in "without the pressure" and tries to "look me in the eye without assuming there is a problem brewing."

I interpret that he tries to keep us ok and always obtaining the right flow but worries that if he doesn't stay on constant watch, I might see him as less than ideal and in fact begin to see him as bad and useless. Paul said, "I completely agree. I picture you could easily be sick and tired of me. If I don't do what I am supposed to in here, work on things, and always be trying to get better, you will tire of me and kick me out." I said, "so, we have to operate at this high raised bar of special behavior at all times or we fail and end up ordinary and inferior." Paul nodded and said, "But, it is hard to be myself, feel safe, and not be unhappy with my progress." I said, "So, besides being scared that I need you to be special at all times, you are scaring yourself with your own demands for perfection and special progress."

As we continued along in his now one year long analytic treatment, Paul began to tell me more about the details of feeling special throughout his life. During his childhood, he was raised by a very religious family and went to church several times a week. Whenever any problems came up or when he told his parents he was upset about something, they always told him to pray about it and remember that "He will be rejoicing in the future because this present day trouble is only earth bound. But, the goodness of God will find him later in life and lift him up to great heights."

Paul explained that when he was being picked on at school or had problems with his sister, his parents seemed to always tell him to "Not pay attention to that because he was going to be taken to a place far above those others and he would feel mighty and realize his greatness." Apparently, it was his mother who usually told Paul most of this. He would routinely go to her for emotional support or help with something and be told to ignore what was going on and look ahead to the days when he would "find out how special and unique he was, that he was destined for something very special." I interpreted, "it sounds like you wanted her to listen to how you felt you were suffering in hell at times but she only talked about the days of heaven that would eventually come." He said "that is a perfect way to sum that up."

Paul had an older sister who was diagnosed as psychotic when she was fifteen. However, Paul tells me that when he looks back, he realizes that his sister acted "very strangely many years before that. She would pick on me, hit me, and call me all sorts of mean and strange names. She would tell me that God was very angry with me and that Satan was coming to get me. I was really scared sometimes after she said that."

Paul told me that in general, his sister was crafty in hiding her abusive behavior from their parents but also Paul thinks his parents "didn't want to see it." So, when he would go to them complaining about her being mean to him, they "didn't usually believe him," "sort of discounted what he said," and told him to "just go out and play and don't worry about it." He was left feeling like they didn't care and just wanted to distract him with thoughts of the future.

But, at the same time, he was interested in what this message meant. Just exactly what was his special and wonderful destiny? He started to think more about that. When Paul was a teen, his sister was completely psychotic and often violent. She beat on him numerous times and the family's focus was often on how to deal with her, what facility to take her to, and what medications were needed at the time. Paul felt he got shuffled to the background once again and he still remembers some of the violent episodes with terror today. A few times, his parents left him alone at home with his sister and she tormented him with verbal abuse and threats of violence. The hours he spent waiting for his parents to return and rescue him still bring him to tears of trauma and rage. But, when his parents came home, Paul said his parents usually "didn't believe it could have been that bad" and seemed to downplay the whole thing. This still hurts Paul as an awful sense of betrayal.

Over time, Paul has felt he can trust me with certain information and certain beliefs he has. Before, he "wasn't sure if I would label him as crazy and lock him up" or "would I listen and try to understand." I interpreted that this anxiety was a duplicate of what he had said about his "betrayal experience" with his parents growing up. He agreed and told me that I seemed to be honestly interested in him and wanting to help but that he "couldn't help but feel I might turn on him in some type of satanic way or if I might be an undercover agent of the government." Whenever Paul reveals these sorts of terrible persecutory phantasies, he is usually quick to reassure me that "he can think to himself that it is ridiculous and not really happening" but that he "feels it to be true in his body." So, intellectually, he was able to stay in touch with reality most of the time or bring himself back to reality for the most part, but emotionally and psychologically he was often teetering on the edge of psychotic breakdown.

Paul told me that he had the idea from both very early in his childhood and still quite actively now in adulthood that he was an "alien insert." He told me that he had always felt very different from others and "had an insight at one point that he was part of an alien master plan." He explained that "these alien forces from a faraway galaxy go from planet to planet to observe and learn. The aliens are just formless energy, so they pick certain people on Earth to have a special part in their grand experiment. At some point, they insert themselves into the mind and body of someone and the person no longer is fully human but not exactly a full alien either. At some point, the alien aspect of the chosen person's mind reports back to the main alien force."

I asked Paul what it was like to realize this as a child. Here, I found it important to simply follow him in this psychotic phantasy and learn more about it. In the counter-transference with such patients, it is easy to become scared, anxious, or shocked and want to do something to bring the patient back to reality. Unfortunately, this would be an acting out of the critical, non-understanding, and rejecting object that he felt pursued by already. So, with patients in this paranoid and fragile state, it is more helpful to stabilize ourselves and try to live within the phantasy long enough to learn more about the nature of how the patient views himself and how he experiences his objects, even if in this delusional way.

Regarding how he felt as a child when he started believing he was part of the alien project, Paul said he was scared at first but then felt special and wondered if he was really supposed to know. He told me that as an adult, he thinks there was a breakdown in the alien's usual procedures, causing him to have "ancient memories of being back with the aliens but then the aliens quickly deleted most of those memories." Paul said he thinks he is unique in that he "knows he is an agent from afar whereas all the other humans that were chosen don't have any idea."

I said, "It also sounds sad that you know you are far from home and alone by yourself without the other aliens. And, you are not really fully human. So, you are caught in this lonely middle ground." Here, I was making an interpretation that addressed the wasteland between the paranoid-schizoid and depressive position that makes up the psychic retreat which Paul seemed to utilize in avoiding massive and overwhelming loss. Paul replied, "I do feel like that sometimes. But, I mostly function as a human so I don't think about it too much. I also worry that they might catch me thinking that and realize I know about them and then they would have to shut me down or something."

Paul went on to explain how sometimes he thinks that instead of this alien idea being correct, instead he might be a "future messiah figure who will eventually rule the planet, in a peaceful way but able to lead everyone to a better way or time." I interpreted, "You still want to have a good parent that you can trust to lead you to the promised land of love, warmth, and safety." Paul looked at me and said, "You are quite clever, you know. You are onto something I think. But, I still think there might be some truth to what I believe, not all the time but sometimes." Interpreting his defense against primitive mourning, I said, "It is scary to give up that special destiny since you might fall far."

He said, "I would be nothing, absolute nothing. That is the problem. I feel I am a broken animal. I am angry I suffered so much in my life but I am convinced that this suffering will lead to a grand and wonderful reward of sorts." I said, "So, you want there to be a tally sheet and you are owed this specialness for all that suffering." He said, "Yes, something like that." I replied, "Maybe to give up that wish, to realize that no special parent will come to rescue you, leaves you feeling crushed and hopeless. So, you hang on to that idea of one day becoming so independent and great you don't even need to be rescued." Paul said, "I am not there yet. I don't want to give it up." I replied, "You want to make sure I understand that and don't rip it away from you too early." He nodded yes.

During other sessions, Paul told me he was and is angry with others around him and "even all the characters in movies and television shows who seem so happy and fine with life. I get very angry because I feel permanently crippled by my painful childhood and the shitty ways my parents treated me or turned their back on me." I said, "You envy others because they seem to have been spared?" He said yes. Then, Paul told me, "My parents never helped me with any of my problems when I was little, even in high school. If I had homework and they didn't understand it, they would say it wasn't important. If I had an emotional problem, they told me to ignore it and think about the future when one day I would rise above everyone else and be rewarded."

After he elaborated on this for a bit, I made the interpretation I had made several times before. I said, "You wanted help with your current hell but they told you to look ahead to the day you get to heaven. That left you ignored and without protection. But, it also made you feel important and better than those people who were hurting you." Paul said, "I just wanted them to pay attention to me right then and help me with the problems I was having, not push it off to this great time in the future. But, it did make me feel important and I looked forward to being this special person who could look down on others and feel superior. I am not proud of that but I did feel that way and still do sometimes."

Telling me more about his "special powers" as a child, Paul said, "When I was ten years old, I realized I could turn the traffic lights to red. I noticed that when I looked at them really hard, they would turn to red. I also noticed that there was a reoccurring pattern of color everywhere I looked. Even up to today, if I take a moment to look around, I become aware that what seemed random before is now an obviously deliberate blending of certain shades of blue and green and sometimes yellow in many objects. I started to notice this several years ago and could see it in cars, buildings, clothing, and even artwork. I started telling people about it and a few said they had noticed it, too. Eventually, I did some Internet research and found that there is actually a website where people from all around the globe have been reporting this phenomenon. So, I am not alone! It appears that this is a fairly common finding that just has never got any mainstream attention or publication. Now, why these patterns exist is another topic altogether but I brought it up as an example of the numerous ways I realized I might have these special powers or abilities."

During another session, Paul told me more about how he has "always felt like a broken animal beyond repair. I must be broken at the core, somehow broken and not functioning because of my childhood traumas. So, when the aliens took my mind over and began a process that would have eventually brought me to some type of honorable or special prominence, this basic flaw, my broken core, messed up the process and prevents me from reaching this end goal. I am stuck in between, never able to reach the place I was destined to be in. This makes me very upset so I try and not give up the hope that one day I might fix myself and be able to continue the journey."

I interpreted, "So, you probably see part of our work here as a way to fix that fundamental flaw. But, it seems very uncomfortable to think you could help yourself and make important changes to better your life and only be a regular human. You end up stuck in between either being a broken flawed loser or this grand wizard. The place in the middle is uncertain and maybe unwanted?" Paul said, "I can intellectually accept that it would be ok or even good to be in that middle place, but another part of me won't give up hope for the road to this promise." I said, "Mother's promise?" He said, "at this point, I can't tell who. Is it me, mom, the alien's, or what? I don't want to give up hope and realize this is all a terrible delusion and that the truth of it all is that I had a shitty childhood and I can do nothing about it."

I interpreted, "So, it is easier to see yourself as temporarily flawed but if you can fix that flaw, then the alien's promise will come true and you can have a happy ending after all. But, that means you have to keep this cosmic tally sheet and always size up if you are either flawed and bad or fantastic and perfect." Paul replied, "I am glad we are talking about these things but it has taken me a long time to trust that it would be ok or helpful to tell you about them. I think the idea that I truly may have an alien presence in me could be critical to understanding some of what I am going through and what to do about it. But, I do worry that you might be part of a selected group of therapists that the government has met with and given a handout that instructs you to contact them if you should even meet with a patient who talks about having an alien presence inside them." I said, "You are worried I will push the secret red button."

Now, never using humor with any patients at any time could be seen as the safest road to take because it avoids the occasional situation when it may backfire and be taken as ammunition in a patient's paranoid or depressive transference state. This can easily happen with paranoid, borderline, or psychotic patients who take you literally and personally. However, I find that it is hard to avoid joking around on occasion and I also have found occasional use of humor to create a sense of mutual understanding, as if we both get the joke. It becomes an "inside" joke and we both temporarily have a common enemy we are fighting. So, it fosters a bit of splitting that can create a moment of collaboration and insight into something that sounds absurd but we also realize is serious and upsetting. But, as I said, this can also backfire.

Basically, I believe that being humorous is usually part of an enactment which can ultimately serve some benefit if properly analyzed, but it is certainly not a technique to deliberately use. As analysts, we avoid these pitfalls and try to not deliberately indulge in them but also try and realize they are inevitable and need to be analyzed for helpful insight when they do occur.

So, to my joking about the red alert button, Paul replied, "Oh no! You have a secret red button?" I realized that at that moment, Paul was completely within his psychotic phantasy of being betrayed by me, the government agent. His alien hybrid identity would be revealed and he would be caught and exterminated. Seeking to stabilize the situation, I said, "No, I definitely do not have a red button. But, my joke not going over so well shows us how anxious and scared you are about being betrayed, judged, and punished. You want to trust me but the feelings of fear and worry are strong."

Paul laughed with relief and said, "Oh good. Well, I know this is all pretty ridiculous, but there is no way of ever really knowing for sure. So, I still think there could be this ongoing presence inside of me and therefore there is this parallel threat to it." I said, "I think that is interesting. You want to be special and have this overseer with you but to have that you always have to look over your shoulder. It is like there is never peace and perfection together. It can quickly turn ugly and be shattered." He nodded in agreement.

During the next session, Paul came in and sat down looking nervous and suspicious. This was common. Many times in the past, he had come in under the strain of trying to figure out "the right topic," "the way to continue the thread from last time," or "the appropriate issue to work on." He pictured me as expecting him to be a timely, hard working, deep thinking, problem-solving, perfect patient. I made this interpretation many times over and we had worked on this transference anxiety until it was much reduced. However, as in this session, it still remained to some degree.

Paul told me, "I think I want to continue to talk about what we were discussing last time." I asked him if he wanted to or if he felt I wanted him to. For awhile, we discussed how he thought I was "sick and tired of all this alien bullshit" and that I probably wanted him "to hurry up and get past all this crazy made up stuff and start living in reality and to get a grip of himself." He was worried I was getting "fed up and losing my patience." I said, "I can see from how you look that you are very nervous about that. You aren't sure if I can tolerate hearing about your desire to escape being so lost, alone, and inferior by being this special, perfect being. You have a hard time believing there is a middle ground and that you could give up your special destiny without descending into hell, without me, someone else, or your special powers to protect you."

Paul was silent for a bit and then said, "I don't want to have to admit to myself that all I had was a shitty lonely time growing up, having to be all by myself facing things that were so scary. I don't want to have to be left with the terrible feeling that there was no one there for me and no one to ever be there and understand me. The promise of being special is a way around that. If I give it up I have nothing and I feel I am nothing. I don't know if I can live with that." I said, "You don't feel you matter to me, your parents, or anyone if you are not super special." Paul replied, "I am afraid of becoming normal. I don't want to have to give up all that I think I am and just end up regular and normal." I said, "You are scared I am going to take away your powers. You are scared I will end up making you an empty normal person who feels lost and alone." Paul agreed with me and added, "I am afraid of that but I also realize the entire system must be questioned. I think one reason I started to believe in this whole alien thing was that I felt so cheated and betrayed by religion and by God. So, I think I sought out a higher being that I could count on, the aliens." I said, "An authority or greater parent you could cling to and go to for help. The aliens were someone who saw you as special." Paul choked up a bit and said yes.

I interpreted his desire for parents who would be there for him and listen to him when he needs help. I said that he must have such strong and mixed feelings about it that he might have a hard time trusting me as someone who cares and listens. Paul said, "Sometimes I feel very grateful because you seem genuinely interested and concerned. Other times, I wonder what your secret agenda might be." I said, "Back to the aliens and all the actors in that story." He nodded. I repeated my earlier comment, "to not be special is to be nothing and have nobody."

Paul choked up and started weeping. He said, "I want someone to be there and someone I can trust. But, you are right. I don't know if I want to give up being special. I am really very scared to give up what I consider my special powers, my superhuman powers. I don't want to just be human." He paused and then added, "Maybe if I can give up my alien powers and become human I might find some human powers. It feels really risky but I think I want to try." Paul began sobbing. He looked at me with sudden anxiety and said, "I am worried you are judging me for crying like a baby, for being so weak and so pitiful. It seems so pitiful for me to break down like this!" I said," It is only human." Paul smiled with relief and allowed himself to cry a bit more.

This awful phantasy of having to give up being special and give up the promise of one day being loved and rewarded to instead face the meaninglessness of being ordinary and useless was the core dilemma for Paul. Patients like him struggle with wanting so much, striving to be special, and waiting to be fixed, loved, and rewarded.

As Searles (1979) notes, hope and change always entails loss. For hope to triumph over despair one must accept the loss of the former idealized hope and realize the calvary will never come and rescue you. But, in doing so, now there is hope that you may be able to rescue yourself and find other more regular, human, and non-idealized figures to assist you in that rescue. This inner source of independent freedom often comes out of the realization that sharing ones despair with another, in the analytic setting, can lead to a firm foundation of new hope, a sense of strength, and a desire to create one's own rewards. By mourning and gradually facing the original despair that has been warded off for so long by this promise of special victory, one can realize that not only are we are all human but that to be human is very special in its own right. To not be all knowing and powerful is not a betrayal, simply part of the human condition. To not know and to have weakness means we can learn, receive, and grow.

Chapter Nine

Lack of Traction in the Analytic Process: Adrift in the Counter-Transference

Some patients are extremely trying to work with and difficult to reach. They have a cold and controlling manner of organizing their objects which seldom allows for genuine emotional connection. Often, we encounter rigid narcissistic defenses involving power and reactive independence with a strong set of conflicts regarding give and take and any sort of need or dependence. Typically, these are borderline and narcissistic patients who operate at either paranoid schizoid (Klein 1946) levels or primitive depressive (Klein 1935, 1940) modes of relating. From these thorny psychological encampments, they react, retreat, and rebel against phantasies of loss that leave them fragmented and desperate.

The acting out in such cases is constant and sharp, making it hard for the analyst to remain empathic, neutral, and objective. Grinberg (1968) has noted that the patient's phantasy or actual experience of separation and loss without adequate mourning and psychological closure is one of the prime triggers in acting out. Part of this acting out is the reaction to feeling overwhelmed by feelings of abandonment and dread which are felt to be rejected by the container object. The patient is left to aimlessly drift in a formless void unless given defensive and temporary form by various methods of acting out. Also, I would add, the absent object of desire, whose absence creates a sense of dread, anger, and sorrow, is avoided by creating an imaginary object of desire through acting out.

The analyst can end up experiencing this very same type of loss and anxiety over separation with thick-skinned or thin-skinned narcissistic patients (Britton 1998) because of their extreme reliance on projective identification. Rosenfeld (1987) believes the thick-skinned narcissist needs to be treated firmly. I agree with this and advocate sensitive confrontations blended with interpretations for a period of time (Waska 2010b) but I also agree with Rosenfeld (1987) that thin-skinned narcissists must be handled in a much more careful and respectful manner. However, there are many patients who embody aspects of both clinical profiles and therefore create very slippery, complex, and vexing situations in the analyst process. This complicated clinical atmosphere can easily create very thorny counter-transference moments that can fail to contain the treatment and even push it to collapse. Other times, these hard-to-reach patients are so hard to engage that treatment failure is simply a matter of time. Regardless, an ongoing study of such transference and counter-transference experiences is vital for the analyst's growth and ability to provide the best he or she can in such no-win scenarios.

The following case highlights the difficulties of working with patients in the borderline and narcissistic realm. These encounters often collapse into a stormy brief treatment with an abrupt end. The case material illustrates the moment-to-moment technical elements of the Kleinian approach as well as the often precarious edge we walk in the counter-transference and the interpretive enactments that can follow.

CASE MATERIAL

Jane only came to see me for two months before she terminated. During this time I did what I could to engage her in an psychoanalytic process but establishing and maintaining analytic contact (Waska 2010a, 2010b) was very difficult because of her intense acting out and my counter-transference reactions to her aggressive, destructive, and defensive methods of narcissistic non-relating.

Jane came to see me for help sorting out issues regarding her current relationship, which she had just ended very abruptly. After five years of living with her boyfriend, she told him she had met someone else who "she really clicked with" and was "going to pursue that path." Jane told me she had felt "somewhat lukewarm" about her relationship for the last couple of years. She described it as "OK, but nothing really exciting or special." She said they had settled into a pattern of predictable activities and socializing that was "fine but seemed to be getting stale. We hang out and do enjoyable activities but that is about it."

Jane was an energetic, well-dressed, attractive forty-year-old woman. She was extremely competitive and aggressive in her workplace, leading a team of salespersons and managing numerous high-powered deals with various customer accounts. Very quickly, I felt I was part of a project she was heading and wanting immediate results from.

Based on this aspect of the transference, I interpreted, "You seem to have a hard time just letting yourself relax here with me and learn about what might be going on emotionally with you. Instead, it looks like you see this as a work project to bang out results from as soon as possible. A problem followed by a solution and then move on to the next challenge."

Jane answered, "What is wrong with that? I approach everything in my life like that. I want to be efficient and not waste time. Why wouldn't I want to do that?"

I said, "Well, this isn't a work goal, it's you. You have feelings and struggles that are more complicated and deserve more time and attention. But, maybe you are not used to seeing yourself that way or letting me see you that way?" She said, "I see what you mean, but why would I?" So, this was the start of a very controlling, concrete type of transference situation in which I was left with the flesh and blood of things and Jane demanded immediate corporate results for the board meeting. This very lopsided dynamic of feelings versus concrete demand was part of the evacuative projective identification process that Jane utilized. She was OK and neutral while all her objects had vulnerable feelings and needs. She did not want to be in this sensitive, dependant place so she made sure to be the opposite.

After five years with her boyfriend, Jane had "fallen" for her new tennis instructor. He was fifteen years younger and married. He had made a pass at her after one of her tennis lessons. She responded immediately and began an affair that involved meeting him for sex as well as frequently attending local tennis tournaments together. After a week or two of this, she told her boyfriend in a very matter-of-fact manner that she "had found her soul mate and thought it best if they break up." Her boyfriend was devastated and asked if he was at fault, what he could do to fix the problem, and if they could go to counseling to work it out. He was willing to forgive her and begged her to not leave. When she said she was "over it and needed to move on," he was angry and after several weeks he moved out. When Jane said she had "fallen" for the new man and had found her "soul mate," I interpreted that these phrases, which normally convey intense feelings and symbolic bliss, sounded more mechanical and matter of fact than emotional. She had a good reason on paper to leave her boyfriend but was not demonstrating it or sharing it with me in the way she talked or related. Jane responded by saying she does feel a lot for him but doesn't want to stay with him and doesn't want to have to spend time going over it "again and again." She said, "I just want to make the change. I know he is upset but I have made up my mind."

Now, hearing all this made me feel very judgmental of Jane. She seemed to just have turned a switch and discarded this person like he was a used tissue. In the counter-transference, I noticed myself thinking she was arrogant, cold, and selfish, and a "bad person." I had to pull myself back from these feelings and remind myself that she had come to me for help with these issues. This was one of the vexing aspects of the transference/counter-transference situation. I was regularly dosed with aspects of Jane's personality that made me completely forget that she had indeed come in and said, "I know I have some sort of problem and I think

I really need to deal with it once and for all. Ever since I started dating, I only stay with the man for a certain amount of time, usually fairly long periods, before I suddenly dump them. I feel bad about it and think there is something wrong with me for doing it, but I also think I shouldn't be unhappy. If it is time to move on, I should. That's just life!"

Jane told me she felt "badly" that every relationship she had ever been in had the same profile. After two, three, four, or five years, she would find herself feeling bored and flat in the relationship. Perhaps there was some communication about it, but mostly without protest Jane just settled into this less-than-satisfied place and felt empty and discontented. Then, she would "spontaneously" meet a man and find him "energetic, smart, good looking, and full of life: a real match." She felt like she had met her "soul mate" and would proceed to leave her boyfriend within the week without much thought about it. She described it, for the most part, as if she was just trading in an old tired piece of her wardrobe for something new and flashy. She would stay with the new model until the next time this pattern occurred. When I made this interpretation, Jane simply agreed with me and added, "Maybe I just have a mini-version of the seven-year itch?"

Jane would tell me she felt bad for the boyfriend and how she knew she had "really hurt his feelings." But, then she would switch back to "realizing it is just part of life to move on when you see something better. You shouldn't prevent yourself from always striving for what you want. Sure, it may hurt others along the way, but that is life as well."

I interpreted this as Jane might be feeling guilty over hurting his feelings but this seemed trumped by her feeling entitled to take what she wanted when she wanted regardless of the consequences. I added that this might be helpful to understand. She went on to tell me she is like that at work and in other settings. Jane said, "I have always been very assertive and never afraid to take what I want. It makes me sound pushy and maybe I am but I don't think there is anything wrong with it." I said, "Part of you seems to think there is something wrong with it because you are coming to see me for help in understanding your behavior." She replied, "Yes. I do want help but mostly I just want the drama to die down and to move on with things." I asked Jane what stopped her from talking with her boyfriend over the years about her unhappiness. She said, "I brought it up sometimes and he knew I wasn't really content. But, I think we just settled into a place where we both tried to be OK with the way it was."

I said, "Maybe it is uncomfortable for you to talk a lot about your feelings with others, whether it be him, me, or others?" She said, "Yes. I can tell you what I am feeling but I don't spend a lot of time sitting around going on about my feelings." Responding to the coarse and flippant way she said this, I said, "You sound like a rough and tough old salt who just wants his beer and TV." Jane said, "Well, that is how I grew up. That was pretty much the way my father was."

In the next few sessions, I learned that Jane grew up not very close with her mother but always spending time with her father. He was "certainly not into talking about feelings. In fact, he was the most unemotional person you could imagine. But, we hung out all the time watching television together. Also, he would come to almost all of my school events. So, we spent tons of time together but rarely talked. We just watched TV programs or sometimes talked about sports."

I said, "So, you tried to be close and when you couldn't find a way to talk with each other, you only had the television to share. It sounds rather cold or distant, maybe lonely at times? In other words, I wonder if you wished he had been able to talk with you more and relate to you more?" Also, you are telling me about how unavailable he was to you emotionally. It seems that now you are a lot like him in some ways. You don't want to bother dealing with your feelings or talking about them with your boyfriend or with me. You want to hang out with a man and do what is fun or practical but nothing else. And, if you get bored, you move on to the next fun man whom you can hang out with."

With seemingly no emotion present in her at all, Jane replied, "Yes. That is exactly true. I have always been that way. I guess it would be good to change, maybe. But, I think people are just the way they are. Also, why should I try and change other people and why should they try and change me?" I said, "Well, you came to me for help in changing these things and to stop your pattern of walking out on men." She said, "Yes, I did. But, I don't think there is much we can do and I don't really know if I want to change. I am happy now with my new boyfriend and it was probably just time to end it with my old boyfriend anyway."

So, over and over, I felt I was being assaulted by her arrogant stance, her apparent lack of desire to change, and her lack of caring for others. I was frustrated at trying to get through to her and never being let in. She would not allow me to come closer and build any kind of connection. So, I ended up feeling compelled to try harder and more aggressively, by making confrontations about how cold she was or how guarded she was being with her feelings. On one hand, this more confrontive approach is helpful with certain narcissistic patients (Waska 2010c) but can also be used in counter-transference enactments to get back at a patient for being withholding and withdrawing.

Jane's need to aggressively emphasize how independent she was made it hard for me to realize that she might have great conflicts about being dependent. Fortunately, she reminded me of this when she said she was very averse to being dependent and "thought that one of her problems was that she was overly dependent on others." Jane said, "I have always been with a man. There has never been a time that I was alone. I don't want to be alone. I hate it and feel like I am losing my mind. I start to feel really lost and lonely. So, dependence is a problem in my life. That is why I don't want to have to come in here, too. I should be able to figure things out for myself and not need to come in here all the time just to know how to run my life."

Jane's persecutory feeling of "having" to come in "all the time" was presented in the same aggressive and dismissive manner. For a moment, I was caught off balance in the counter-transference and debated with her about how once-a-week treatment was not "all the time." Fortunately, I regained my analytic focus and interpreted her anxiety over being attached to me. However, this was all a very to-and-fro, slippery situation that made the going tough and added to the overall mutual acting out.

Jane's fluctuating moods and this back and forth way of seeing self and other continued throughout the short period of time I knew her. At one point, her new boyfriend was abrasive and rude to her and she was "shocked." She told me, "I should have known. Actually, it doesn't surprise me. But, now that I see him for what he is I realize I don't need that kind of grief in my life. I have stopped seeing him. I told my boyfriend it is over and that we could get back together. I am done and ready to go back to the way things were."

Here, I was again struck by the incredible lack of empathy and the sheer arrogance of the stance she took. Interpreting the projective identification process, I said, "I wonder if you are surprised and hurt but feel too hurt or embarrassed to talk about it?" Jane said, with complete indifference, "No. I just don't want to be with him anymore. I misjudged him but we all make mistakes."

The next session, Jane said she was "in a state of panic. I feel very anxious and really empty or lost inside. I feel like everything is off balance." I asked her what was wrong. She explained that her boyfriend hadn't simply taken her back without any issue. In fact, he told her he was going to move out for a month and "think things over and figure out if he wanted to be with her anymore." He was angry and wasn't sure he could get over it.

Jane was devastated. She said she couldn't bear the idea of being alone. Now, both men were unavailable to her. She talked about a lifelong "fear of being alone, a dread of having to be alone without anyone." She also talked about how she "knew this was a problem and led her to being overly dependent on men and that she wanted to not have to look to men to fulfill herself. She wanted to be able to operate by herself and not need anyone." I interpreted that she was so upset and feeling so desperate without anyone that she was reacting by wanting to never need anyone. I said, "You must feel weak or less than when you need someone so much. So, it looks like you are lashing back and saying you are above all that and need no one." She said, "Well, I don't want to need anyone. But right now, I am crumbling. I don't know if I can function. I can't sleep and I don't eat anything. I feel lost."

I said, "You haven't looked at our relationship as a resource. You don't like depending on me either. But, this might actually be a good time to increase the frequency of our meetings." To my surprise in the moment, but not so much later upon reflection, she responded immediately. She said, "I think that sounds like a good idea. I need it. It will help me get through this." It was the "get though this" that felt selfish. I felt like a Band-Aid she would use and then discard.

I said, "I think meeting more often will help you to feel more stable *and* will give us more time to learn about you and your struggles. But, it is also important to notice how back and forth you can feel, one minute not wanting me or other men in your life, not needing us at all and the next moment really feeling lost without us. Let's see if we can figure that out without having to resort to any immediate rash reactions. In other words, let's make sure to talk about things before pulling the plug or before rushing in." Jane replied, "That sounds good. I think this is a good idea." So, we began meeting twice a week.

At this point, I found myself thinking more about Jane's childhood. She seemed to not be very interested in her mother but considered her "OK in most departments and we got along fine." But, Jane was very drawn to her father and felt they "had a very close relationship." In my mind, their relationship was very close, almost. From her own description, she was able to spend time with him and receive comfort from him, but in a very narrow and restrictive manner. They could "hang out and watch TV" but not much else. It seemed that not much was ever said between them except for comments about the TV programs. Any comments or discussion about each other, their relationship, or feelings were "out of the question."

In the counter-transference, I began to have an image of a very deadened or mummified father that Jane could sit with and spend time with, but never truly engage with. There was no life between them, only the satisfaction of a compromised companionship. I pictured the father as emotionally mute, casting an emotional silence over Jane, leaving her always searching for a hint of life and sound. And, she tries to act like she was OK without. The more I thought about them in this way, the more interpretations I made in this direction. I did not believe what she told me or my own counter-transference vision to be an actual record of the real interaction from Jane's childhood but more of a product of her core phantasy state being introduced to me in the counter-transference via projective identification.

I interpreted that this father/daughter image was the way she related in the transference and her relationship with the other two men in her life. Jane plainly and simply agreed. She told me, "Yes. That is pretty much the way it was. And, as far as how I feel now, I don't think I am searching for anything abnormal, just someone special who is a good match for me. I never spoke with my father about feelings. Never. And, that never happened too much with my boyfriend. But, it's all too late for that. I just want to be with someone who likes the things I like and I can have fun with." I said, "Like you had with your father, no talking but lots of hanging out and having fun." She said, "Yes."

So, here I felt frustrated and wanted to convince Jane about the importance of feelings and the need to communicate with others about them. I found myself making accusatory interpretations about how cold and cut-off she was from me and others, pushing us all away to avoid feeling weak or dependent. I said she seemed to just want to have power over her objects regardless of the consequences. I added that this must feel good at first as she gets her way and only answers to herself. But, in the end, she must feel empty and alone. Like a steel door closing, Jane would reply, "Yes. I like having it my way. You are right about all of that. That is the way I have always been and I don't see how I would change or even if I want to change."

I was making verbal judgments and pushy recommendations that were accurate in fact but attacking in form. In between, I was able to pull back and reflect a bit on what I thought might be happening. I began to realize that there seemed to be a rapid cycling of projective identification evacuations and role inductions that created a very rigid pattern of relating. I thought that Jane was identifying with her TV father who couldn't provide much and seemed like a dead or mummified object who refused to give or come to life. I pictured her placing all men in this role as a sort of payback. Her narcissistic attack and need to control was so that she could now be the withdrawn, cold father instead of having to endure being the shutout dismissed child. She was so dependent and desperate for her father's love that she turned the tables and let the men in her life suffer with having to try and reach her and connect with her.

So, I began to think of how Jane was being the cold, distant father, leaving me frustrated and angry. I thought of how she was perhaps evoking in me her own desire to rail against this deadened object, trying to convince the comatose or atrophied object of the importance of empathy, love, and the value of feelings. I pictured her feeling lost without enough love and communication with her various boyfriends and then retaliating by leaving them, hoping to link up with a better model, one that was alive and giving.

After attending twice a week for two weeks, Jane announced, "I want to only come in once a week. I don't need any more than that. I want to depend on myself, not on you and therapy for everything. Besides, I feel better now and don't need this." I asked her what had changed and found out that she had visited her boyfriend and felt he wanted to be with her again even though he still wanted some time away to think things through. She said, "I know he wants to be with me now so that seems settled." Also, Jane had started seeing the other man again and sleeping with him at her boyfriend's apartment while he was away thinking things over. I asked her if he knew about this and she said, "Of course not."

I felt used and thrown away again. I felt outraged and angry. While I did a decent job of tempering that, my feelings still came out in my remarks. I said, "You needed me to get you through the loneliness and despair for two weeks but now you have traded me in for a better model, in fact two new models. You seem to need to use men to make sure you don't feel so alone and lost." Jane said, "I know I do that. That is my pattern."

I said, "You say that like you don't care and don't want to change. I am sure part of you does care. But, it looks like once you have what you need to feel better, you don't feel anxious so you don't see why you would need to explore more or change more." She replied, "Exactly." Jane's completely concrete dismissal allowed no differences, no reflection, no growth, and no vulnerability or dependence. It left me speechless. For her to be different would naturally involve disappointment, give and take, and risk of loss, but would also bring on the possibility of love, trust, and fulfillment. This was out of the question at this time in her life. She wanted control and so things had to stay timeless and frozen in the tomb of her past. Thus, the limits on our relationship left us with only this desperate, angry child and this cold, entitled father. The only other flexibility was that we could trade places occasionally.

Two weeks later, she was still seeing the other man behind the back of her boyfriend. Jane said she was looking forward to having her boyfriend move back in with her but had no real plans to break it off with the other man. At the same time, she said she wasn't so impressed with the new guy anymore and may stop seeing him. Her boyfriend was telling her how much he still loved her and while he was "never sure he could trust her again," he wanted to make a go of it.

Jane said, "If he can't ever trust me, then I don't see the point. I know I caused that but if he can't move past that I don't think I want to be a part of that. I don't know if I want to continue seeing him." I said, "You keep throwing us all away. You need us then you don't. It is very hard to remain connected to us all when your feelings fluctuate between desperation, resentment, and boredom." Predictably, Jane agreed.

Here, on reflection, I wish I had also interpreted her possible anxiety over losing control of her boyfriend and realizing she was the one who messed it all up. In other words, perhaps she was rigidly defending against massive shame, guilt, and remorse of a persecutory variety. But, I suspect her response to that approach would have been the same because I did make such references along the way to other situations and she predictably agreed and then dismissively moved on to another topic.

Over the next couple of sessions, I interpreted how she at times played out the role of her distant father, pushing me and her other men aside, ignoring us and hurting us. Then, I commented, she switched to playing out the role of the desperate child needing closeness and some kind of guaranteed comfort but that only brings on anger and resentment at having to need anyone. So, she then switches to her claim of total independence and superiority. I interpreted that she sets things up with us in the transference so as I get a good taste of the rejected child while she gets to be the controlling, rejecting father. I told her I was sure she felt I was being controlling at times as well, making her feel like an angry, dependent child.

Taking it all in very literally, Jane agreed and said she should be able to come as often as she wants and not have to do it my way. I said that she was asking for my help but then feeling it was restrictive and useless so she rebelled against it. Jane said, "Well, I do feel it is restrictive and useless." Somewhat irritated, I drifted into an interpretive enactment. I said, "You seem to be most comfortable being selfish and not allowing yourself to be vulnerable to the shared dialogue of a back and forth. You want to call the shots, you are only in it for yourself, and everyone else is expendable."

On one hand, this type of confrontive and firm interpretive approach is part of an effective therapeutic approach Kleinians use with certain narcissistic patients (Waska 2010b). However, as with any specific interpretive approach, it can become partly or totally tainted by an underlying counter-transference issue. So, when I said these very direct and confrontive comments, they were both accurate and therapeutically valid. However, I also was acting out the counter-transference feelings I had by blaming and judging her.

Regarding my saying she treated everyone as expendable, Jane replied, "It is sort of funny. You just described my role at work again. I see others as only as good as what they can do for me and otherwise I get rid of them. But, you are right. I am that way in general. I have always been that way. I am selfish. I won't ever change." I interpreted her sense of rebellion in the "I won't ever change." She said, "No. It is just who I am and I don't see that ever changing. People don't change."

At this point, in the counter-transference, I felt disgusted, hopeless, angry, and controlled. I felt unable to reach Jane and frustrated at how much she kept me at a distance. I felt completely cornered, controlled, and aghast at how entitled and selfish she appeared to be. I say "appeared" because in the midst of all my counter-transference reactions, I still thought of her as a person who was suffering and who needed help. I was still willing to try and help her but felt completely blocked. I also felt sad and sorry for her, given her lifelong pattern of trying to fill this empty void inside her.

Indeed, when I reflected on this session, I felt Jane was so angry that she had endured a father object who would not budge and would not ever be available that in the transference she felt that she "sure as hell wouldn't give me anything either." If she had to suffer then, I would have to suffer now.

Given my decades of work with borderline and narcissistic patients who fit this very difficult, traumatized, volatile and concrete profile, I knew it was only a matter of time before she probably quit. In fact, I felt that certainty after the first few weeks of working with Jane. But, now I knew it was looming near. I felt unable to get thought to her and make any connection whatsoever. When I realized this might be the heart of the transference, I tried to interpret just that. She dismissed it. When I realized my constantly trying to get through and trying harder and harder might be the enactment itself, I stayed quiet and simply available. But, this went nowhere. In fact, she told me "therapy is useless and goes nowhere. I get nothing out of it and I can think for myself better than wasting my time coming here."

When I tried to explore or interpret all of these states as working together in a doomed to fail sort of transference, where each one of us ended up feeling helpless and hopeless and unable to depend on each other, Jane told me she "definitely understood what I meant and agrees with it. But, it doesn't matter because I can take care of myself just fine and I realize now all I did with my boyfriend was make a simple mistake in judgment. Now, I see what I really need in life and I will go forward and get it. If I want to see the other guy, that is what I will do. Life is too short. I don't want to be with anyone that I don't want to be with. If I don't get anything out of the relationship, why should I stay in it?"

I asked her if she was also talking about how she saw our relationship. She said yes and informed me that she would not be coming back again. She told me that a friend had recommended another therapist and she was "going to try that person." I said, "It feels like you are dropping me for the next best thing, just like you dropped your boyfriend for the other guy. Instead of just doing that, maybe it would help to spend some time talking about what I am not giving you and what you're frustrated about here." She said, "No thanks. I have made my decision." With that, Jane's short stay in analytic treatment ended.

Discussion

I felt Jane had grown tired of being with another dead or mummified object and moved on to another object that appeared to contain life, hope, and attention in the way she wanted it. She had used me up and was ready to go on to the next object. She fed on male objects until she tired of the taste or felt she had gobbled up all there was to have and then moved on to the next plate. My overall view of Jane's transference and her lifelong phantasy struggle was that of feeling she was barely connected to her father by a superficial thread of "hanging out" and TV watching but when it came to emotional fulfillment and support, she was left with a deadened or comatose object that didn't seem able or willing to interact with her. So, there was a mutual interest that sustained them but Jane was locked out of the life of the relationship, her father's heart.

The presence of a selfish, deadened object that was unavailable and without emotional meaning seemed to plague Jane's upbringing and her internal life as an adult. She, in turn, seemed to go on to become this comatose, cutoff person who would let you in a little if you were willing to hang out with her and do things she enjoyed. But, sooner or later, she grew bored of you or rejecting if you had differences or opposing needs. Again, I thought this might have been her sense of abandonment with her father and the source of the extreme panic she felt when suddenly without her boyfriend and the new man. So, I conceptualized the transference as this identification and projection with and of a cold and empty father container, dead to others unless they went along with what he/she wanted. In the counter-transference, I was overcome by this feeling and fought back, demanding she let me in. When she didn't, I protested by essentially calling her names, "selfish," "impatient," and "cold" much as she probably felt toward her internalized father object.

Since most analysts in private practice see a great deal of disturbed patients who for a variety of reasons only attend for a few sessions or perhaps a few months before abruptly aborting treatment, it is helpful to try to understand the clinical profile of such encounters. This involves a study of the dynamic makeup of the patient's internal conflicts and the resulting counter-transference reactions evoked within the analyst.

Jane seemed to fluctuate between a need/fear object relational conflict and a narcissistic self-sufficiency stance (Adler 1991) in which dependency is devalued and avoided. Indeed, she used a manic defense in which she, in phantasy, believed she had appropriated all the needed emotional nourishment for her father/boyfriend/analyst that she needed and now was totally self-sufficient (Grotstein 2010). In the paranoid-schizoid position (Klein 1946), life is very concrete and without much flexibility. There is little or no concern for the object except for if it goes away and this feels very persecutory. In other words, the object's value is a selfish concern (Ogden 1991). Although Jane did bring up her sense of guilt and remorse on occasion, this was a primitive state of depressive (Klein 1935, 1940) guilt in which she was more worried about the consequences to her from her actions than to the impact on her objects. And, she used manic control to dismiss the severity or meaning of her actions, saying it was "just life" and "even if people get hurt, that is the way things are and everyone should just move on." All of these extreme states of mind made it very difficult to establish analytic contact (Waska 2007, 2010a, 2010b) and my own counter-transference issues made it difficult to maintain that contact when it briefly emerged.

In conclusion, this case illustrates a very difficult treatment that never really got off the ground with a patient in the borderline and narcissistic spectrum. Her paranoid and primitive depressive phantasies were such that I was rapidly pulled in and acted out certain aspects of her internal conflicts. The locked door of her heart and mind invited me to bang on the door, demanding entrance. Although this certainly had an oedipal quality to it, as far as her not being allowed into her father's mind and heart, I saw this as much more fragmented and developmentally more regressed, perhaps a comatose father defense against a dead mother anxiety. Jane's narcissistic way of not relating to me evoked a strong countertransference of both withdrawal and protest.

In the end, I think I was able to make many accurate and sometimes helpful interpretations. However, I think I also managed to step into a mutual acting out of her core conflicts and in the process became yet one more out of reach and unappealing object in her long history of failed connections. She was extremely difficult to work with but I did not make that situation any more pliable.

If anything, I provided a pit stop, an emotional foxhole for temporary reprieve from her immediate as well as historical downpour of persecutory and primitive depressive anxieties. By discarding me, she was back in temporary control of her graveyard objects, but ultimately still having to live her life among the dead and unavailable.

Chapter Ten
Closing

In this volume, I have taken the reader on an in-depth examination of some of the more baffling and thorny clinical challenges encountered in psychoanalytic practice with more disturbed patients, particularly those more distressed depressive and narcissistic individuals. I have brought a sharp focus to several key themes and issues that characterize some of the most confusing and taxing aspects of conducting psychoanalysis with these harder-to-reach individuals. Using a remarkably accessible, here-and-now, moment-to-moment view of what takes place in the course of psychoanalytic treatment, I have shown the step-by-step process of working with patients who suffer from rather profound, long standing, and resistant conditions of the mind.

Part One of this book illuminates the baffling and complex nature of patients who have little sense of internal security, integration, or trust. The as-if personality, the graveyard sentry, the depressive patient, and those who struggle with persecutory guilt and primitive loss are some of the daunting and elusive psychological profiles examined in detail. The essence of self and object conflict and the complications of phantasies regarding love, hate, and knowledge were discussed in a manner that allowed the reader to gain a greater theoretical and clinical insight into how to work with patients who represent our most trying therapeutic encounters.

I believe I have provided a very clear picture of not only those interventions that do not work but a glimpse of those psychoanalytic approaches within the Kleinian school that offer these types of patients a chance of greater internal integration, inner fulfillment, and the opportunity to feel more whole, stable, and confident about the nature of the self and its relationship to others.

In Part Two of this book, the focus shifted to the Kleinian approach with patients within the narcissistic spectrum of experience. Here, issues of demand, entitlement, and specialness were examined as well as some of the underlying phantasies of envy, persecutory mourning, and internal fragmentation as the result of excessive projective identification.

Throughout the entire book, I revealed much about my own personal struggle in the counter-transference with the more hard to reach patient. The counter-transference was shown to be a potentially dangerous area of acting out in which the analyst ends up making blind stabs at advancing the treatment combined with a jungle of justifications for the analyst's own reactions to and confusions about the patient. The feelings of love, hate, and the need to know and learn are universal and as such become the very bedrock of all transference and counter-transference problems. These possible pitfalls in the counter-transference are even more common and potentially more damaging with the more severely neurotic, borderline, or narcissistic patients profiled throughout this book.

However, I have provided a great deal of clinical and theoretical evidence in the book for the positive and careful use of counter-transference. I believe the counter-transference serves as a valuable and critical component in all psychoanalytic treatments but is especially useful or even necessary in the treatment of more disturbed patients. To examine this area of technique, I have provided honest and direct case material that shows how I sometimes did falter or fail to move the treatment forward due to my counter-transference acting out. But, I have also shown how my continuous commitment to closely monitoring my counter-transference feelings and thoughts often provided me with the ability to better translate the exact nature of the patient's conflict and to then bring to bear the best interpretive approach to help the patient work through their anxieties and face the fundamental dread and the joy of change and integration.

Bibliography

1. Adler, G. (1991). Counter-Transference Issues in the Treatment of Borderline and Narcissistic Personality Disorders, *Modern Psychoanalysis*, 16: (1) 37–64.
2. Ahumada, J. (2004). Musings on Neville Symington's Clinical Presentation. *International Journal of Psycho-Analysis*, 85: (2) 262–264.
3. Akhtar, S. (2002). Forgiveness: Origins, Dynamics, Psychopathology, and Technical Relevance. *Psychoanalytic Quarterly*, 71: (2) 175–212.
4. Alvarez, A. (2010). Levels of Analytic Work and Levels of Pathology: The Work of Calibration. *International Journal of Psychoanalysis*, 91: 859–878.
5. Andkjær Olsen, O. (2004). Depression and Reparation as Themes in Melanie Klein's Analysis of the Painter Ruth Weber. *Scandinavian Psychoanalytic Review*, 27: (1) 34–42.
6. Andresen, J. (1996). An Origin of the Inhibition of Imagination. *Contemporary Psychoanalysis*. 32: 307.
7. Bauer, G. (1993). *The Analysis of the Transference in the Here and Now*, Aronson, New York.
8. Bass, A. (1997). The Problem of Concreteness. *Psychoanalytic Quarterly*, 4: 642–682.
9. Billow, R. (2000). From Counter-Transference to Passion. *Psychoanalytic Quarterly*, 1: 93–120.
10. Bion, W. R. (1959). Attacks on Linking. *International Journal of Psychoanalysis*, 40: 308–315.
11. Bion, W. (1962). *Learning from Experience*, London, Heinemann.
12. Bion, W. (1966). *Bulletin of the British Psychoanalytic Society*, 5.
13. Britton, R. (1989). The Missing Link: Parental Sexuality in the Oedipus Complex. In: *The Oedipus Complex Today: Clinical Implications*, pp. 83–101.
14. Britton, R. (1992). The Oedipus Situation and the Depressive Position. In: *Clinical Lectures on Klein and Bion, New Library of Psychoanalysis*, 14: 34–45.
15. Britton, R. (1998). *Belief and Imagination: Explorations in Psychoanalysis*, London, Routledge.
16. Britton, R. (2000). Hyper-Subjectivity and Hyper-Objectivity in Narcissistic Disorders. *Fort Da*, 2: 53–64.

17. Britton, R. (2008). He Thinks Himself Impaired: The Pathologically Envious Personality. In *Envy and Gratitude Revisited,* edited by Priscilla Roth and Alessandra Lemma, Karnac, London.
18. Caper, R. (1996). Play, Experimentation and Creativity. *International Journal of Psycho-Analysis,* 77: 859–869.
19. Caper, R. (1997). A Mind of One's Own. *International Journal of Psycho-Analysis,* 78: 265–278.
20. Caper, R. (2008). Envy, Narcissism, and the Destructive Instinct. In *Envy and Gratitude Revisited,* edited by Priscilla Roth and Alessandra Lemma, Karnac, London, 35–49.
21. Cartwright, D. (2010). *Containing States of Mind,* Routledge, London.
22. Chessick, R. (1994). What Brings About Change in Psychoanalytic Treatment? *Psychoanalytic Review,* 81: (2) 279–300.
23. Cooper, S. (2010). *A Disturbance in the Field: Essays in Transference-Countertransference Engagement,* Taylor and Francis, New York.
24. Deutsch, H. (1942). Some Forms of Emotional Disturbance and Their Relationship to Schizophrenia. *Psychoanalytic Quarterly,* 11: 301–321.
25. Diamond, D. (2004). Attachment Disorganization: The Reunion of Attachment Theory and Psychoanalysis. *Psychoanalytic Psychology,* 21: (2) 276–299.
26. Eizirik, C. (2010). Panel Report: Analytic Practice: Convergences and Divergences. *International Journal of Psychoanalysis,* 91: 371–375.
27. Feldman, M. (1989). The Oedipus Complex: Clinical Manifestations. In *The Oedipus Complex Today,* edited by John Steiner, London, Karnac.
28. Feldman, M. (2008). Envy and the Negative Therapeutic Reaction. In *Envy and Gratitude Revisited,* edited by Priscilla Roth and Alessandra Lemma, London: Karnac, 168–185.
29. Ferenczi, S. (1925). Contra-Indications to the Active Psychoanalytic Technique. In *Further Contributions to the Theory and Technique of Psychoanalysis,* edited by J. Rickman, London: Hogarth, 1950, 217–230.
30. Fonagy, P. (2008). Being Envious of Envy and Gratitude, in *Envy and Gratitude Revisited,* edited by Priscilla Roth and Alessandra Lemma, London: Karnac, 201–210.
31. Freud, S. (1914). *Remembering, Repeating, and Working Through,* S.E. 12, 145–156.
32. Freud, S. (1925). *An Autobiographical Study,* S.E. 20, 7–74.
33. Gill, M. (1979). The Analysis of the Transference. *Journal of the American Psychoanalytic Association,* 27S: 263–288.
34. Green, A. (1983). *On Private Madness,* Hogarth: London.

35. Grinberg, L. (1962). On a Specific Aspect of Countertransference Due to the Patient's Projective Identification. *International Journal of Psycho-Analysis*, 43: 436–440.
36. Grinberg, L. (1964). Two Kinds of Guilt—Their Relations with Normal and Pathological Aspects of Mourning. *International Journal of Psychoanalysis*, 45: 366–371.
37. Grinberg, L. (1968). On Acting Out and Its Role in the Psychoanalytic Process. *International Journal of Psycho-Analysis*, 49: 171–178.
38. Grotstein, J. (1983). Deciphering the Schizophrenic Experience. *Psychoanalytic Inquiry*, 3:1, 37–69.
39. Grotstein, J. (1987). An Object Relations Perspective. In *Techniques of Working with Resistances*, edited by Donald Milman and George Goldman, New York: Aronson.
40. Grotstein, J. (2010a). *But at the Same Time and on Another Level: Psychoanalytic Theory and Technique in the Kleinian/Bionian Mode, Volume 1*, London: Karnac.
41. Grotstein, J. (2010b). *But at the Same Time and on Another Level: Psychoanalytic Theory and Technique in the Kleinian/Bionian Mode, Volume 2*, London: Karnac.
42. Guntrip, H. (1969). *Schizoid Phenomenon, Object Relations, and the Self*, New York: IUP.
43. Haft, J. (2005). "On My Way Here, I Passed a Man with a Scab": Understanding a Case of Severe Obsessive-Compulsive Disorder. *Psychoanalytic Quarterly*, 74: (4) 1101–1126.
44. Hamilton, N. G. (1990). The Containing Function and the Analyst's Projective Identification. *International Journal of Psychoanalysis*, 71: 445–454.
45. Heimannn, P. (1956). Dynamics of Transference Interpretations. *International Journal of Psychoanalysis*, 37: 303–310.
46. Hinshelwood, R. (2004). Contrasting Clinical Techniques: A British Kleinian, Contemporary Freudian and Latin American Kleinian Discuss Clinical Material. *International Journal of Psycho-Analysis*, 85: (5) 1257–1260.
47. Horner, A. (1987). Object Relations and Transference Resistance. In *Techniques of Working with Resistances*, edited by Donald Milman and George Goldman, New York: Aronson.
48. Joseph, B. (1959). An Aspect of the Repetition Compulsion. *International Journal of Psycho-Analysis*, 40: 213–222.
49. Joseph, B. (1982). Addiction to Near-Death. *International Journal of Psychoanalysis*, 63: 449–456.
50. Joseph, B. (1985). Transference: The Total Situation. *International Journal of Psychoanalysis*, 66: 447–454.
51. Joseph, B. (1987). Projective Identification: Clinical Aspects. In *Projection, Identification, Projective Identification*, edited by J. Sandler, Madison, CT: International Universities Press.

52. Joseph, B. (1989). *Psychic Equilibrium and Psychic Change: Selected Papers of Betty Joseph,* edited by Michael Feldman and Elizabeth Bott Spillius, The New Library of Psychoanalysis, London and New York: Tavistock/Routledge.
53. Joseph, B. (2000). Agreeableness as Obstacle. *International Journal of Psycho-Analysis,* 81: (4) 641–649.
54. Klein, M. (1935). A Contribution to the Psychogenesis of Manic-Depressive States. *International Journal of Psycho-Analysis,* 16: 145–174.
55. Klein, M. (1940). Mourning and Its Relation to Manic-Depressive States. *International Journal of Psycho-Analysis,* 21: 125–153.
56. Klein, M. (1946). Notes on Some Schizoid Mechanisms. *International Journal of Psycho-Analysis,* 27: 99–110.
57. Klein, M. (1950). On the Criteria for the Termination of a Psycho-Analysis. *International Journal of Psycho-Analysis,* 31: 78–80.
58. Klein, M. (1952). The Origins of Transference. *International Journal of Psycho-Analysis,* 33: 433–438.
59. Klein, M. (1975). *Envy and Gratitude and Other Works 1946–1963,* edited by M. Masud R. Khan. The International Psycho-Analytical Library, Vol. 104, 346 pages. London: The Hogarth Press and the Institute of Psycho-Analysis.
60. Lamann-Adamo, V. (2006). Aspects of a Compliant Container: Considering Narcissistic Personality Configurations. *International Journal of Psychoanalysis,* 87: 369–382.
61. Lemma, A. (2008). Keeping Envy in Mind. In *Envy and Gratitude Revisited,* edited by Priscilla Roth and Alessandra Lemma, London: Karnac, 92–108.
62. Lopez-Corvo, R. E. (1994). *Self-Envy: Therapy and the Dividend Internal World.* Northvale, NJ/ London: Aronson.
63. Lussier, A. (1999). In *The Dead Mother: The Work of Andre Green,* Routledge, London.
64. Malcolm, R. (1990). As-If: The Phenomenon of Not Learning. *International Journal of Psycho-Analysis,* 71: 385–392.
65. Malin, A. & Grotstein, J. (1966). Projective Identification in the Therapeutic Process. *International Journal of Psychoanalysis,* 47: 26.
66. Marilyn, C. (2001). Nonphysical Touch: Modes of Containment and Communication Within the Analytic Process. *Psychoanalytic Quarterly,* 70: (2) 387–416.
67. Mitchell, S. (1995). Interaction in the Kleinian and Interpersonal Traditions. *Contemporary Psychoanalysis,* 31: 65.
68. Moser-Ha, H. (2001). Working through Envy: Some Technical Issues. *International Journal of Psychoanalysis,* 82: 713–726.
69. Neuenschwander Escosteguy Carneiro, M. (2006). From Acting to Communicating: The Analysis of a Boy with a Pathological Organization. *International Journal of Psycho-Analysis,* 87: (3) 681–701.

70. Newman, K. (1988). Counter-Transference: Its Role in Facilitating the Use of the Object. *Annuals of Psychoanalysis*, 16: 251–285.
71. Ogden, T. (1990). On the Structure of Experience. In *Master Clinicians on Treating the Regressed Patient*, edited by B. Boyer and P. Giovacchini, New York: Aronson.
72. Ogden, T. (1991). Analyzing the Matrix of Transference. *International Journal of Psycho-Analysis*, 72: 593–605.
73. Ogden, T. (1996). Reconsidering Three Aspects of Psychoanalytic Technique. *International Journal of Psycho-Analysis*, 77: 883–899.
74. Ogden, T. (1997). Reverie and Interpretation. *Psychoanalytic Quarterly*, 4: 567–595.
75. Ogden, T. (1999). *The Dead Mother: The Work of Andre Green*, Routledge, London.
76. Oremland, J. (1995). The Concept of Interaction. *Journal of the American Psychoanalytic Association*, 43: (2) 525–537.
77. O'Shaughnessy, E. (1964). The Absent Object. *Journal of Child Psychotherapy*, 1: (2) 134–143.
78. O'Shaughnessy, E. (2001). The Dead Mother: The Work of Andre Green, A Review. *International Journal of Psychoanalysis*, 82: 619–621.
79. O'Shaughnessy, E. (2008). On Gratitude. In *Envy and Gratitude Revisited*, edited by Priscilla Roth and Alessandra Lemma, London: Karnac.
80. Racker, H. (1957). The Meanings and Uses of Countertransference. *Psychoanalytic Quarterly*, 26: 303–357.
81. Racker, H. (1960). A Study of Some Early Conflicts through Their Return in the Patient's Relation with the Interpretation. *International Journal of Psychoanalysis*, 15: 47–58.
82. Rather, L. (2001). Collaborating with the Unconscious Other: The Analysand's Capacity for Creative Thinking. *International Journal of Psycho-Analysis*, 82: (3) 515–531.
83. Rey, J. (1988). That Which Patients Bring to Analysis. *International Journal of Psycho-Analysis*, 69: 457–470.
84. Riviere, J. (1936). A Contribution to the Analysis of the Negative Therapeutic Reaction. *International Journal of Psycho-Analysis*, 17: 304–320.
85. Rosenfeld, H. (1971). A Clinical Approach to the Psychoanalytic Theory of the Life and Death Instincts: An Investigation into the Aggressive Aspects of Narcissism. *International Journal of Psycho-Analysis*, 52: 169–178.
86. Rosenfeld, H. (1987). *Impasse and Interpretation: Therapeutic and Anti-therapeutic Factors in the Psychoanalytic Treatment of Psychotic, Borderline, and Neurotic Patients. New Library of Psychoanalysis Vol. 1*, London: Tavistock.

87. Roth, P. (2001). Mapping the Landscape: Levels of Transference Interpretation. *International Journal of Psycho-Analysis,* 82: (3) 533–543.
88. Rusbridger, R. (2004). Elements of the Oedipus Complex: A Kleinian Account. *International Journal of Psycho-Analysis,* 85: (3) 731–747.
89. Roth, P. (2001). Mapping the Landscape: Levels of Transference Interpretation. *International Journal of Psycho-Analysis,* 82: (3) 533–543.
90. Safá-Gerard, D. (1998). Bearable and Unbearable Guilt: A Kleinian Perspective. *Psychoanalytic Quarterly,* 67: (3) 351–378.
91. Searles, H. (1978). Psychoanalytic Therapy with the Borderline Adult. In *New Perspectives in Psychotherapy of the Borderline Adult,* edited by James Masterson, Brunner/Mazel, New York.
92. Searles, H. (1979). The Development of Mature Hope in the Patient-Therapist Relationship, in *Countertransference and Related Subjects,* New York: IUP.
93. Segal, H. (1962). The Curative Factors in Psycho-Analysis. *International Journal of Psycho-Analysis,* 43: 212–217.
94. Segal, H. (1973) *Introduction to the Work of Melanie Klein, 2nd ed.* London: Hogarth Press.
95. Segal, H. (1982) Early Infantile Development as Reflected in a Psychoanalytic Process: Steps in Integration. *International Journal of Psychoanalysis,* 63: 15–22.
96. Segal, H. (1993). On the Clinical Usefulness of the Concept of Death Instinct. *International Journal of Psycho-Analysis,* 74: 55–61.
97. Segal, H. (1998). Manic Reparation. In *The Contemporary Kleinians of London,* edited by Roy Schafer, Madison, CT: International Universities Press, 441.
98. Sekoff, J. (1999) in *The Dead Mother: The Work of Andre Green,* Routledge, London.
99. Shafer, R. (1995). Aloneness in the Countertransference. *Psychoanalytic Quarterly,* 64: 496–516.
100. Sodre, I. (2008). On Envy and the Hatred of Love. In *Envy and Gratitude Revisited,* edited by Priscilla Roth and Alessandra Lemma, London: Karnac, 19–34.
101. Spillius, E. (1993). Varieties of Envious Experiences, *International Journal of Psychoanalysis,* 74: 1199–1272.
102. Steiner, J. (1987). The Interplay between Pathological Organizations and the Paranoid-Schizoid and Depressive Positions. *International Journal of Psycho-Analysis,* 68: 69–80.
103. Steiner, J. (1990). Pathological Organizations as Obstacles to Mourning: The Role of Unbearable Guilt. *International Journal of Psycho-Analysis,* 71: 87–94.

104. Steiner, J. (1993). *Psychic Retreats: Pathological Organizations of the Personality in Psychotic, Neurotic, and Borderline Patients*, London: Routledge.
105. Steiner, J. (1996). The Aim of Psychoanalysis in Theory and in Practice, *International Journal of Psychoanalysis*, 77: 1073–1084.
106. Steiner, J. (2000). Containment, Enactment and Communication. *International Journal of Psycho-Analysis*, 81: (2) 245–255.
107. Steiner, J. (2001). Response. *International Journal of Psycho-Analysis*, 82: (1) 173–174.
108. Steiner, J. (2004). Gaze, Dominance and Humiliation in the Schreber Case. *International Journal of Psycho-Analysis*, 85: (2) 269–284.
109. Steiner, J. (2006). Interpretive Enactments and the Analytic Setting. *International Journal of Psychoanalysis*, 87: 315–320.
110. Steiner, J. (2008a). Transference to the Analyst as an Excluded Observer. *International Journal of Psychoanalysis*, 89: 39–54.
111. Steiner, J. (2008b). The Repetition Compulsion. In *Envy and Gratitude Revisited*, edited by Priscilla Roth and Alessandra Lemma, London: Karnac, 137–151.
112. Waska, R. (2004). *Projective Identification: The Kleinian Interpretation*, London: Brunner/Rutledge.
113. Waska, R. (2006). *The Danger of Change: The Kleinian Approach with Patients who Experience Progress as Trauma*, London: Brunner/Rutledge.
114. Waska, R. (2007). *The Concept of Analytic Contact: A Kleinian Approach to Reaching the Hard to Reach Patient*, London: Brunner/Rutledge.
115. Waska, R. (2010a). *Selected Theoretical and Clinical Issues in Psychoanalytic Psychotherapy: A Modern Kleinian Approach to Analytic Contact*, New York: Novoscience.
116. Waska, R. (2010b). *The Modern Kleinian Approach to Psychoanalysis: Clinical Illustrations*, New York: Jason Aronson.
117. Waska, R. (2010c). *Love, Hate, and Knowledge: The Kleinian Method of Analytic Contact and the Future of Psychoanalysis*, London: Karnac.
118. Waska, R. (2010d). *Moments of Uncertainty in Psychoanalytic Practice: Interpreting Within the Matrix of Projective Identification, Counter-Transference, and Enactment*. Columbia University Press.
119. Waska, R. (2010e). *Treating Severe Depressive and Persecutory Anxieties States: Using Analytic Contact to Transform the Unbearable*, London: Karnac.
120. Weib, H. (2008). Romantic Perversion: The Role of Envy in the Creation of a Timeless Universe. In *Envy and Gratitude Revisited*, edited by Priscilla Roth and Alessandra Lemma, London: Karnac, 152–167.

121. Weintrobe, S. (2004). Links between Grievance, Complaint, and Different Forms of Entitlement. *International Journal of Psycho-Analysis*, 85: (1) 83–96.
122. Wilson, E. (2009). The Internal Obstructive Object, *Psychoanalytic Quarterly*, 78: (3) 791.
123. Zeavin, L. (2005). Knowing and Not Knowing: The Analyst's Pregnancy. *Psychoanalytic Quarterly*, 74: (3) 703–735.

Index

About the Author

Robert Waska MFT, PhD is a 1999 graduate of the Institute for Psychoanalytic Studies, an International Psychoanalytical Association affiliate organization. He conducts a full-time private psychoanalytic practice for individuals and couples in San Francisco and Marin County, California. In addition, he has taught classes and supervised therapists in the Bay Area and has presented papers in the U.S. and internationally.

Dr. Waska is the author of eleven published textbooks on Kleinian psychoanalytic theory and technique, is a contributing author for two psychology texts, and has published more than ninety articles in professional journals. He also serves on the review committee for several journals and book publishers. In addition, Dr. Waska is an artist who creates unique combinations of photography, poetry, and digital design.

His clinical work, now thirty years in the making, focuses on contemporary Kleinian topics, including projective identification, loss, borderline and psychotic states, the practical realities of psychoanalytic practice in the modern world, and the establishment of analytic contact with difficult, hard-to-reach patients. He emphasizes the moment-to-moment understanding of transference and phantasy as the vehicle for gradual integration and mastery of unconscious conflict between self and other.

Correspondence:

Dr. Waska
P.O. Box 2769
San Anselmo, CA 94979 USA